TRADE ISSUES, POLICIES AND LAWS

U.S.-SINGAPORE FREE TRADE AGREEMENT AFTER FIVE YEARS

TRADE ISSUES, POLICIES AND LAWS

Additional books in this series can be found on Nova's website
under the Series tab.

Additional E-books in this series can be found on Nova's website
under the E-books tab.

ASIAN POLITICAL, ECONOMIC AND SECURITY ISSUES

Additional books in this series can be found on Nova's website
under the Series tab.

Additional E-books in this series can be found on Nova's website
under the E-books tab.

TRADE ISSUES, POLICIES AND LAWS

U.S.-SINGAPORE FREE TRADE AGREEMENT AFTER FIVE YEARS

ROBERT E. FLEMCHAK
EDITOR

Nova Science Publishers, Inc.
New York

NOTICE TO THE READER

The Publisher has taken reasonable care in the preparation of this book, but makes no expressed or implied warranty of any kind and assumes no responsibility for any errors or omissions. No liability is assumed for incidental or consequential damages in connection with or arising out of information contained in this book. The Publisher shall not be liable for any special, consequential, or exemplary damages resulting, in whole or in part, from the readers' use of, or reliance upon, this material. Any parts of this book based on government reports are so indicated and copyright is claimed for those parts to the extent applicable to compilations of such works.

Independent verification should be sought for any data, advice or recommendations contained in this book. In addition, no responsibility is assumed by the publisher for any injury and/or damage to persons or property arising from any methods, products, instructions, ideas or otherwise contained in this publication.

This publication is designed to provide accurate and authoritative information with regard to the subject matter covered herein. It is sold with the clear understanding that the Publisher is not engaged in rendering legal or any other professional services. If legal or any other expert assistance is required, the services of a competent person should be sought. FROM A DECLARATION OF PARTICIPANTS JOINTLY ADOPTED BY A COMMITTEE OF THE AMERICAN BAR ASSOCIATION AND A COMMITTEE OF PUBLISHERS.

Additional color graphics may be available in the e-book version of this book.

LIBRARY OF CONGRESS CATALOGING-IN-PUBLICATION DATA

U.S.-Singapore Free Trade Agreement after five years / editor, Robert E. Flemchak.
    p. cm.
  Includes index.
  ISBN 978-1-61122-350-7 (hardcover)
  1. Free trade--United States. 2. Tariff--Law and legislation--United States. 3. Free trade--Singapore. 4. Tariff--Law and legislation--Singapore. 5. United States--Commerce--Singapore. 6. Singapore--Commerce--United States. 7. United States. United States-Singapore Free Trade Agreement Implementation Act. I. Flemchak, Robert E. II. Title: US-Singapore Free Trade Agreement after five years.
  HF1756.U48 2011
  382'.97305957--dc22
                    2011003169

Published by Nova Science Publishers, Inc. ✛ New York

CONTENTS

PREFACE

The U.S.-Singapore FTA has taken on new importance in trade policy because the United States is engaged in negotiations to join the Trans-Pacific Partnership (TPP). In addition, the U.S.-Singapore FTA has provided greater access for U.S. companies, has been instrumental in increasing bilateral trade, and has provided reassurance to Singaporeans of U.S. interest in the country. As a city-state, Singapore operates as an entrepot with essentially free trade. Under the FTA, concessions dealt mainly with providing greater access for American service providers and with strengthening the business environment in areas such as the protection of intellectual property rights and access to government procurement. This book examines the U.S.-Singapore Free Trade Agreement in detail, as well as the documented effects after five years

Chapter 1 - The U.S.-Singapore Free Trade Agreement (FTA) (P.L. 108-78) went into effect on January 1, 2004. This report provides an overview of the major trade and economic effects of the FTA over the three years ending in 2006. It also includes detailed information on key provisions of the agreement and legislative action.

The U.S.-Singapore FTA has taken on new importance in trade policy because the United States is engaged in negotiations to join the Trans-Pacific Partnership (TPP). The TPP negotiations are the first major market-opening initiative of the Obama Administration. On December 14, 2009, United States Trade Representative Ron Kirk notified Congress of the intent to enter into the TPP negotiations. The objective is to shape a high-standard, broad-based regional free trade agreement with Australia, Brunei Darussalam, Chile, New Zealand, Peru, Singapore, and Vietnam. The first round of negotiations began March 15, 2010, in Sydney, Australia.

The U.S.-Singapore FTA has provided greater access for U.S. companies, has been instrumental in increasing bilateral trade, and has provided reassurance to Singaporeans of U.S. interest in the country. As a city-state, Singapore operates as an entrepot with essentially free trade. Under the FTA, concessions dealt mainly with providing greater access for American service providers and with strengthening the business environment in areas such as the protection of intellectual property rights and access to government procurement.

In 2009, the United States ran a $6.6 billion surplus in its balance of merchandise trade with Singapore, up from $1.4 billion in 2003, but down from the $12.0 billion in 2008. U.S. exports of goods to Singapore surged from $16.6 billion in 2003 to a peak of $27.9 billion in 2008 before declining to $22.3 billion in 2009. Even with this rapid increase in U.S. exports to Singapore, the U.S. share of Singapore's imports has declined from 16% in 2003 to 12% in 2009. The main reason for this is that Singapore's overall trade is booming. Still, Singapore imports more from the United States ($28.5 billion) than from China ($26.0 billion).The U.S. balance of trade in services with Singapore declined from a surplus of $4.0 billion in 2001 to $1.2 billion 2005 but has risen to $4.2 billion in 2008. A significant increase has been in income from U.S. direct investments in Singapore. U.S. access to the Singaporean market for multinational corporations seems to have been enhanced considerably under the FTA. U.S. income from assets in Singapore rose from $6.7 billion in 2003 to $21.1 billion by 2008.

On the U.S. import side (Singapore's exports), a noteworthy development is that U.S. imports of pharmaceuticals from Singapore have risen from $0.09 billion in 2003 to $3.0 billion in 2007 before declining to $2.0 billion in 2008. Singapore has developed as a regional center for multinational pharmaceutical companies. This apparently was partly triggered by provisions in the FTA that required Singapore to strengthen its intellectual property protection.

Chapter 2 - The Government of the United States and the Government of the Republic of Singapore ("the Parties"),

Recognizing their longstanding friendship and important trade and investment relationship;

Recognizing that open and competitive markets are the key drivers of economic efficiency, innovation and wealth creation;

Recognizing the importance of ongoing liberalization of trade in goods and services at the multilateral level;

Aware of the growing importance of trade and investment for the economies of the Asia-Pacific region;

Reaffirming their rights, obligations and undertakings under the Marrakesh Agreement Establishing the World Trade Organization, and other multilateral, regional, and bilateral agreements and arrangements to which they are both Parties;

Recognizing that economic development, social development, and environmental protection are interdependent and mutually reinforcing components of sustainable development, and that an open and non-discriminatory multilateral trading system can play a major role in achieving sustainable development;

In: U.S.-Singapore Free Trade Agreement after Five Years   ISBN: 978-1-61122-350-7
Editor: Robert E. Flemchak   © 2011 Nova Science Publishers, Inc.

Chapter 1

THE U.S.-SINGAPORE FREE TRADE AGREEMENT: EFFECTS AFTER FIVE YEARS

Dick K. Nanto

SUMMARY

The U.S.-Singapore Free Trade Agreement (FTA) (P.L. 108-78) went into effect on January 1, 2004. This report provides an overview of the major trade and economic effects of the FTA over the three years ending in 2006. It also includes detailed information on key provisions of the agreement and legislative action.

The U.S.-Singapore FTA has taken on new importance in trade policy because the United States is engaged in negotiations to join the Trans-Pacific Partnership (TPP). The TPP negotiations are the first major market-opening initiative of the Obama Administration. On December 14, 2009, United States Trade Representative Ron Kirk notified Congress of the intent to enter into the TPP negotiations. The objective is to shape a high-standard, broad-based regional free trade agreement with Australia, Brunei Darussalam, Chile, New Zealand, Peru, Singapore, and Vietnam. The first round of negotiations began March 15, 2010, in Sydney, Australia.

The U.S.-Singapore FTA has provided greater access for U.S. companies, has been instrumental in increasing bilateral trade, and has provided reassurance to Singaporeans of U.S. interest in the country. As a city-state, Singapore operates as an entrepot with essentially free trade. Under the FTA, concessions dealt mainly with providing greater access for American service providers and with strengthening the business environment in areas such as the protection of intellectual property rights and access to government procurement.

In 2009, the United States ran a $6.6 billion surplus in its balance of merchandise trade with Singapore, up from $1.4 billion in 2003, but down from the $12.0 billion in 2008. U.S. exports of goods to Singapore surged from $16.6 billion in 2003 to a peak of $27.9 billion in 2008 before declining to $22.3 billion in 2009. Even with this rapid increase in U.S. exports to Singapore, the U.S. share of Singapore's imports has declined from 16% in 2003 to 12% in 2009. The main reason for this is that Singapore's overall trade is booming. Still, Singapore imports more from the United States ($28.5 billion) than from China ($26.0 billion).The U.S. balance of trade in services with Singapore declined from a surplus of $4.0 billion in 2001 to $1.2 billion 2005 but has risen to $4.2 billion in 2008. A significant increase has been in income from U.S. direct investments in Singapore. U.S. access to the Singaporean market for multinational corporations seems to have been enhanced considerably under the FTA. U.S. income from assets in Singapore rose from $6.7 billion in 2003 to $21.1 billion by 2008.

On the U.S. import side (Singapore's exports), a noteworthy development is that U.S. imports of pharmaceuticals from Singapore have risen from $0.09 billion in 2003 to $3.0 billion in 2007 before declining to $2.0 billion in 2008. Singapore has developed as a regional center for multinational pharmaceutical companies. This apparently was partly triggered by provisions in the FTA that required Singapore to strengthen its intellectual property protection.

Negotiations for the U.S.-Singapore Free Trade Agreement were launched under the Clinton Administration in December 2000. The FTA became the fifth such agreement the United States has signed and the first with an Asian country.

The U.S.-Singapore Free Trade Agreement (P.L. 108-78) went into effect on January 1, 2004. This report provides an overview of the major trade and economic developments Tfollowing the FTA over the five years ending in January 2010. It also includes selected information on key provisions of the agreement. As the United States and Singapore adjust to the provisions of the FTA, it becomes increasingly difficult to separate out the effects of the FTA from that which has occurred because of other economic forces. The effects of the global financial crisis and recession of 2008-2009 have had a major downward effect on trade flows, but some general conclusions still can be drawn.

The U.S.-Singapore FTA has taken on new importance in trade policy because the United States is engaged in negotiations to join the Trans-Pacific Partnership (TPP). The TPP negotiations are the first major market-opening initiative of the Obama Administration. On December 14, 2009, United States Trade Representative Ron Kirk notified Congress of the intent to enter into the TPP negotiations. The objective is to shape a high-standard, broad-based regional free trade agreement with Australia, Brunei Darussalam, Chile, New Zealand, Peru, Singapore, and Vietnam. The first round of negotiations began March 15, 2010, in Sydney, Australia. Singapore, Chile, Brunei, and New Zealand are the original members of the pact. The United States, Australia, Peru, and Vietnam are seeking to join. The United States already has FTAs with Singapore, Chile, Australia, and Peru. The TPP could become the basis for a Free Trade Area of the Asia-Pacific over the long term.[1]

The U.S.-Singapore FTA essentially eliminated tariffs on all goods traded between the two countries. It also included market access measures and other provisions related to trade in services, investment, rules of origin, intellectual property rights, government procurement, licensing of professionals, telecommunications, worker rights, the environment, capital controls, and dispute settlement.

The FTA has provided greater access for U.S. companies, has been instrumental in increasing bilateral trade, and has provided reassurance to Singaporeans of U.S. interest in the country at a time when many in the region perceived that the United States had been focused on the Middle East and "neglecting" Asia. The FTA seems to have benefitted overall bilateral relations. The FTA has provided certain advantages to American businesses, but since Singapore has FTAs with many other nations, those advantages often are extended to other nations as well.

As a city-state, Singapore operates as an *entrepot* and shipping center and basically has free trade with almost all countries. It imposes import restrictions on only a handful of goods. Under the FTA, Singapore made concessions that dealt mainly with providing greater access for American service providers (particularly financial services) and with strengthening the business environment in areas such as the protection of intellectual property rights and access to government procurement.

In 2009, the United States ran a $6.6 billion surplus in its balance of merchandise trade with Singapore, up from $1.4 billion in 2003, but down from the $12.0 billion in 2008. U.S. exports of goods to Singapore surged from $16.6 billion in 2003 to a peak of $27.9 billion in 2008 before declining to $22.3 billion in 2009. Major U.S. exports to Singapore include machinery, electrical machinery, aircraft, optical and medical instruments, plastic, and mineral fuel oil. U.S. trade with Singapore has increased faster than anticipated before the FTA.

Even with this rapid increase in U.S. exports to Singapore, however, the U.S. share of Singapore's imports has declined from 16% in 2003 to 12% in 2009.[2] The main reason for this is that Singapore's overall trade is booming. Still, Singapore imports more from the United States ($28.5 billion) than from China ($26.0 billion). Malaysia is Singapore's top source of imports, while the United States is second, and China is third. Imports from China, however, have been rising rapidly, and China has passed Japan as a source of imports.

The U.S. balance of trade in services with Singapore declined from a surplus of $4.0 billion in 2001 to $1.2 billion in 2005 but rose to $4.2 billion in 2008. While U.S. receipts of royalties and license fees ($3.2 billion) and exports of other private services ($4.2 billion) have increased, so have U.S. payments for other private services ($2.1 billion) and for travel and transportation ($1.3 billion). A significant increase has been in income from U.S. direct investments in Singapore. U.S. access to the Singaporean market for multinational corporations seems to have been enhanced considerably under the FTA. U.S. income from assets in Singapore rose from $6.7 billion in 2003 to $21.1 billion by 2008. As an example of U.S. service providers in Singapore under the FTA, Citibank has been able to expand its operations there (it has 50% of the credit card market), offer innovative products (such as biometric identification for bill paying), and partner with the subway system to issue credit cards that double as subway fare cards and to locate branches and ATM terminals in and around subway stations.

On the U.S. import side (Singapore's exports), a noteworthy development is that U.S. imports of pharmaceuticals from Singapore have risen dramatically from $0.09 billion in 2003 to $3.0 billion in 2007 before declining to $2.0 billion in 2008. In 2008, Singapore was the seventh largest supplier of pharmaceuticals to the United States. The FTA did not lower the U.S. tariff rate for pharmaceuticals, since such products already enter the United States duty free. What appears to have occurred has been the development of Singapore as a regional center for multinational pharmaceutical companies. This apparently was partly triggered by provisions in the FTA that required Singapore to strengthen its intellectual property protection. The Singaporean government also has provided incentives for multinational biomedical companies to locate research and production in the country. Most of the major pharmaceutical companies of the world have established subsidiaries in Singapore and are exporting part of their production.

Singapore has relatively high labor standards. It ratified the International Labor Organization's Minimum Age Convention in 2005. This brought the number of ILO

Conventions the country has ratified to more than 20, including Core Conventions that cover child labor, forced labor, collective bargaining, and equal remuneration.

As a city state with 3.4 million people and an area roughly the size of the Washington, DC, area inside the Beltway, Singapore's environmental challenges relate primarily to industrial pollution (strictly regulated), urbanization, and preservation of natural areas. The country touts itself as a garden city. It recycles all waste water, appears clean, and uses variable tolls to alleviate traffic congestion. The United States has not formally raised environmental or labor issues with Singapore under the FTA.

For details on the content of the FTA, see CRS Report RL31789, *The U.S.-Singapore Free Trade Agreement*, by Dick K. Nanto.

TRADE IN GOODS

Since the U.S.-Singapore FTA came into effect in January 2004, U.S. trade with Singapore has boomed. As shown in **Figure 1**, U.S. exports of merchandise to Singapore rose by 68% from $16.6 billion in 2003 to a peak of $27.9 billion in 2008 before the global financial crisis depressed world trade in 2009. In 2009, U.S. exports to Singapore were at $22.3 billion. U.S. imports from Singapore increased by a lesser 22% to go from $15.1 billion in 2003 to a peak of $18.4 billion in 2007 before declining to $15.7 billion in 2009 or approximately the same level as prior to the FTA. The U.S. trade surplus with Singapore rose from $1.4 billion in 2003 to a peak of $12.0 billion in 2008 before declining to $6.6 billion in 2009.

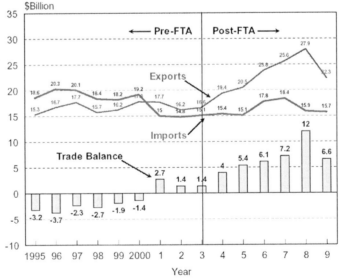

Source: Congressional Research Service. Data from U.S. Bureau of Economic Analysis accessed through Global Trade Atlas.

Figure 1. U.S. Merchandise Exports to, Imports from, and Trade Balance with Singapore

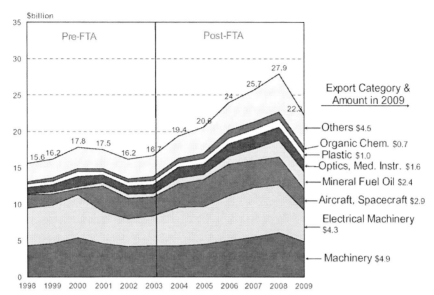

Source: Data from U.S. Department of Commerce on f.a.s. Basis.

Figure 2. Leading U.S. Exports to Singapore by Category

Major U.S. exports to Singapore include machinery, electrical machinery, aircraft/spacecraft, mineral fuel and oil, optical and medical instruments, plastic, and organic chemicals. As shown in Figure 2, U.S. exports of each of these products have risen since the U.S.-Singapore FTA took effect in January 2004, although they declined in 2009 because of the global financial crisis. The highly developed nature of the city-state's economy can be seen in the major U.S. exports there. They consist primarily of industrial and scientific machinery and materials.

The rising surplus in merchandise trade with Singapore, however, masks other underlying trends that do not bode as well for the United States. Although Singapore's share of U.S. exports to the world has remained at about 2.3% to 2.1%, Singapore's imports from the United States have been declining relative to those from many other countries of the world. As shown in **Table 1**, in 2001, the United States accounted for 16.4% of Singapore's imports. By 2009, that share had fallen to 12%, despite the rapid growth in U.S. exports there. Still, Singapore imports more from the United States ($28.5 billion) than from China ($26.0 billion). Malaysia is Singapore's top source of imports, while the United States is second, and China is third. Imports from China, however, have been rising rapidly, and China has passed Japan as a source of imports.

The surplus in the U.S. balance of merchandise trade with Singapore runs contrary to a commonly held perception that free trade agreements lead to larger U.S. deficits in trade. The perception seems to be generated mostly by U.S. trade with its immediate neighbors, Canada and Mexico. As shown in **Figure 3**, in 2009, the United States ran trade surpluses with Australia, Singapore, Chile, the Dominican Republic, Morocco, and seven other FTA countries, while it ran deficits with Mexico, Canada, Israel, Costa Rica, and Nicaragua.

During the FTA talks with Singapore, negotiations were intense over that country's import restrictions on a few products. Even though Singapore is largely a free-trade nation, it has restrictions on imports of specific controlled items (including chewing gum) and has import duties on beer, stout, and a local beverage called *samsu*. Under the FTA, Singapore allowed imports from the United States of chewing gum with "therapeutic value" (excluding nicotine gum) to be sold in pharmacies. The country also dropped all duties on beer, stout, and *samsu* from the United States.

Table 1. Singapore's Import Market Shares by Import Source (Percent of Total Imports)

Rank	Import Source	2001	2003	2006	2009
1	Malaysia	17.3	15.8	13.1	11.6
2	United States	16.4	13.1	12.5	11.3
3	China	6.2	8.1	11.4	10.1
4	Japan	13.9	11.3	8.3	7.6
5	Indonesia	7.1[a]	6.1	6.2	5.8
6	Korea, South	3.3	3.6	4.4	5.7
7	Taiwan	4.3	4.8	6.4	5.2
8	France	1.8	1.8	2.2	3.4
9	Thailand	4.4	4.0	3.7	3.4
10	Saudi Arabia	3.6	2.9	3.9	3.3
	Rest of world	23.4	28.5	30.2	36.0

Source: Underlying data from Global Trade Atlas
a. Estimated.

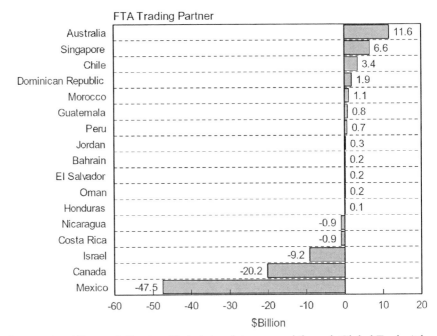

Source: Congressional Research Service. Underlying data accessed through Global Trade Atlas.
Notes: The United States has signed free trade agreements with Columbia, Panama, and South Korea that have not been approved by Congress and implemented.

Figure 3. U.S. Balance of Merchandise Trade with FTA Partner Countries

Under the FTA, U.S. exports of beer (made from malt, Harmonized System code 2203) rose from $0.352 million in 2003 to $0.648 million in 2005 but was at $0.505 million in 2009. As a share of Singapore's total imports of beer, however, in 2009, the United States accounted for about 0.5% of the total and ranked 18th among all sources of beer imports. The top six sources were Malaysia, Mexico, Belgium, the Netherlands, Thailand, and South Korea.[3] Among these countries, only Thailand and South Korea have free trade agreements with Singapore.

With respect to chewing gum, the data on Singaporean imports do not show appreciable imports from the United States. In 2009, out of a total of $850,309 in chewing gum imports (HS 170410), none came from the United States. $627,016 in chewing gum came from Indonesia and $112,907 that came from South Korea. As for imports from the United States in previous years, in 2005, Singapore imported $1,298 and 2006, $246 worth of American chewing gum.[4]

TRADE AND MARKET ACCESS IN SERVICES

U.S. business interests point out that the greatest potential effect of the U.S.-Singapore FTA is likely to be increased access by U.S. companies to Singapore's market in services. Services are provided in two ways: in cross-border transactions and from subsidiaries in the trading partner's economy. Services such as insurance, shipping, provision of intellectual property, and travel often are sold across borders and are counted as exports and imports. Other services, such as accounting, legal services, and banking often are provided directly to the consumer through overseas subsidiaries of U.S. companies. These transactions usually do not appear as exports or imports, although the repatriation of profits from such activity is counted as an income flow.

The United States has traditionally run a surplus in its balance of services trade with Singapore. This is shown in **Figure 4**. Under the FTA, this balance declined from $4.0 billion in 2001 to $2.6 billion in 2006 but has risen to $4.2 billion in 2009. Among the four components of trade in services, the United States ran surpluses in two and deficits in two. In royalties and license fees, the U.S. surplus increased from $2.5 billion in 2001 to $3.1 billion in 2008. Some of this rise in fees for intellectual property likely can be attributed to strengthened intellectual property protection in Singapore resulting from the FTA. In other private services, the U.S. surplus has fluctuated with a fall from $1.9 billion in 2001 to $0.7 billion in 2006 but a rise to $2.2 billion in 2008. In military and government transactions, the trade balance varies from year to year. It was -$0.04 billion in 2001, -$0.2 billion in 2006, and -$0.6 billion in 2008. In travel and transportation, the balance trends toward an increasingly large U.S. deficit. Most of this is in transportation, particularly shipping, as well as in passenger fares and travel. This negative balance grew from -$0.3 billion in 2001 to -$1.0 billion in 2006 but diminished to -$0.4 billion as the global financial crisis curtailed shipping and tourism.

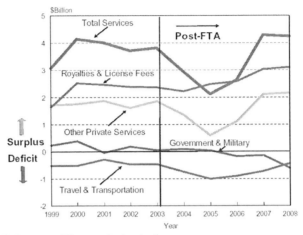

Source: Data from U.S. Bureau of Economic Analysis

Figure 4. U.S. Balance of Trade with Singapore in Services and Its Components

Increased market access in services under an FTA, therefore, may or may not result in an improvement in the U.S. bilateral trade balance in services. It depends on what kind of service is being traded and the relative comparative advantage of each country. U.S. service providers, moreover, may find it more advantageous under the increased access and strengthened intellectual property regime engendered by an FTA to locate a subsidiary in the FTA partner country. This may reduce U.S. exports of private services but also may increase royalties and payments from use of intellectual property and earnings from operations in the host country. In the Singapore case, U.S. income from assets owned in Singapore increased from $3.9 billion in 2001 to $6.7 billion in 2003, and after the FTA jumped to $14.3 billion in 2006 and $21.1 billion in 2008.[5] In 2008, Singaporean investors earned $6.3 billion on their assets in the United States for a $14.8 billion surplus for the United States. This is more than triple the U.S. surplus in trade in services.

Financial Services

In financial services, Singapore made several key concessions under the FTA. In 2007, the government lifted the ban on new licenses for full-service and wholesale American banks. Licensed full-service banks from the United States (two as of 2007) are now able to offer all their services at an unlimited number of locations. Under the first two years of the FTA, U.S.-licensed full-service banks were able to operate at up to 30 customer service locations (branches or off-premise ATMs). Non-U.S. full-service foreign banks have been allowed to operate at a combined 25 locations. Locally incorporated subsidiaries of U.S. banks are able to apply for access to the local automated teller machine (ATM) network on commercial terms, and branches of U.S. banks were to obtain access to the ATM network by 2008.[6]

Citibank, in particular, has been expanding its presence in Singapore. From four branches in 2004, it now has eleven full-service branches and more planned.[7] It was the first in Singapore to introduce a biometric payment system that allows payments without credit cards based on fingerprint identification. It also has joined with the Singapore MRT subway system to provide credit cards that double as subway tickets and to locate ATMs and branches in and around subway stations.[8] Citibank has a 50% share of the Singapore credit card market.[9] As of mid-2006, Citibank along with the other major foreign banks had created their own ATM network[10] rather than join that of the local banks. American banks are allowed under the FTA to enter the domestic ATM network if financial considerations warrant such a move.

Legal Services

In general, foreigners in Singapore cannot practice Singapore law (without local credentials), employ Singapore lawyers to practice Singapore law, or litigate in local courts. Since June 2004, however, U.S. and other foreign lawyers have been allowed to represent parties in arbitration in Singapore without the need for a Singapore attorney to be present. U.S. law firms can provide legal services with respect to Singapore law only through a joint venture or formal alliance with a Singapore law firm.[11] Under the FTA, Singapore has recognized law degrees from Harvard University, Columbia University, New York University, and the University of Michigan for the purpose of admission to practice law in Singapore. Also, since October 2006, graduates of these universities who are ranked among the top 70% of their graduating class may be admitted to the Singapore bar.[12]

ELECTRONIC COMMERCE

The FTA contains state-of-the-art provisions on electronic commerce, including national treatment and most-favored-nation obligations for products delivered electronically, affirmation that services disciplines cover all services delivered electronically, and permanent duty-free status of products delivered electronically.

INTELLECTUAL PROPERTY RIGHTS (IPR) PROTECTION

The FTA provided the impetus for the Singapore government to amend its laws to create one of the strongest IPR regimes in Asia.[13] In July 2004, amendments to the Trademarks Act, the Patents Act, the Layout Designs of Integrated Circuits Act, Registered Designs Act, a new Plant Varieties Protection Act, and a new Manufacture of Optical Discs Act came into effect. This was followed in 2005 by an amended Copyright Act and Broadcasting Act. Singapore also has implemented or ratified various international conventions or treaties dealing with IPRs.

Singaporean officials have indicated that the provisions in the FTA that strengthened IPR protection in Singapore have attracted foreign business investments. Recently, Microsoft, Pfizer, ISIS Pharmaceuticals, Motorola, Genentech, and Lucas Films have made new investments in operations in Singapore.[14]

In January 2010, the World Intellectual Property Organization (WIPO) of the United Nation established an office in Singapore to handle some of WIPO's dispute resolution activities. The Singapore office is to administer and facilitate hearings in cases conducted under WIPO arbitration rules and to provide training and advice on procedures such as arbitration, mediation and expert determination. The Singapore Office of WIPO aims to cater to regional needs and to make WIPO's experience and expertise in intellectual property alternative dispute resolution more accessible in the Asia-Pacific Region.[15]

INVESTMENTS

The U.S.-Singapore FTA provides for national and most-favored nation treatment for foreign investors. Investors have the right to make financial transfers freely and without delay. The FTA also provides for disciplines on performance requirements, for international law standards in the case of expropriation, and for access to binding international arbitration. In 2006, Singapore was the third largest destination for U.S. foreign direct investment in the Asia Pacific. U.S. direct investment (cumulative position) in Singapore was $40.8 billion in 2001, $51.1 billion in 2003, $81.9 billion in 2006, and $106.5 billion in 2008. By comparison, in 2008, it was $88.5 billion in Australia, $79.2 billion in Japan, $51.5 billion in Hong Kong, and $45.7 billion in China.[16]

According to the U.S. Department of Commerce, in 2004 and 2005, one of the strongest increases in the value added of overseas affiliates of U.S. multinational corporations was in manufacturing operations in Singapore. The attractiveness of the country as a "manufacturing base for the Asia-Pacific region was heightened by the enactment of the United States-Singapore Free Trade Agreement, which facilitates the shipment of inputs to production from the United States." In 2005, U.S. affiliates in Singapore accounted for 15% of Singapore's GDP, up from 13.2% in 2004 and second only to the share in GDP of U.S. affiliates in Ireland (18.5%). In 2005, U.S. non-bank affiliates in Singapore employed 123,600 persons, held assets of $150.7 billion, had sales of $162.7 billion, and generated net income of $18.7 billion. This net income in Singapore exceed that by U.S. non-bank affiliates in Japan ($15.0 billion), Australia ($13.0 billion), or China ($7.9 billion) for the same year.[17]

U.S. IMPORTS FROM SINGAPORE

Just as U.S. exports to Singapore have increased since the U.S.-Singapore FTA came into effect in 2004, so also have U.S. imports from Singapore. After the FTA, Imports rose by 22% from $15.1 billion in 2003 to $18.4 billion in 2007 (not adjusted for inflation) but as the global financial crisis curtailed international trade, imports from Singapore declined to $15.7 billion in 2008 and $15.7 in 2009. Since the FTA, therefore, U.S. exports have increased considerably more than U.S. imports.

By sector, the growth rates for imports vary considerably. **Figure 5** shows the average annual growth rates for the four years prior to and for the five years after the FTA was implemented for the top 40 products (by 2-digit Harmonized System code) imported from Singapore. In 2009, the value of these products ranged from a low of $3.9 million for nickel to $4,639.6 million for machinery. Imports from Singapore are concentrated in the top six categories each with amounts exceeding $1 billion. Together these six accounted for 91% of the total imports from Singapore in 2009.

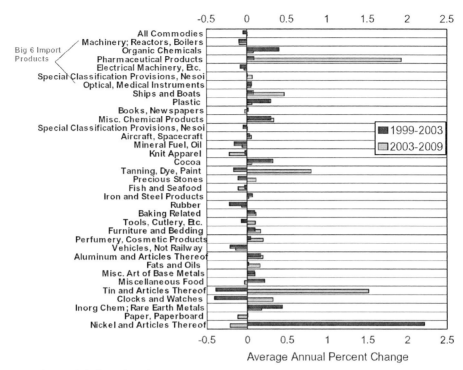

Source: Data from Global Trade Atlas

Figure 5. Average Annual Growth Rates in Top 40 U.S. Imports from Singapore Pre- and Post-FTA

One of the concerns expressed during consideration of the FTA was that it would increase significantly imports of textiles and apparel from Singapore. This has not occurred. In 2009, there were no imports of knitted or crocheted fabrics. Since 2003, imports of woven apparel fell by 39% per year from $38 million to $3 million in 2009, and imports of knit apparel likewise fell by 22% per year from $233 million to $68 million.

The most significant gains have been in U.S. imports of pharmaceuticals from Singapore. Imports of such products jumped from $0.09 billion in 2003 to $3.0 billion in 2007, although they declined to $2.0 billion in 2009.[18] Singapore is the ninth largest supplier of pharmaceuticals to the United States, behind Belgium, Israel, and Switzerland, but ahead of Italy, Japan, and India. The vast majority (95%) of these imports ($1.9 billion) were cardiovascular medicaments (HS 3004909120).

The increase in imports of pharmaceuticals from Singapore cannot be attributed to a reduction in U.S. tariffs under the FTA. Pharmaceuticals already enter the United States duty free. Rather what appears to have occurred is the development of Singapore as a regional center for multinational pharmaceutical companies—both for manufacturing and for research and development. Two major factors have contributed to this. The first is the strengthening of intellectual property protection and new or revised laws in Singapore. The second is the development of a biomedical industrial park (Tuas Medical Park) for pharmaceutical companies to locate production and other facilities plus a research complex called Biopolis that houses biomedical research institutes, councils, and related organizations.

Multinational companies have come to dominate the manufacture of pharmaceuticals in Singapore. These include Merck Sharp and Dohme, Aventis, GlaxoSmithKline, Pfizer,

Schering-Plough, Wyeth, and Eli Lilly.[19] Singapore is increasingly becoming a base for both regional and global pharmaceutical production for a growing number of multinational companies. The government goal is to have at least ten multinational pharmaceutical manufacturing facilities operational in Singapore by 2010. Much of the production is for export, particularly to North America and Europe. Exports from other Asian countries also flow into Singapore for re-export. The country exports more pharmaceuticals than any other "Asian Tiger" economy (Hong Kong, Taiwan, and South Korea).[20]

Before the FTA, a sizable proportion of Singapore's pharmaceutical exports were transshipments from other countries. While such re-exports continue to increase, exports of domestic production now dominate. **Figure 6** shows Singapore's global exports of pharmaceuticals and the rapid increase in domestic exports relative to re-exports. From 2002 to 2006, the re-export share of all pharmaceutical exports dropped from 60% to 11%.

BALANCE OF TRADE BY SECTORS

In the modern globalized economy, much trade is intra-industry. The old economic model of trade in which each country specializes in certain products and exchanges them for others in which it has a comparative disadvantage only remotely resembles trade between industrialized economies populated by multinational enterprises. In many cases, the United States both imports and exports products in the same sector. Some of this trade may occur within a manufacturer's supply chain that may straddle several countries. For example, an electronic product may be designed and marketed in the United States, but final assembly may be in Singapore using components from the United States as well as from other economies in the region. The U.S. balance of trade in goods with Singapore is shown in **Figure 7** by two-digit Harmonized System codes.

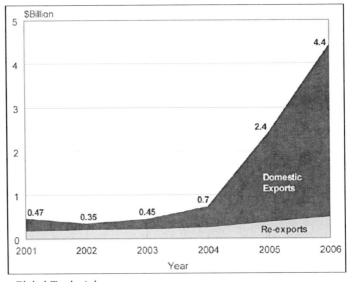

Source: Data from Global Trade Atlas

Figure 6. Singapore's Exports of Pharmaceutical Products by Origin

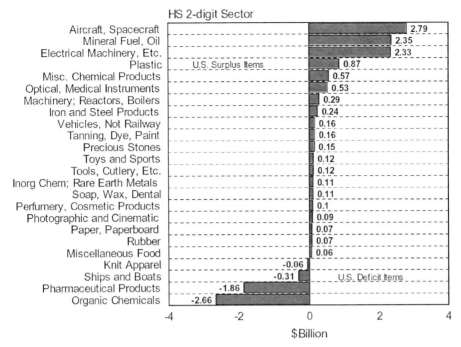

HS 2-digit Sector

Source: Data from Global Trade Atlas
Note: Includes sectors with either a surplus or deficit greater than $50 million.

Figure 7. U.S.-Singapore Balance of Trade by Major Surplus and Deficit Sectors, 2009

The balance of trade by sectors also indicates how trade with Singapore may be affecting sectoral employment in the United States. The first observation is that the U.S. aerospace products, mineral fuel and oil, and electrical machinery producers are doing well in Singapore. The U.S. trade surplus in each exceeds $2.3 billion. The largest U.S. sectoral deficits in trade are in organic chemicals (-$2.7 billion) and pharmaceutical products (-$1.9 billion). Most other sectors are experiencing either small surpluses or small deficits in bilateral trade—less than $1 billion. (The sectors not shown in **Figure 7** had balances with an absolute value of less than $60 million.)

LABOR ISSUES

In the U.S.-Singapore FTA, labor obligations are part of the core text of the trade agreement. Both parties were to reaffirm their obligations as members of the International Labor Organization, and they are to strive to ensure that their domestic laws provide for labor standards consistent with internationally recognized labor principles. The agreement also contains language that it is inappropriate to weaken or reduce domestic labor protections to encourage trade or investment. The agreement further requires parties to effectively enforce their own domestic labor laws. This obligation is to be enforceable through the agreement's dispute settlement procedures.

Singapore has ratified 24 ILO Conventions (20 in force), including five Core Conventions that cover child labor (ratified in 2001); forced labor; collective bargaining, and equal remuneration (ratified in 2002). The country ratified the Minimum Age Convention in November 2005 after the FTA went into effect. Unless otherwise indicated, the other conventions were ratified in 1965. (The United States has ratified 14 ILO Conventions [12 in force] including 2 [Forced Labor and Child Labor] of the five Core Conventions.)[21]

In 2009 Singapore's national labor force was made up of approximately 2.99 million workers of which about 500,000 were unionized and represented by 68 unions. Almost all of the unions (which represent virtually all of the union members) were affiliated with the National Trade Union Congress (NTUC), an umbrella organization with a close relationship with the government.

In a 2009 study of the U.S.-Singapore FTA, the Government Accountability Office concluded the following:[22]

> Singapore generally had strong protections for workers going into the FTA and has since improved them. As a high-income economy, Singapore provides good working conditions and a broad range of social benefits for most of its workers, and U.S. officials involved in the negotiations said changes in Singapore's labor laws were not needed to conclude the FTA. The International Trade Union Confederation (ITUC) reports that there are some restrictions on unions in Singapore's labor laws, but many of the restrictions are not applied in practice. U.S. FTA negotiators were initially concerned by Singapore's lack of a minimum wage law, but these concerns were allayed by an understanding of Singapore's unique system for determining wage increases through the annual recommendations of a National Wages Council that is composed of government, trade union, and employer representatives. U.S. embassy officials said Singapore has made changes in its laws to improve worker protections since the FTA took force. The embassy officials stated that, for example, a workplace safety and health act was enacted to provide safety protections to a broader range of workers.

> State's 2008 human rights report indicates that Singapore's Ministry of Manpower effectively enforced its laws and regulations on working conditions, safety and health standards, and child labor. (p. 37)

> No U.S. activity or assistance on labor has been provided since the FTA went into effect, according to ILAB (U.S. Bureau of International Labor Affairs) officials. Singapore has high labor standards and relatively few labor problems, as indicated in the FTA labor rights report. U.S. officials told us that because Singapore's labor laws and enforcement systems were good, they did not see a need for extensive cooperation and, furthermore, Singapore had not requested it.... Despite the provisions in the labor cooperation annex and the expectations of negotiators in both countries, neither U.S. nor Singapore government officials were aware of any technical cooperation activities concerning labor since the FTA was implemented. However, Singaporean officials told us they were cooperating on labor issues with other trade partners, such as the Trans-Pacific Strategic Economic Partnership that also includes Chile, New Zealand, and Brunei Darussalam. (p. 44)

ENVIRONMENTAL ISSUES

In the U.S.-Singapore FTA, both parties agreed to ensure that their domestic environmental laws provide for high levels of environmental protection and that they are to strive to continue to improve such laws. They are not to weaken or reduce domestic environmental protections to encourage trade or investment. The agreement also requires that parties effectively enforce their own domestic environmental laws. This obligation is to be enforceable through the agreement's dispute settlement procedures.

Since Singapore is an island (3.4 million population) the size of the Washington, DC, area inside the Beltway, it has virtually no natural resources. Its environmental issues are characteristic of a highly urbanized city. It has no problems associated with mining, forestry, or large-scale agriculture. Singapore touts itself as the "garden city of the East." It is relatively clean, ordered, and well-planned. Waste water is purified and recycled. The restricted space available in the country raises issues pertaining to industrial pollution (tightly regulated), urbanization, and the protection of the few natural areas still existing. Vehicular traffic is alleviated by charging special tolls to travel into the inner city during rush hours and by levying taxes and other fees on new or used cars.[23]

CARGO SECURITY

The closer economic links established under the FTA appear to have assisted in areas such as cargo security. In December 2007, Singapore announced that it was to conduct a six-month trial project under the Secure Freight Initiative. Under this initiative, 100% of U.S.-bound shipping containers are to be scanned for nuclear or radiological materials before being loaded on ships. Singapore is to be one of seven ports participating in the trial.[24]

The Ports Command in Singapore already had been cooperating with the United States in various security initiatives. It now scans about 15% of the 24 million cargo containers that pass through its ports, and it is able to scan an incoming container truck in less than one minute. In March 2003, Singapore was the first country to sign on to the U.S.-sponsored Cargo Security Initiative.[25]

OTHER EFFECTS

The U.S.-Singapore FTA also generated non-economic effects. At a time when many in Southeast Asia perceive that the United States is distracted by events in the Middle East and not paying enough attention to Asia, the FTA provided some degree of reassurance of U.S. interest in the region. It also created a bandwagon effect as Malaysia, Thailand, and South Korea soon followed with negotiations of their own for an FTA with the United States. Singapore has supported the U.S.-backed proposal to create a Free Trade Area of the Asia Pacific under the Asia Pacific Economic Cooperation forum. It also has aggressively been concluding other FTAs that eventually could form the basis for this proposed free trade area.

In addition, the closer economic ties under the U.S.-Singapore FTA contributed to more diplomatic and military cooperation with Singapore. In July 2005, the United States and Singapore signed a Strategic Framework Agreement that extended bilateral cooperation to defense and security. Located in the midst of several secular Muslim nations, Singapore has been active in cooperating with the United States in political and security cooperation in the global counterterrorism campaign.

Singapore has been at the forefront of cooperating with neighboring countries and the United States to enhance maritime security in nearby waters, especially in the Strait of

Malacca where terrorist threats and piracy have been problems. Singapore also has cooperated extensively to ensure the security of cargo bound for the United States. Singapore also continues to welcome port visits by the U.S. Navy and allows U.S. aircraft carriers to use the special pier at its naval base built especially to accommodate such large ships.[26]

In 2007, when Buddhist-led demonstrations erupted in Burma, Singapore held the Chair of ASEAN, the Association of Southeast Asian Nations, of which Burma/Myanmar is a member. Despite the tradition of non-interference in domestic affairs of the member states, Singapore supported investigation of the protests in Burma by the Special U.N. Envoy to Myanmar Ibrahim Gambari. Singapore also continued its bilateral and multilateral intelligence and law enforcement cooperation to investigate terrorist groups with a focus on Jemaah Islamiya, a group that had plotted to carry out attacks in Singapore in the past.[27]

End Notes

[1] Office of the U.S. Trade Representative, *U.S. Engagement with the Trans-Pacific Partnership: Action to Date*, Washington, DC, December 14, 2009. "New Trans-Pacific Partnership Talks to Take Center Stage in 2010," *International Trade Reporter*, January 21, 2010. See also CRS Report R40502, *The Trans-Pacific Strategic Economic Partnership Agreement*, by Ian F. Fergusson and Bruce Vaughn.

[2] Data sources for this introductory overview are provided in later sections of this report.

[3] Data are from Global Trade Atlas.

[4] Data are from Global Trade Atlas. CRS attempted to obtain export data from a major U.S. chewing gum company, but it declined to cooperate. Likewise, the International Chewing Gum association would not provide CRS with data on exports to Singapore.

[5] U.S. Bureau of Economic Analysis. Balance of payments data by country. Some of these assets may be in securities.

[6] U.S. Trade Representative. *2007 National Trade Estimate Report on Foreign Trade Barriers*. Online version at http://www.ustr.gov/Document_Library/Reports_Publications/2007/2007_NTE_Report/Section_Index.html.

[7] See Citibank Singapore website at http://www.citibank.com.sg.

[8] Citigroup Inc. *Citibank Singapore Expands its Customer Touchpoint Network by 60% with SMRT Partnership*. Press Release, July 16, 2007.

[9] Citibank Offers First Travel Card in Region. *The Straits Times*, August 18, 2007, p. S31.

[10] ATM5 is the shared ATM network of ABN AMRO, Citibank, HSBC, Maybank and Standard Chartered. Banks.

[11] As of October 2005, 16 of the 64 foreign law firms in Singapore were from the United States.

[12] U.S. Trade Representative, *2007 National Trade Estimate Report.*

[13] For details, see Economist Intelligence Unit. Singapore: Licensing and Intellectual Property. EIU ViewsWire, New York, July 6, 2007.

[14] Meetings with government officials in Singapore, August 2007.

[15] The Bureau of National Affairs, Inc. , "WIPO to Set Up Office in Singapore," *International Trade Reporter*, August 20, 2009.

[16] U.S. Bureau of Economic Analysis. On a historical cost basis.

[17] Mataloni, Ray. Operations of U.S. Multinational Companies in 2005. *Survey of Current Business*, November 2007. pp. 48-49, 51, 58.

[18] Data are from the U.S. Department of Commerce. Note that according to Singaporean trade data, in 2009, Singapore exported a total of $4,685 million in pharmaceuticals of which $1,417 million went to Canada, $786 million to the Netherlands, and $695 million to the United States.

[19] The Singapore Association of Pharmaceutical Industries lists 34 companies as members.

[20] Espicom Business Intelligence Ltd. The Pharmaceutical Market: Singapore. November 2006. (Report description).

[21] International Labour Organization. See website at http://www.ilo.org.

[22] U.S. Government Accountability Office, *International Trade, Four Free Trade Agreements GAO Reviewed Have Resulted in Commercial Benefits, but Challenges on Labor and Environment Remain*, GAO-09-439, July 2009, p. 37.

[23] Tan, Alan K.J. "Preliminary Assessment of Singapore's Environmental Law." United Nations Online Network in Public Administration and Finance report. June 24, 2007.

[24] U.S. Embassy, Singapore. Singapore Participates in Six-month Trial Project to Scan Shipping Containers Bound for the United States under Secure Freight Initiative. Press Release. December 17, 2007.

[25] U.S. Customs and Border Protection. Singapore to Scan U.S.-Bound Cargo as Part of Secure Freight Initiative. Press Release, December 17, 2007. Maritime and Port Authority of Singapore. "A Port's Role," Presentation at the International Association of Ports and Harbors Asia/Oceania Regional Meeting, February 1-2, 2007.

[26] Although, Singapore did send some 191 troops—mostly sailors on a ship—to Iraq in 2003, it withdrew them in March 2005 because the small size of Singapore's Navy made the one ship critical in the rotation of duties at home.

[27] U.S. Department of State, Office of the Coordinator for Counterterrorism. *Country Reports on Terrorism*, April 30, 2007.

In: U.S.-Singapore Free Trade Agreement after Five Years
ISBN: 978-1-61122-350-7
Editor: Robert E. Flemchak
© 2011 Nova Science Publishers, Inc.

Chapter 2

UNITED STATES - SINGAPORE FREE TRADE AGREEMENT

Robert E. Flemchak

The Government of the United States and the Government of the Republic of Singapore ("the Parties"),

Recognizing their longstanding friendship and important trade and investment relationship;

Recognizing that open and competitive markets are the key drivers of economic efficiency, innovation and wealth creation;

Recognizing the importance of ongoing liberalization of trade in goods and services at the multilateral level;

Aware of the growing importance of trade and investment for the economies of the Asia-Pacific region;

Reaffirming their rights, obligations and undertakings under the Marrakesh Agreement Establishing the World Trade Organization, and other multilateral, regional, and bilateral agreements and arrangements to which they are both Parties;

Recognizing that economic development, social development, and environmental protection are interdependent and mutually reinforcing components of sustainable development, and that an open and non-discriminatory multilateral trading system can play a major role in achieving sustainable development;

Reaffirming their commitment to achieving the Asia-Pacific Economic Co-operation goals of free and open trade and investment;

Reaffirming their commitment to securing trade liberalization and an outward-looking approach to trade and investment;

Reaffirming their shared commitment to facilitating bilateral trade through removing or reducing technical, sanitary and phytosanitary barriers to the movement of goods between the Parties;

Desiring to promote competition;

Desiring to promote transparency and to eliminate bribery and corruption in business transactions;

Recognizing that liberalized trade in goods and services will assist the expansion of trade and investment flows, raise the standard of living, and create new employment opportunities in their respective territories;

Desiring to expand trade in services on a mutually advantageous basis, under conditions of transparency and progressive liberalization, with the aim of securing an overall balance of rights and obligations, while recognizing the rights of each Party to regulate, and to introduce new regulations, giving due respect to national policy objectives;

Reaffirming the importance of pursuing the above in a manner consistent with the protection and enhancement of the environment, including through regional environmental cooperative activities and implementation of multilateral environmental agreements to which they are both parties; and

Affirming their commitment to encourage the accession to this Agreement by other States in order to further the liberalization of trade in goods and services between States;

Have *agreed* as follows:

1. ESTABLISHMENT OF A FREE TRADE AREA AND DEFINITIONS

Article 1.1: General

1. The Parties to this Agreement, consistent with Article XXIV of GATT 1994 and Article V of GATS, hereby establish a free trade area in accordance with the provisions of this Agreement.
2. The Parties reaffirm their existing rights and obligations with respect to each other under existing bilateral and multilateral agreements to which both Parties are party, including the WTO Agreement.
3. This Agreement shall not be construed to derogate from any international legal obligation between the Parties that entitles goods or services, or suppliers of goods or services, to treatment more favorable than that accorded by this Agreement.

Article 1.2: General Definitions

For purposes of this Agreement, unless otherwise specified:

1. **Customs Valuation Agreement** means the WTO Agreement on Implementation of Article VII of the General Agreement on Tariffs and Trade 1994;
2. **days** means calendar days;
3. **enterprise** means any entity constituted or organized under applicable law, whether or not for profit, and whether privately-owned or governmentally-owned, including any corporation, trust, partnership, sole proprietorship, joint venture or other association;
4. **enterprise of a Party** means an enterprise constituted or organized under the law of a Party;
5. **GATS** means the General Agreement on Trade in Services;
6. **GATT 1994** means the General Agreement on Tariffs and Trade 1994;
7. **goods of a Party** means domestic products as these are understood in GATT 1994 or such goods as the Parties may agree, and includes originating goods of that Party;
8. **government procurement** means the process by which a government obtains the use of or acquires goods or services, or any combination thereof, for governmental purposes and not with a view to commercial sale or resale, or use in the production or supply of goods or services for commercial sale or resale;
9. **measure** includes any law, regulation, procedure, requirement or practice;
10. **national** means a natural person referred to in Annex 1A;
11. **originating good** has the meaning established in Chapter 3 (Rules of Origin);
12. **person** means a natural person or enterprise;
13. **person of a Party** means a national or an enterprise of a Party;
14. **territory** means for a Party the territory of that Party as set out in Annex 1A;
15. **TRIPS Agreement** means the Agreement on Trade-Related Aspects of Intellectual Property Rights;
16. **WTO** means the World Trade Organization; and
17. **WTO Agreement** means the Marrakesh Agreement Establishing the World Trade Organization.

Annex 1A. Certain Definitions

For purposes of this Agreement:

1. **national** means:
    (a) with respect to Singapore, any person who is a citizen within the meaning of its Constitution and domestic laws; and
    (b) with respect to the United States, national of the United States as defined in Title III of the Immigration and Nationality Act.
2. **territory** means:

(a) with respect to Singapore, its land territory, internal waters and territorial sea as well as the maritime zones beyond the territorial sea, including the seabed and subsoil, over which the Republic of Singapore exercises sovereign rights or jurisdiction under its national laws and international law for the purpose of exploration and exploitation of the natural resources of such areas; and

(b) with respect to the United States,

    (i) the customs territory of the United States which includes the 50 states, the District of Columbia and Puerto Rico;

    (ii) the foreign trade zones located in the United States and Puerto Rico; and

    (iii) any areas beyond the territorial seas of the United States within which, in accordance with international law and its domestic law, the United States may exercise rights with respect to the seabed and subsoil and their natural resources.

2. NATIONAL TREATMENT AND MARKET ACCESS FOR GOODS

Article 2.1: National Treatment

Each Party shall accord national treatment to the goods of the other Party in accordance with Article III of GATT 1994, including its interpretative notes. To this end, Article III of GATT 1994 and its interpretative notes are incorporated into and made a part of this Agreement, subject to Annex 2A.

Article 2.2: Elimination of Duties

1. Except as otherwise provided in this Agreement, each Party shall progressively eliminate its customs duties on originating goods of the other Party in accordance with Annexes 2B (U.S. Schedule) and 2C (Singapore Schedule).

2. A Party shall not increase an existing customs duty or introduce a new customs duty on imports of an originating good, other than as permitted by this Agreement, subject to Annex 2A.

3. Upon request by any Party, the Parties shall consult to consider accelerating the elimination of customs duties as set out in their respective schedules. An agreement by the Parties to accelerate the elimination of customs duties on an originating good shall be treated as an amendment to Annexes 2B and 2C, and shall enter into force after the Parties have exchanged written notification certifying that they have completed necessary internal legal procedures and on such date or dates as may be agreed between them.

Article 2.3: Customs Value

Each Party shall apply the provisions of the Customs Valuation Agreement for the purposes of determining the customs value of goods traded between the Parties.

Article 2.4: Export Tax

A Party shall not adopt or maintain any duty, tax or other charge on the export of any good to the territory of the other Party.

Article 2.5: Temporary Admission

1. Each Party shall grant duty-free temporary admission for the following goods, imported by or for the use of a resident of the other Party:
    (a) professional equipment, including software and broadcasting and cinematographic equipment, necessary for carrying out the business activity, trade, or profession of a business person who qualifies for temporary entry pursuant to the laws of the importing country; and
    (b) goods intended for display or demonstration at exhibitions, fairs, or similar events, including commercial samples for the solicitation of orders, and advertising films.
2. A Party shall not condition the duty-free temporary admission of a good referred to in paragraph 1, other than to require that such good:
    (a) be used solely by or under the personal supervision of a resident of the other Party in the exercise of the business activity, trade, or profession of that person;
    (b) not be sold or leased or consumed while in its territory;
    (c) be accompanied by a security in an amount no greater than the charges that would otherwise be owed on entry or final importation, releasable on exportation of the good;
    (d) be capable of identification when exported;
    (e) be exported on the departure of that person or within such other period of time as is reasonably related to the purpose of the temporary admission, to a maximum period of three years from the date of importation;
    (f) be imported in no greater quantity than is reasonable for its intended use; and
    (g) be otherwise admissible into the Party's territory under its laws.
3. If any condition that a Party imposes under paragraph 2 has not been fulfilled, the Party may apply the customs duty and any other charge that would normally be owed on entry or final importation of the good.
4. Each Party, through its Customs authorities, shall adopt procedures providing for the expeditious release of the goods described in paragraph 1. To the extent possible, when such goods accompany a resident of the other Party seeking temporary entry, and are imported by that person for use in the exercise of a business activity, trade, or profession of that person, the procedures shall allow for the goods to be released simultaneously with the entry of that person subject to the necessary documentation required by the Customs authorities of the importing Party.
5. Each Party shall, at the request of the person concerned and for reasons deemed valid by its Customs authorities, extend the time limit for temporary admission beyond the period initially fixed.
6. Each Party shall permit temporarily admitted goods to be exported through a customs port other than that through which they were imported.

7. Each Party shall relieve the importer of liability for failure to export a temporarily admitted good upon presentation of satisfactory proof to the Party's Customs authorities that the good has been destroyed within the original time limit for temporary admission or any lawful extension. Prior approval will have to be sought from the Customs authorities of the importing Party before the good can be so destroyed.

Article 2.6: Goods Re-Entered after Repair or Alteration

1. A Party shall not apply a customs duty to a good, regardless of its origin, that re-enters its territory after that good has been exported temporarily from its territory to the territory of the other Party for repair or alteration, regardless of whether such repair or alteration could be performed in its territory.
2. A Party shall not apply a customs duty to a good, regardless of its origin, imported temporarily from the territory of the other Party for repair or alteration.
3. For purposes of this Article:
    (a) the repairs or alterations shall not destroy the essential characteristics of the good, or change it into a different commercial item;
    (b) operations carried out to transform unfinished goods into finished goods shall not be considered repairs or alterations; and
    (c) parts or pieces of the goods may be subject to repairs or alterations.

Article 2.7: Import and Export Restrictions

1. Except as otherwise provided in this Agreement, a Party shall not adopt or maintain any prohibition or restriction on the importation of any good of the other Party or on the exportation or sale for export of any good destined for the territory of the other Party, except in accordance with Article XI of GATT 1994, including its interpretative notes, and to this end Article XI of GATT 1994, including its interpretative notes, is incorporated into and made a part of this Agreement.
2. The Parties understand that the GATT 1994 rights and obligations incorporated by paragraph 1 prohibit, in any circumstances in which any other form of restriction is prohibited, export price requirements and, except as permitted in enforcement of countervailing and antidumping orders and undertakings, import price requirements.
3. In the event that a Party adopts or maintains a prohibition or restriction on the importation from or exportation to a non-Party of a good, nothing in this Agreement shall be construed to prevent the Party from:
    (a) limiting or prohibiting the importation from the territory of the other Party of such good of that non-Party; or
    (b) requiring as a condition of export of such good of the Party to the territory of the other Party, that the good not be re-exported to the non-Party, directly or indirectly, without being consumed in the territory of the other Party.
4. Paragraphs 1 through 3 shall not apply to the measures set out in Annex 2A.
5. Nothing in this Article shall be construed to affect a Party's rights and obligations under the WTO Agreement on Textiles and Clothing.

Article 2.8: Merchandise Processing Fee

A Party shall not adopt or maintain a merchandise processing fee for originating goods.

Article 2.9: Distilled Spirits

Singapore shall harmonize its excise taxes on imported and domestic distilled spirits. Such harmonization of the aforesaid excise duties shall be carried out in stages and shall be completed by 2005.

Article 2.10: Broadcasting Apparatus

A Party shall not maintain any import ban on broadcasting apparatus, including satellite dishes.

Article 2.11: Chewing Gum

Singapore shall allow the importation of chewing gum with therapeutic value for sale and supply, and may subject such products to laws and regulations relating to health products.

Article 2.12: Tariff Treatment of Non-Originating Cotton and Man-Made Fiber Apparel Goods (Tariff Preference Levels)

1. Subject to paragraphs 3 and 4, the United States shall apply the applicable rate of duty under paragraph 2 to imports of cotton or man-made fiber apparel goods provided for in Chapters 61 and 62 of the Harmonized System and covered by the U.S. categories listed in Annex 2B that are both cut (or knit to shape) and sewn or otherwise assembled in Singapore from fabric or yarn produced or obtained outside the territory of a Party, and that meet the applicable conditions for preferential tariff treatment under this Agreement, other than the condition that they be originating goods.

2. The rate of duty applicable to goods described in paragraph 1 is the United States most-favored-nation rate of duty reduced in five equal annual increments, beginning on the date this Article enters into force, such that the rate of duty shall be zero beginning on the first day of the fifth year after that date .

3. Paragraph 1 shall not apply to imports of goods described in that paragraph in quantities greater than:
   (a) 25,000,000 square meter equivalents ("SME") in the first year following entry into force of this Article;
   (b) 21,875,000 SME in the second year following entry into force of this Article;
   (c) 18,750,000 SME in the third year following entry into force of this Article;
   (d) 15,625,000 SME in the fourth year following entry into force of this Article;
   (e) 12,500,000 SME in the fifth year following entry into force of this Article;
   (f) 9,375,000 SME in the sixth year following entry into force of this Article;
   (g) 6,250,000 SME in the seventh year following entry into force of this Article; and
   (h) 3,125,000 SME in the eighth year following entry into force of this Article.

For purposes of this paragraph, quantities of textile and apparel goods shall be converted into SME according to the conversion factors set forth in Annex 2D.

4. This Article shall cease to apply beginning on the date that is nine years after entry into force of this Article.

Article 2.13: Definitions

For purposes of this Chapter, **customs duty** includes any customs or import duty and a charge of any kind imposed in connection with the importation of a good, including any form of surtax or surcharge in connection with such importation, but does not include any:

(a) charge equivalent to an internal tax imposed consistently with Article III:2 of GATT 1994 in respect of the like domestic good or in respect of goods from which the imported good has been manufactured or produced in whole or in part;

(b) antidumping or countervailing duty that is applied pursuant to a Party's domestic law;

(c) fee or other charge in connection with importation commensurate with the cost of services rendered; or

(d) duty imposed pursuant to Article 5 of the WTO Agreement on Agriculture.

Annex 2A. Application of Chapter 2: National Treatment and Market Access for Goods

Articles 2.1, 2.2, and 2.7 shall not apply to:

(a) controls by the United States on the export of logs of all species;

(b)

(i) measures under existing provisions of the Merchant Marine Act of 1920, 46 App. U.S.C. § 883; the Passenger Vessel Act, 46 App. U.S.C. §§ 289, 292 and 316; and 46 U.S.C. § 12108, to the extent that such measures were mandatory legislation at the time of the United States' accession to the General Agreement on Tariffs and Trade 1947 and have not been amended so as to decrease their conformity with Part II of GATT 1947;

(ii) the continuation or prompt renewal of a non-conforming provision of any statute referred to in clause (i); and

(iii) the amendment to a non-conforming provision of any statute referred to in subparagraph (b)(i) to the extent that the amendment does not decrease the conformity of the provision with Articles 2.1 and 2.7;

(c) actions authorized by the Dispute Settlement Body of the WTO.

Annex 2B

The U.S. Schedule to Annex 2B attached as a separate volume.

Annex 2C

The Singapore Schedule to Annex 2C attached as a separate volume.

Annex 2D. Conversion Factors

The following conversion factors shall be used to calculate quantities in SME for purposes of Article 2.12.

U.S. Category	Conversion Factor	Description	Primary Unit of Measure
237	19.20	PLAYSUITS, SUNSUITS, ETC	DZ
239	6.30	BABIES' GARMENTS & CLOTHING ACCESS.	KG
330	1.40	COTTON HANDKERCHIEFS	DZ
331	2.90	COTTON GLOVES AND MITTENS	DPR
332	3.80	COTTON HOSIERY	DPR
333	30.30	M&B SUITTYPE COATS, COTTON	DZ
334	34.50	OTHER M&B COATS, COTTON	DZ
335	34.50	W&G COTTON COATS	DZ
336	37.90	COTTON DRESSES	DZ
338	6.00	M&B COTTON KNIT SHIRTS	DZ
339	6.00	W&G COTTON KNIT SHIRTS/BLOUSES	DZ
340	20.10	M&B COTTON SHIRTS, NOT KNIT	DZ
341	12.10	W&G COTTON SHIRTS/BLOUSES,NOT KNIT	DZ
342	14.90	COTTON SKIRTS	DZ
345	30.80	COTTON SWEATERS	DZ
347	14.90	M&B COTTON TROUSERS/BREECHES/SHORTS	DZ
348	14.90	W&G COTTON TROUSERS/BREECHES/SHORTS	DZ
349	4.00	BRASSIERES, OTHER BODY SUPPORT GARMENTS	DZ
350	42.60	COTTON DRESSING GOWNS, ROBES ETC. DZ	
351	43.50	COTTON NIGHTWEAR/PAJAMAS	DZ
352	9.20	COTTON UNDERWEAR	DZ
353	34.50	M&B COTTON DOWNFILLED COATS	DZ
354	34.50	W&G COTTON DOWNFILLED COATS	DZ
359	8.50	OTHER COTTON APPAREL	KG
630	1.40	MMF HANDKERCHIEFS	DZ
631	2.90	MMF GLOVES AND MITTENS	DPR
632	3.80	MMF HOSIERY	DPR

Table. (Continued)

U.S. Category	Conversion Factor	Description	Primary Unit of Measure
633	30.30	M&B MMF SUITTYPE COATS	DZ
634	34.50	OTHER M&B MMF COATS	DZ
635	34.50	W&G MMF COATS	DZ
636	37.90	MMF DRESSES	DZ
638	15.00	M&B MMF KNIT SHIRTS	DZ
639	12.50	W&G MMF KNIT SHIRTS & BLOUSES	DZ
640	20.10	M&B NOT-KNIT MMF SHIRTS	DZ
641	12.10	W&G NOT-KNIT MMF SHIRTS & BLOUSES	DZ
642	14.90	MMF SKIRTS	DZ
643	3.76	M&B MMF SUITS	NO
644	3.76	W&G MMF SUITS	NO
645	30.80	M&B MMF SWEATERS	DZ
646	30.80	W&G MMF SWEATERS	DZ
647	14.90	M&B MMF TROUSERS/BREECHES/SHORTS	DZ
648	14.90	W&G MMF TROUSERS/BREECHES/SHORTS	DZ
649	4.00	MMF BRAS & OTHER BODY SUPPORT GARMENTS	DZ
650	42.60	MMF ROBES, DRESSING GOWNS, ETC.	DZ
651	43.50	MMF NIGHTWEAR & PAJAMAS	DZ
652	13.40	MMF UNDERWEAR	DZ
653	34.50	M&B MMF DOWNFILLED COATS	DZ
654	34.50	W&G MMF DOWNFILLED COATS	DZ
659	14.40	OTHER MMF APPAREL	KG

3. RULES OF ORIGIN

Section A: Origin Determination

Article 3.1: Originating Goods

For purposes of this Agreement, an **originating good** means a good:

(a) wholly obtained or produced entirely in the territory of one or both of the Parties; or
(b) that has satisfied the requirements specified in Annex 3A; or
(c) otherwise provided as an originating good under this Chapter.

Article 3.2: Treatment of Certain Products

1. Each Party shall provide that a good listed in Annex 3B is an originating good when imported into its territory from the territory of the other Party.

2. Within six months after entry into force of this Agreement, the Parties shall meet to explore the expansion of the product coverage of Annex 3B. The Parties shall consult regularly to review the operation of this Article and consider the addition of goods to Annex 3B.[3-1]

Article 3.3: De Minimis

1. Each Party shall provide that a good that does not undergo a change in tariff classification pursuant to Annex 3A is nonetheless an originating good if:
   (a) the value of all non-originating materials used in the production of the good that do not undergo the required change in tariff classification does not exceed 10 percent of the adjusted value of the good; and
   (b) the good meets all other applicable criteria set forth in this Chapter for qualifying as an originating good.

   The value of such non-originating materials shall, however, be included in the value of non-originating materials for any applicable regional value content requirement for the good.

2. Paragraph 1 does not apply to:
   (a) a non-originating material provided for in chapter 4 of the Harmonized System or in subheading 1901.90 that is used in the production of a good provided for in chapter 4 of the Harmonized System;
   (b) a non-originating material provided for in chapter 4 of the Harmonized System or in subheading 1901.90 that is used in the production of a good provided for in the following provisions: subheadings 1901.10, 1901.20 or 1901.90; heading 2105; or subheadings 2106.90, 2202.90, or 2309.90;
   (c) a non-originating material provided for in heading 0805 or subheadings 2009.11 through 2009.30 that is used in the production of a good provided for in subheadings 2009.11 through 2009.30, or subheadings 2106.90 or 2202.90;
   (d) a non-originating material provided for in chapter 15 of the Harmonized System that is used in the production of a good provided for in headings 1501 through 1508, 1512, 1514 or 1515;
   (e) a non-originating material provided for in heading 1701 that is used in the production of a good provided for in headings 1701 through 1703;
   (f) a non-originating material provided for in chapter 17 of the Harmonized System or heading 1805 that is used in the production of a good provided for in subheading 1806.10;
   (g) a non-originating material provided for in headings 2203 through 2208 that is used in the production of a good provided for in headings 2207 or 2208; and
   (h) a non-originating material used in the production of a good provided for in Chapters 1 through 21 of the Harmonized System unless the non-originating material is provided for in a different subheading than the good for which origin is being determined under this Article.

For purposes of this paragraph, **heading** and **subheading** mean, respectively, a heading and subheading of the Harmonized System.

3. A textile or apparel good provided for in Chapters 50 through 63 of the Harmonized System that is not an originating good, because certain fibers or yarns used in the production of the component of the good that determines the tariff classification of the good do not undergo an applicable change in tariff classification set out in Annex 3A, shall nonetheless be considered to be an originating good if the total weight of all such fibers or yarns in that component is not more than seven percent of the total weight of that component. Notwithstanding the preceding sentence, a textile or apparel good containing elastomeric yarns in the component of the good that determines the tariff classification of the good shall be an originating good only if such yarns are wholly formed in the territory of a Party.

Article 3.4: Accumulation

1. Originating materials from the territory of a Party, used in the production of a good in the territory of the other Party, shall be considered to originate in the territory of the other Party.
2. A good is an originating good when it is produced in the territory of one or both Parties by one or more producers, provided that the good satisfies the requirements in Article 3.1 and all other applicable requirements of this Chapter.

Article 3.5: Regional Value Content

Where Annex 3A refers to a regional value content, each Party shall provide that the regional value content of a good shall be calculated on the basis of one of the following methods:

(a) Build-down Method

$$RVC = \frac{AV - VNM}{AV} \times 100$$

where
RVC is the regional value content, expressed as a percentage;
AV is the adjusted value, and
VNM is the value of non-originating materials that are acquired and used by the producer in the production of the good.

(b) Build-up Method

$$RVC = \frac{VOM}{AV} \times 100$$

where
RVC is the regional value content, expressed as a percentage;
AV is the adjusted value; and
VOM is the value of originating materials that are acquired or self-produced, and used by the producer in the production of the good.

Article 3.6: Value of Materials

1. Each Party shall provide that for purposes of calculating the regional value content of a good and for purposes of applying the de minimis rule, the value of a material is:

    (a) for a material imported by the producer of the good, the adjusted value of the material;

    (b) for a material acquired in the territory where the good is produced, except for materials within the meaning of subparagraph (c), the adjusted value of the material; or

    (c) for a material that is self-produced, or where the relationship between the producer of the good and the seller of the material influenced the price actually paid or payable for the material, including a material obtained without charge, the sum of:

        (i) all expenses incurred in the production of the material, including general expenses; and

        (ii) an amount for profit.

2. Each Party shall provide that the value of materials may be adjusted as follows:

    (a) for originating materials, the following expenses may be added to the value of the material if not included under paragraph 1:

        (i) the costs of freight, insurance, packing, and all other costs incurred in transporting the material to the location of the producer;

        (ii) duties, taxes and customs brokerage fees on the material paid in the territory of one or more of the Parties, other than duties and taxes that are waived, refunded, refundable or otherwise recoverable, including credit against duty or tax paid or payable; and

        (iii) the cost of waste and spoilage resulting from the use of the material in the production of the good, less the value of renewable scrap or by-product; and

    (b) for non-originating materials, where included under paragraph 1, the following expenses may be deducted from the value of the material:

        (i) the costs of freight, insurance, packing, and all other costs incurred in transporting the material to the location of the producer;

        (ii) duties, taxes, and customs brokerage fees on the material paid in the territory of one or more of the Parties, other than duties and taxes that are waived, refunded, refundable, or otherwise recoverable, including credit against duty or tax paid or payable;

        (iii) the cost of waste and spoilage resulting from the use of the material in the production of the good, less the value of renewable scrap or by-products;

        (iv) the cost of processing incurred in the territory of a Party in the production of the non-originating material; and

        (v) the cost of originating materials used in the production of the non-originating material in the territory of a Party.

Article 3.7: Accessories, Spare Parts, and Tools

Each Party shall provide that accessories, spare parts, or tools delivered with a good that form part of the good's standard accessories, spare parts, or tools, shall be treated as originating goods if the good is an originating good, and shall be disregarded in determining whether all the non-originating materials used in the production of the good undergo the applicable change in tariff classification, provided that:

(a) the accessories, spare parts, or tools are not invoiced separately from the good;
(b) the quantities and value of the accessories, spare parts, or tools are customary for the good; and
(c) if the good is subject to a regional value content requirement, the value of the accessories, spare parts, or tools shall be taken into account as originating or non-originating materials, as the case may be, in calculating the regional value content of the good.

Article 3.8: Fungible Goods and Materials

1. Each Party shall provide that the determination of whether fungible goods or materials are originating goods shall be made either by physical segregation of each good or material or through the use of any inventory management method, such as averaging, last-in, first-out, or first-in, first out, recognized in the generally accepted accounting principles of the Party in which the production is performed or otherwise accepted by the Party in which the production is performed.

2. Each Party shall provide that that an inventory management method selected under paragraph 1 for particular fungible goods or materials shall continue to be used for those fungible goods or materials throughout the fiscal year of the person that selected the inventory management method.

Article 3.9: Packaging Materials and Containers for Retail Sale

Each Party shall provide that packaging materials and containers in which a good is packaged for retail sale, if classified with the good, shall be disregarded in determining whether all the non-originating materials used in the production of the good undergo the applicable change in tariff classification set out in Annex 3A and, if the good is subject to a regional value-content requirement, the value of such packaging materials and containers shall be taken into account as originating or non-originating materials, as the case may be, in calculating the regional value content of the good.

Article 3.10: Packing Materials and Containers for Shipment

Each Party shall provide that packing materials and containers in which a good is packed for shipment shall be disregarded in determining whether:

(a) the non-originating materials used in the production of the good undergo an applicable change in tariff classification set out in Annex 3A; and
(b) the good satisfies a regional value content requirement.

Article 3.11: Indirect Materials

Each Party shall provide that an indirect material shall be treated as an originating material without regard to where it is produced and its value shall be the cost registered in the accounting records of the producer of the good.

Article 3.12: Third Country Transportation

A good shall not be considered to be an originating good if the good undergoes subsequent production or any other operation outside the territories of the Parties, other than unloading, reloading, or any other operation necessary to preserve it in good condition or to transport the good to the territory of a Party.

Section B: Supporting Information and Verification

Article 3.13: Claims for Preferential Treatment

1. Each Party shall provide that an importer may make a claim for preferential treatment under this Agreement based on the importer's knowledge or on information in the importer's possession that the good qualifies as an originating good.
2. Each Party may require that an importer be prepared to submit, upon request, a statement setting forth the reasons that the good qualifies as an originating good, including pertinent cost and manufacturing information. The statement need not be in a prescribed format, and may be submitted electronically, where feasible.

Article 3.14: Obligations Relating to Importations

1. Each Party shall grant any claim for preferential treatment under this Agreement made in accordance with this Section, unless the Party possesses information that the claim is invalid.
2. A Party may deny preferential treatment under this Agreement to an imported good if the importer fails to comply with any requirement of this Chapter.
3. If a Party denies a claim for preferential treatment under this Agreement, it shall issue a written determination containing findings of fact and the legal basis for the determination.
4. The importing Party shall not subject an importer to any penalty for making an invalid claim for preferential treatment if the importer:
   (a) upon becoming aware that such claim is not valid, promptly and voluntarily corrects the claim and pays any duty owing; and
   (b) in any event, corrects the claim and pays any duty owing within a period determined by the Party, which shall be at least one year from submission of the invalid claim.

Article 3.15: Record Keeping Requirement

Each Party may require that importers maintain for up to five years after the date of importation records relating to the importation of the good, and may require that an importer provide, upon request, records which are necessary to demonstrate that a good qualifies as an originating good, as stipulated in Article 3.13.2, including records concerning:

(a) the purchase of, cost of, value of, and payment for, the good;
(b) the purchase of, cost of, value of, and payment for, all materials, including indirect materials, used in the production of the good; and
(c) the production of the good in the form in which the good is exported.

Article 3.16: Verification

For purposes of determining whether a good imported into its territory from the territory of the other Party qualifies as an originating good, a Party may conduct a verification by means of:

(a) requests for information from the importer;
(b) written requests for information to an exporter or a producer in the territory of the other Party;
(c) requests for the importer to arrange for the producer or exporter to provide information directly to the Party conducting the verification;
(d) information received directly by the importing Party from an exporter or a producer as a result of a process described in Article 3.13.2;
(e) visits to the premises of an exporter or a producer in the territory of the other Party, in accordance with any procedures that the Parties jointly adopt pertaining to the verification; or
(f) such other procedures as the Parties may agree.

Article 3.17: Certain Apparel Goods

Notwithstanding any other provision of this Agreement, the United States shall consider an apparel good listed in Chapter 61 or 62 of Annex 3A to be an originating good if it is both cut (or knit to shape) and sewn or otherwise assembled in one or both Parties from fabric or yarn, regardless of origin, designated by the appropriate U.S. government authority as fabric or yarn not available in commercial quantities in a timely manner in the United States. Such designation must have been made in a notice published in the Federal Register of the United States identifying apparel goods made from such fabric or yarn as eligible for entry into the United States under subheading 9819.11.24 or 9820.11.27 of the Harmonized Tariff Schedule of the United States as of November 15, 2002. For purposes of this Article, reference in such a notice to yarn or fabric formed in the United States shall be deemed to include yarn or fabric formed in either Party.

Section C: Consultation and Modifications

Article 3.18: Consultation and Modifications

1. The Parties shall consult and cooperate to ensure that this Chapter is applied in an effective and uniform manner.
2. The Parties shall consult regularly to discuss necessary amendments to this Chapter and its Annexes, taking into account developments in technology, production processes, and other related matters, pursuant to Article 20.3 (Consultations).
3. Within six months after entry into force of this Agreement, the Parties shall meet:
   (a) to consider possible modifications to Annex 3A, including an assessment of the operation and use of the RVC;
   (b) the addition of products to Annex 3B; and
   (c) to review and consider possible modifications to Annex 3C.
4.
   (a) On the request of either Party, the Parties shall consult:
       (i) to consider whether the rules of origin applicable to particular textile or apparel goods under this Chapter should be revised to address availability of supply of fibers, yarns or fabrics in the territories of the Parties; or
       (ii) to review the rules of origin applicable to particular textile or apparel goods in light of
           (A) the effects of increasing global competition,
           (B) the termination of the WTO Agreement on Textiles and Clothing and the full integration of the textile and apparel sector into GATT 1994, and
           (C) eventual harmonization of rules of origin pursuant to Part IV of the WTO Agreement on Rules of Origin.
   (b) In the consultations referred to in subparagraph (a)(i), each Party shall consider all data presented by the other Party showing substantial production in its territory of a particular fiber, yarn or fabric. The Parties shall consider that substantial production has been shown if a Party demonstrates that its domestic producers are capable of supplying commercial quantities of the fiber, yarn or fabric in a timely manner.
   (c) The Parties shall endeavor to conclude consultations under subparagraph (a)(i) within 60 days of receipt of a request by one Party from the other Party. An amended rule of origin agreed to by the Parties shall supersede any prior rule of origin under this Agreement for the textile or apparel goods at issue, on approval by the Parties in accordance with Article 21.8 (Amendments).
   (d) In consultations under subparagraph (a)(ii), the Parties shall give particular consideration to operative rules in other economic association or integration agreements and developments relating to textile and apparel production and trade.

Section D: Definitions

Article 3.19: Definitions

For purposes of this Chapter:

1. **adjusted value** means the value determined under Articles 1 through 8, Article 15, and the corresponding interpretative notes of the Customs Valuation Agreement, as adjusted to exclude any costs, charges, or expenses incurred for transportation, insurance, and related services incident to the international shipment of the merchandise from the country of exportation to the place of importation;
2. **fungible goods or materials** means goods or materials that are interchangeable for commercial purposes and whose properties are essentially identical;
3. **generally accepted accounting principles** means the recognized consensus or substantial authoritative support in the territory of a Party, with respect to the recording of revenues, expenses, costs, assets, and liabilities, the disclosure of information and the preparation of financial statements. These standards may encompass broad guidelines of general application as well as detailed standards, practices, and procedures;
4. **goods wholly obtained or produced entirely in the territory of one or both of the Parties** means goods that are:
    (a) mineral goods extracted there;
    (b) vegetable goods, as such goods are defined in the Harmonized System, harvested there;
    (c) live animals born and raised there;
    (d) goods obtained from hunting, trapping, fishing, or aquaculture conducted there;
    (e) goods (fish, shellfish, and other marine life) taken from the sea by vessels registered or recorded with a Party and flying its flag;
    (f) goods produced exclusively from products referred to in paragraph (e) on board factory ships registered or recorded with a Party and flying its flag;
    (g) goods taken by a Party, or a person of a Party, from the seabed or beneath the seabed outside territorial waters, provided that the Party has rights to exploit such seabed;
    (h) goods taken from outer space, provided they are obtained by a Party or a person of a Party and not processed in the territory of a non-Party;
    (i) waste and scrap derived from
        (i) production there; or
        (ii) used goods collected there, provided such goods are fit only for the recovery of raw materials;
    (j) recovered goods derived there from used goods; or
    (k) goods produced there exclusively from goods referred to in (a) through (i) above, or from their derivatives, at any stage of production.
5. **Harmonized System** means the Harmonized Commodity Description and Coding System;
6. **indirect material** means a good used in the production, testing or inspection of a good but not physically incorporated into the good, or a good used in the

maintenance of buildings or the operation of equipment associated with the production of a good, including:

(a) fuel and energy;

(b) tools, dies, and molds;

(c) spare parts and materials used in the maintenance of equipment and buildings;

(d) lubricants, greases, compounding materials, and other materials used in production or used to operate equipment and buildings;

(e) gloves, glasses, footwear, clothing, safety equipment, and supplies;

(f) equipment, devices, and supplies used for testing or inspecting the goods;

(g) catalysts and solvents; and

(h) any other goods that are not incorporated into the good but whose use in the production of the good can reasonably be demonstrated to be a part of that production;

7. **material** means a good that is used in the production of another good;

8. **material that is self-produced** means a good, such as a part or ingredient, produced by the producer and used by the producer in the production of another good

9. **non-originating material** means a material that has not satisfied the requirements of this Chapter;

10. **preferential treatment** means the customs duty rate and treatment under Article 2.8 (Merchandise Processing Fee) that is applicable to an originating good pursuant to this Agreement;

11. **producer** means a person who grows, raises, mines, harvests, fishes, traps, hunts, manufactures, processes, assembles or disassembles a good;

12. **production** means growing, raising, mining, harvesting, fishing, trapping, hunting, manufacturing, processing, assembling or disassembling a good;

13. **recovered goods** means materials in the form of individual parts that result from:

(a) the complete disassembly of used goods into individual parts; and

(b) the cleaning, inspecting, or testing, and as necessary for improvement to sound working condition one or more of the following processes: welding, flame spraying, surface machining, knurling, plating, sleeving, and rewinding in order for such parts to be assembled with other parts, including other recovered parts in the production of a remanufactured good of Annex 3C;

14. **remanufactured good** means an industrial good assembled in the territory of a Party, designated under Annex 3C, that:

(a) is entirely or partially comprised of recovered goods;

(b) has the same life expectancy and meets the same performance standards as a new good; and

(c) enjoys the same factory warranty as such a new good; and

15. **used** means used or consumed in the production of goods.

Section E: Application and Interpretation

Article 3.20: Application and Interpretation

For purposes of this Chapter:

(a) the basis for tariff classification is the Harmonized System;

(b) any cost and value referred to in this Chapter shall be recorded and maintained in accordance with the generally accepted accounting principles applicable in the territory of the Party in which the good is produced.

Annex 3A. Product-Specific Rules

Annex 3A is attached as a separate volume.

Annex 3B. Integrated Sourcing Initiative

Annex 3B is attached as a separate volume.

4. CUSTOMS ADMINISTRATION

Article 4.1: Publication and Notification

1. Each Party shall ensure that its laws, regulations, guidelines, procedures, and administrative rulings governing customs matters are promptly published, either on the Internet or in print form.

2. Each Party shall designate, establish, and maintain one or more inquiry points to address inquiries from interested persons pertaining to customs matters, and shall make available on the Internet information concerning procedures for making such inquiries.

3. To the extent possible, each Party shall:
    (a) publish in advance any regulation governing customs matters that it proposes to adopt; and
    (b) provide interested persons and the other Party a reasonable opportunity to comment on such proposed regulations.

4. Nothing in this Article shall require a Party to publish law enforcement procedures and internal operational guidelines including those related to conducting risk analysis and targeting technologies, if the Party considers that publication would impede law enforcement.

Article 4.2: Administration

1. Each Party shall administer in a uniform, impartial, and reasonable manner all its laws, regulations, decisions, and rulings governing customs matters.

2. Each Party shall ensure that its laws and regulations governing customs matters are not prepared, adopted, or applied with a view to or with the effect of creating arbitrary or unwarranted procedural obstacles to international trade.

Article 4.3: Advance Rulings

1. Each Party shall provide for the issuance of written advance rulings to a person described in subparagraph 2(a) concerning tariff classification, questions arising from the application of the Customs Valuation Agreement, country of origin, and the qualification of a good as an originating good under this Agreement.

2. Each Party shall adopt or maintain procedures for the issuance of advance rulings that:

    (a) provide that an importer in its territory or an exporter or producer in the territory of the other Party may request such a ruling prior to the importation in question;

    (b) include a detailed description of the information required to process a request for an advance ruling; and

    (c) provide that the advance ruling be based on the facts and circumstances presented by the person requesting the ruling.

3. Each Party shall provide that its customs authorities:

    (a) may request, at any time during the course of evaluating a request for an advance ruling, additional information necessary to evaluate the request;

    (b) shall issue the advance ruling expeditiously, and within 120 days after obtaining all necessary information; and

    (c) shall provide, upon request of the person who requested the advance ruling, a full explanation of the reasons for the ruling.

4. Subject to paragraph 5, each Party shall apply an advance ruling to importations into its territory beginning on the date of issuance of the ruling or such date as may be specified in the ruling. The treatment provided by the advance ruling shall be applied to importations without regard to the identity of the importer, exporter, or producer, provided that the facts and circumstances are identical in all material respects.

5. A Party may modify or revoke an advance ruling upon a determination that the ruling was based on an error of fact or law, or if there is a change in law consistent with this Agreement, a material fact, or circumstances on which the ruling is based. The issuing Party shall postpone the effective date of such modification or revocation for a period of not less than 60 days where the person to whom the ruling was issued has relied in good faith on that ruling.

Article 4.4: Review and Appeal

1. With respect to determinations relating to customs matters, each Party shall provide that importers in its territory have access to:

    (a) at least one level of administrative review of determinations by its customs authorities independent of the official or office responsible for the decision under review;[4-1] and

    (b) judicial review of decisions taken at the final level of administrative review.

Article 4.5: Cooperation

1. Each Party shall endeavor to provide the other Party with advance notice of any significant modification of administrative policy or other similar development related to its laws or regulations governing importations that is likely to substantially affect the operation of this Agreement.

2. The Parties shall through their competent authorities and in accordance with this Chapter, cooperate in achieving compliance with their respective laws or regulations pertaining to:

    (a) implementation and operation of this Agreement;

    (b) restrictions and prohibitions on imports or exports; and

    (c) other issues that the Parties may agree.

3. Where a Party has a reasonable suspicion of unlawful activity related to its laws or regulations governing importations, it may request the other Party to provide the following types of information pertaining to trade transactions relevant to that activity that took place no more than five years before the date of the request, or from the date of discovery of the apparent offense in cases of fraud and in other cases on which the Parties may agree:

    (a) the name and address of the importer, exporter, manufacturer, buyer, vendor, broker, or transporter;

    (b) shipping information relating to container number, size, port of loading before arrival, destination port after departure, name of vessel and carrier, the country of origin, place of export, mode of transportation, port of entry of the goods, and cargo description; and

    (c) classification number, quantity, unit of measure, declared value, and tariff treatment.

    The requesting Party shall make its request in writing; shall specify the grounds for reasonable suspicion and the purposes for which the information is sought; and shall identify the requested information with sufficient specificity for the other party to locate and provide the information. For example, the requesting Party may identify the importer, exporter, country of origin, the time period, port or ports of entry, cargo description, or Harmonized System number applicable to the importation or exportation in question.

4. For purposes of paragraph 3, a reasonable suspicion of unlawful activity means a suspicion based on one or more of the following types of relevant factual information obtained from public or private sources:

    (a) historical evidence that a specific importer, exporter, manufacturer, producer, or other company involved in the movement of goods from the territory of one Party to the territory of the other Party has not complied with a Party's laws or regulations governing importations;

    (b) historical evidence that some or all of the enterprises involved in the movement from the territory of one Party to the territory of the other Party of goods within a specific product sector where goods are moving from the territory of one Party to the territory of the other Party has not complied with a Party's laws or regulations governing importations; or

(c) other information that the Parties agree is sufficient in the context of a particular request.

5. The other Party shall respond by providing available information that is material to the request.

6. Each Party shall also endeavor to provide the other Party with any other information that would assist in determining whether imports from or exports to the other Party are in compliance with applicable domestic laws or regulations governing importations, including those related to the prevention or investigation of unlawful shipments.

7. The Parties shall endeavor to provide each other technical advice and assistance for the purpose of improving risk assessment techniques, simplifying and expediting customs procedures, advancing the technical skill of personnel, and enhancing the use of technologies that can lead to improved compliance with laws or regulations governing importations.

8 The Parties shall use their best efforts to explore additional avenues of cooperation for the purpose of enhancing each Party's ability to enforce its laws or regulations governing importations, including by examining the establishment and maintenance of other channels of communication to facilitate the secure and rapid exchange of information, and considering efforts to improve effective coordination on importation issues, building upon the mechanisms established in this Article and the cooperation established under any other relevant agreements.

Article 4.6: Confidentiality

1. Where a Party providing information to the other Party in accordance with this Chapter designates the information as confidential, the other Party shall maintain the confidentiality of the information. The Party providing the information may require written assurances from the other Party prior to forwarding information that such information will be held in confidence, used only for the purposes requested, and not disclosed without specific permission of the Party providing the information, in accordance with its laws and regulations, except where the Parties agree that the information may be used or disclosed for law enforcement purposes or in the context of judicial proceedings.

2. A Party may decline to provide information requested by the other Party where the other Party has failed to act in conformity with the assurances referred to in paragraph 1.

3. Each Party shall maintain procedures to ensure that confidential information, including information the disclosure of which could prejudice the competitive position of the person providing the information, submitted in connection with the Party's administration of its import and export laws is entitled to treatment as confidential information and protected from unauthorized disclosure.

Article 4.7: Penalties

Each Party shall adopt or maintain measures that provide for the imposition of civil or administrative penalties and, where appropriate, criminal penalties, for violations of its customs laws and regulations governing classification, valuation, country of origin, and eligibility for preferential treatment under this Agreement.

Article 4.8: Release and Security

1. Each Party shall adopt or maintain procedures:
   (a) providing for the release of goods within a period of time no greater than that required to ensure compliance with its customs laws;
   (b) allowing, to the extent possible, goods to be released within 48 hours of arrival;
   (c) allowing, to the extent possible, goods to be released at the point of arrival, without interim transfer to customs warehouses or other locations; and
   (d) allowing importers who have complied with the procedures that the Party may have relating to the determination of value and payment of duty to withdraw goods from customs, but may require importers to provide security as a condition to the release of goods, when such security is required to ensure that obligations arising from the entry of the goods will be fulfilled.

2. Each Party shall:
   (a) ensure that the amount of any security is no greater than that required to ensure that obligations arising from the importation of the goods will be fulfilled, and, where applicable, not in excess of the amount chargeable, based on tariff rates under domestic and international law, including this Agreement, and on valuation in accordance with the Customs Valuation Agreement;
   (b) ensure that any security shall be discharged as soon as possible after its customs authorities are satisfied that the obligations arising from the importation of the goods have been fulfilled; and
   (c) shall adopt procedures allowing:
      (i) importers to provide security such as bank guarantees, bonds, or other non-cash financial instruments;
      (ii) importers that regularly enter goods to provide security such as standing bank guarantees, continuous bonds or other non-cash financial instruments covering multiple entries; and
      (iii) importers to provide security in any other forms specified by its customs authorities.

Article 4.9: Risk Assessment

Each Party shall employ risk management systems that enable its customs authorities to concentrate inspection activities on high-risk goods and that facilitate the movement of low-risk goods, including systems which allow for the processing of information regarding an importation prior to the arrival of the imported goods.

Article 4.10: Express Shipments

Each Party shall ensure efficient clearance of all shipments, while maintaining appropriate control and customs selection. In the event that a Party's existing system does not ensure efficient clearance, it should adopt procedures to expedite express shipments. Such procedures shall:

(a) provide for pre-arrival processing of information related to express shipments;

(b) permit, as a condition for release, the submission of a single document in the form that the Party considers appropriate, such as a single manifest or a single declaration, covering all of the goods in the shipment by an express service company, through, if possible, electronic means;

(c) provide, where possible, for deferred payment of duties, taxes, and fees with appropriate guarantees;

(d) minimize, to the extent possible, the documentation required for the release of express shipments; and

(e) allow, in normal circumstances, for an express shipment to be released within six hours of the submission of necessary customs documentation.

Article 4.11: Definitions

For purposes of this Chapter, **customs matters** means matters pertaining to the classification and valuation of goods for customs duty purposes, rates of duty, country of origin, and eligibility for preferential treatment under this Agreement, and all other procedural and substantive requirements, restrictions, and prohibitions on imports or exports, including such matters pertaining to goods imported or exported by or on behalf of travelers. Customs matters do not include matters pertaining to antidumping or countervailing duties.

5. TEXTILES AND APPAREL

Article 5.1: Scope

1. This Chapter applies to measures adopted or maintained by a Party, including administrative, judicial, and enforcement actions by a Party, and to cooperation between the Parties, relating to trade in textile and apparel goods.

2. Singapore's obligations under this Chapter with respect to enterprises cover:

 (a) conduct of enterprises in Singapore, including:

   (i) production, processing, or manipulation of textile or apparel goods in its territory, including in a free trade zone,

   (ii) importation of such goods into its territory, including into a free trade zone or

   (iii) exportation of such goods from its territory, including from a free trade zone; and

 (b) conduct of enterprises operating under the Outward Processing Arrangement, as well as maintenance of records and documents by such enterprises in Singapore that may be relevant to determining the existence or extent of circumvention.

3. In the event of any inconsistency between this Chapter and another Chapter of this Agreement, this Chapter shall prevail to the extent of the inconsistency.

Article 5.2: Anti-Circumvention

1. The details of cooperation on matters relating to textile and apparel goods are as stated in this Chapter. Each Party shall take necessary and appropriate measures, including administrative, judicial and enforcement action:
   (a) to aggressively enforce its laws relating to circumvention;
   (b) to actively cooperate with the other Party in the enforcement of the other Party's laws relating to circumvention; and
   (c) to prevent circumvention.
2. In furtherance of paragraph 1, each Party shall maintain or adopt laws that:
   (a) authorize its officials to take action to deter circumvention and to carry out obligations under this Chapter relating to information sharing; and
   (b) establish criminal penalties, and civil or administrative penalties, that effectively deter circumvention.

Article 5.3: Monitoring

1. Singapore shall establish and maintain programs to monitor the importation, production, exportation, and processing or manipulation in a free trade zone of textile and apparel goods, as specified in this Article. These programs shall provide the information necessary for each Party to ascertain whether a violation of its laws relating to trade in textile and apparel goods or an act of circumvention is occurring or has occurred.
2. Singapore shall institute a registration system covering all enterprises operating in its territory or operating under the Outward Processing Arrangement and that are engaged in the production of textile or apparel goods or the export to the United States of such goods that a person claims as originating goods or marks as products of Singapore.
3. Singapore shall register enterprises under the system described in paragraph 2 for terms of up to two years, subject to renewals of up to two years at a time. Singapore shall not authorize a textile or apparel good that a person claims as an originating good or marks as a product of Singapore to be exported to the United States unless the good is produced by a registered enterprise and exported by a registered enterprise.
4. Singapore shall establish and maintain a program to verify that textile and apparel goods that a person claims as originating goods or marks as products of Singapore and that are exported to the United States are produced by registered enterprises. This program shall include on-site government inspections of such enterprises at least twice a year and without prior notice to verify that they comply with laws of Singapore relating to trade in textile and apparel goods and that their production of and capability to produce such goods are consistent with claims regarding the origin of such goods. Under this program, Singapore shall provide to the United States:

(a) within 14 days of the completion of each such inspection, a written report regarding the results of that inspection, including any conduct discovered as a result of the inspection that Singapore believes to be a violation of either Party's laws relating to circumvention, and

(b) each year, a written report summarizing the results of all such inspections on an enterprise-by-enterprise basis.

The first report under subparagraph (b) shall be submitted no later than 12 months after this Chapter takes effect. Singapore shall designate any information in reports under subparagraph (a) or (b) that it considers to be confidential.

5. For each shipment of textile or apparel goods that a registered enterprise produces for exportation to the United States or exports to the United States, Singapore shall require the enterprise to maintain in Singapore records relating to such production or exportation for a period of five years from the date on which such records are created. Singapore also shall require each registered enterprise that produces textile or apparel goods to maintain in Singapore records relating to its production capabilities in general, the number of persons it employs, and any other records and information sufficient to allow officials of each Party to verify the enterprise's production and exportation of textile or apparel goods, including:

(a) records demonstrating that the materials used to produce or assemble textile and apparel goods were obtained or produced by the enterprise and were available for production, such as:

(i) bills of lading from the persons that supplied the materials;

(ii) customs clearance records or equivalent records if the materials were imported into Singapore; and

(iii) transaction records, including:

(A) commercial invoices, if the materials were purchased,

(B) transfer records,

(C) mill certificates if the materials were spun, extruded (for yarns) or woven, knitted or formed by any other fabric forming process (for example, tufting) by an enterprise of Singapore,

(D) production records if the registered enterprise produced the materials, and

(E) purchase orders if the materials were imported from a foreign producer, broker, trader, or other intermediary;

(b) with respect to textile and apparel goods the enterprise has produced that are claimed as originating goods or marked as products of Singapore, production records that substantiate the claim or marking, such as:

(i) cutting records for products assembled from cut components;

(ii) assembly or production records that the production manager maintains on the factory floor that document daily production, including workers' daily production records, wage records, production steps, and sewing tickets; and

(iii) employee time cards, payment records, or other documentation showing which employees were working, how long they worked, and what work they performed during the period the goods were produced;

(c) with respect to textile and apparel goods that a subcontractor has produced in whole or in part for the enterprise and that are claimed as originating goods or marked as products of Singapore, records that substantiate the claim, such as:

    (i) cutting records for products assembled from cut components;

    (ii) if partially assembled by the subcontractor, production records documenting the partial assembly;

    (iii) bills of lading; and

    (iv) transfer documents to the shipper or primary contractor and proof of payment by the shipper or primary contractor for the work done; and

(d) records establishing which production processes took place outside the territory of Singapore, if a portion of the processing or operations was conducted there under the Outward Processing Arrangement, such as:

    (i) records demonstrating export from Singapore of materials, components, subassemblies or finished goods for processing; and

    (ii) customs records or records containing equivalent information, such as cargo manifests, showing re-importation into Singapore of the goods after processing.

6. Singapore shall establish and maintain a program to ensure that textile and apparel goods that are imported into or exported from Singapore or that are processed or manipulated in a free trade zone in Singapore en route to the United States are marked with the correct country of origin and that the documents accompanying the goods accurately describe the goods. This program shall provide for:

(a) immediate referral by Singapore officials of suspected violations of either Party's laws relating to intentional circumvention to the appropriate enforcement authorities; and

(b) not later than 14 days after the resolution of the matter,[5-1] issuance by Singapore to the United States of a written report of

    (i) each violation of a law of Singapore relating to circumvention, including a failure to maintain or produce records, and

    (ii) any other act of circumvention; involving textile or apparel goods destined for the United States, occurring in the territory of Singapore, and resulting in enforcement action by Singapore. In each case, the report shall state the enforcement action taken and the ultimate resolution of the matter. Singapore shall designate in the report any information it considers to be confidential, except that, at a minimum, Singapore may not designate the name of any enterprise that its enforcement authorities have determined to have engaged in circumvention.

Article 5.4: Cooperation

General

1. In furtherance of Article 5.2.1(b), on request, a Party shall, in a manner consistent with its laws and procedures,

(a) promptly obtain from an enterprise and provide to the other Party, to the extent available, all correspondence, reports, bills of lading, invoices, order confirmations, and other documents or information, relevant to circumvention, that the requesting Party considers may have taken place; and

(b) facilitate the gathering by the other Party's enforcement authorities of information relevant to circumvention, including, as appropriate, by conducting site visits or establishing contacts with persons in the Party's territory.

Any request for cooperation under this Article shall be made in writing and shall include a brief statement of the matter at issue and the cooperation requested.

Site Visits

2. A Party seeking to conduct site visits in the territory of the other Party shall provide a written request to the host Party's competent authority not less than14 days before the proposed dates of the visits. The request shall identify the number of enterprises to be visited, the proposed dates of the visits, and the reason for the visits, but need not specify the identities of the enterprises to be visited.

3. The competent authority shall be prohibited from informing any person, other than officials of the host Party directly responsible for organizing the site visits, of the request and its contents. The host Party shall prohibit those officials and any other person in its territory from notifying an enterprise in advance of a visit. The responsible officials of the host Party shall seek permission to conduct a site visit from a responsible person at the enterprise at the time of the visit.

4. Responsible officials of the Party seeking to conduct site visits in the territory of the other Party shall conduct such visits together with responsible officials of the host Party and in accordance with the laws of the host Party. On completion of a site visit, the requesting Party shall brief the responsible officials of the host Party and shall subsequently provide to that Party a written report of the results of the visit. The written report shall include:

(a) the name of the enterprise visited;

(b) for each shipment checked, information discovered relating to circumvention;

(c) observations made at the enterprise relating to circumvention; and

(d) as relevant, an assessment of whether the enterprise is maintaining records of the type described in Article 5.3.5 and can demonstrate that its production of and capability to produce textile or apparel goods is consistent with claims that the textile or apparel goods it produces or has produced are originating goods or products of the host Party.

5. If the responsible person at an enterprise proposed to be visited denies permission for the site visit to occur:

(a) the visit shall not occur;

(b) the host Party shall not issue any visas or export licenses that may be required to accompany textile or apparel goods that the enterprise produces or exports when such goods are exported to the requesting Party, until the host Party determines that the enterprise's production of and capability to produce such goods is consistent with claims that textile or apparel goods it produces or has produced are originating goods or products of the host Party; and

(c) the requesting Party may deny entry of textile or apparel goods produced or exported by the enterprise until that Party determines that the enterprise's production of and capability to produce such goods is consistent with claims that textile or apparel goods it produces or has produced are originating goods or products of the host Party.

6. Permission for a site visit shall be deemed to have been denied if the enterprise does not allow the responsible officials of the requesting Party access to:

(a) the enterprise's premises, including its production and storage areas and any other facilities;

(b) any production records relating to:

(i)   textile or apparel goods that have been exported to the territory of the requesting Party;

(ii) the enterprise's production capabilities in general; and

(iii) number of persons the enterprise employs; and

(c) any other records or information, including records and information of the type described in Article 5.3, relevant to a determination of whether the enterprise's production of and capability to produce textile or apparel goods are consistent with claims that the textile and apparel goods it produces or has produced are originating goods or products of the host Party.

Establishing Facts

7. If a Party suspects that circumvention has occurred, on its request the other Party shall facilitate the gathering of the facts necessary for the requesting Party to determine whether circumvention has occurred. If a Party determines that circumvention has occurred, on its request the other Party shall facilitate the requesting Party's establishment of any additional facts necessary to take enforcement action and to prevent circumvention. This paragraph applies to circumvention or suspected circumvention with regard to importation, exportation, processing or manipulation in a free trade zone, or transshipment.[5-2]

8. If a Party requests the other Party to examine transshipped textile or apparel goods, its officials shall endeavor to examine such goods.[5-3]

9. When a Party makes a request under paragraph 7 with respect to a particular shipment, it shall, to the extent possible, notify the other Party of: the importer, the exporter, the country of origin, the dates on which the shipment was entered, the port or ports of entry, and the cargo description or Harmonized System subheading of the goods.

Article 5.5: Enforcement

1. In furtherance of Article 5.2.1, each Party shall vigorously investigate claims of violations of laws relating to circumvention and, where appropriate, bring enforcement action to address any such violations.

2. If Singapore discovers conduct by an enterprise that it suspects is a violation of either Party's laws relating to circumvention, and the conduct has not been noted in a report

under Article 5.3.4, Singapore shall note the conduct in a report provided to the United States not later than 14 days after the discovery. If Singapore suspects that the conduct noted in a report under either the first sentence of this paragraph or Article 5.3.4 involves intentional circumvention, it shall immediately investigate and report the results of the investigation to the United States within 14 days of the conclusion of the investigation. In that case, Singapore shall also immediately initiate a detailed review of all textile and apparel goods that the enterprise has produced for exportation to the United States or exported to the United States during the six months preceding the date that Singapore discovered the conduct. Singapore shall prepare a report describing the results of that review and shall transmit that report to the United States no later than 60 days after it provides the report called for under the first sentence of this paragraph or under Article 5.3.4. The Parties may agree, in light of the facts of a particular review, to extend this 60-day period.

3. A report describing the results of a review of textile and apparel goods conducted pursuant to paragraph 2 shall include the following:
    (a) the name and address of the enterprise investigated;
    (b) the nature of the suspected violation (for example, failure to maintain adequate production records, or making false statements relating to country of origin or production);
    (c) a brief description of the evidence of a violation;
    (d) any penalty imposed or other action taken;
    (e) the identification numbers of the visas or export licenses corresponding to the goods and of all visas or export licenses that Singapore has issued to the enterprise during the 12 months before the date on which the conduct was discovered. If no visa or export license numbers are available, the report shall include the invoice number and date of export for each exportation of goods to the United States;
    (f) the product category, description, and quantity of the goods included in the exportations to the United States; and
    (g) purchase orders, bills of lading, contracts, payment records, invoices, and other records indicating the origin of the goods included in the exportations to the United States, and information identifying the importer of those goods in the United States, if Singapore possesses such information.

4. If Singapore finds that an enterprise has engaged in intentional circumvention, it shall take effective enforcement action, which shall include denying permission for an appropriate period for textile or apparel goods that the enterprise produces or exports to be exported to the United States.

5.
    (a) If a Party finds that an enterprise in its territory or operating under the Outward Processing Arrangement:
        (i) has failed to maintain or produce records in accordance with the Party's laws adopted or maintained in accordance with this Chapter,[5-4] or
        (ii) has engaged in conduct inconsistent with the Party's law that was intended to or did in fact result in circumvention, and if the Party requires a visa or export license to accompany exportations of textile or apparel goods to the territory of the other Party, then beginning on the date of the finding, the

Party shall not issue, for a period at least as long as the applicable period described in paragraph 6, such a visa or export license to the enterprise.

(b) If the United States finds that an enterprise of Singapore has engaged in intentional circumvention, then beginning on the date of the finding it may deny entry into the United States, during a period no longer than the applicable period described in paragraph 6, of textile or apparel goods that the enterprise has produced or exported.

6.

(a) With respect to a first finding under paragraph 5(a) or a first finding under paragraph 5(b), the applicable period is six months.

(b) With respect to a second finding under paragraph 5(a) or a second finding under paragraph 5(b), the applicable period is two years.

(c) With respect to any further finding under paragraph 5(a) or 5(b), the applicable period shall be two years, except that where measures a Party imposed with respect to the enterprise as a result of an earlier finding under paragraph 5(a) or 5(b) are still in effect, the applicable period shall be extended by the period remaining before those measures expire.

Article 5.6: Information Sharing

1. Within three months after the date this Chapter takes effect, Singapore shall notify the United States in writing of the names of all registered enterprises. Thereafter, Singapore shall provide the names of any newly registered, de-registered, or re-registered enterprises in written, quarterly updates to the United States.

2. At the time Singapore notifies the United States of a registered enterprise, it shall supply profile information to the United States regarding the enterprise, and shall update the information annually. This information shall include:

(a) name of the enterprise;

(b) address of the enterprise and locations of its facilities in Singapore, and, for an enterprise operating under the Outward Processing Arrangement, location of its facilities, whether in Singapore or outside of Singapore, involved in the production of textile or apparel goods claimed to be originating goods or marked as products of Singapore or export of such goods to the United States;

(c) telephone number, fax number, and e-mail address;

(d) statement of whether the enterprise is owned by Singapore persons, non-Singapore persons, or both;

(e) names of:
   (i) the directors and their respective positions within the enterprise, and
   (ii) the owners, in the case of an enterprise that is not incorporated;

(f) number of workers, skill sets (occupations), wages, hours of work, and minimum age for employment;

(g) number and type of machines the enterprise uses to produce textile or apparel goods;

(h) production capacity of the enterprise and identification of textile or apparel goods the enterprise produces; and

(i) names of customers in the United States.

Article 5.7: Confidentiality

1. Except as otherwise provided in this Chapter, each Party shall maintain the confidentiality of non-publicly available information, including business confidential information, that the other Party provides to it in accordance with this Chapter and has designated as confidential, unless the Party that provided the information gives permission for the information to be publicly disclosed.

2. A Party shall not disclose to a non-Party for law enforcement purposes or in connection with judicial proceedings information relating to intentional circumvention that the other Party has provided to the Party pursuant to Article 5.3, 5.4, 5.5 or 5.6, unless the other Party consents to the disclosure.

3.
    (a) Subject to subparagraph (b), nothing in this Chapter shall prevent a Party from making public the name of an enterprise that the Party has found to have engaged in intentional circumvention or that has failed to demonstrate its production of or capability to produce textile or apparel goods as provided under this Chapter.

    (b) If a Party makes public the name of an enterprise as described in sub-paragraph (a) and the finding underlying the disclosure is based on information provided by the other Party pursuant to Article 5.3, 5.4, 5.5 or 5.6, the Party making the disclosure shall not disclose the information provided by the other Party or the fact that it based its finding on information provided by the other Party, unless the other Party consents to the disclosure of such information or such fact.

4. If a Party considers that the other Party has not maintained the confidentiality of information as required under this Article, it may make a written request to the other Party for consultations. The Parties shall consult within 30 days after the request is delivered with a view to agreeing on appropriate steps to ensure compliance with this Article.

Article 5.8: Consultations and Related Matters

1. A Party may request consultations with the other Party under this Article, with a view to seeking a mutually satisfactory solution, if it believes that:
    (a) the other Party is not complying with the terms of this Agreement relating to textile and apparel goods;
    (b) circumvention relating to trade between the Parties is occurring; or
    (c) the other Party is failing to effectively enforce its laws regarding circumvention.
    Unless the Parties agree otherwise, they shall commence consultations within 30 days of a Party's receipt of a written request by the other Party and conclude consultations within 90 days of the Party's receipt of the written request.

2. If the Parties are unable to reach a mutually satisfactory solution under paragraph 1 and the United States has presented to Singapore clear evidence that circumvention has occurred, the United States may reduce the quantity of textile and apparel goods that may be imported into its territory from Singapore by an amount not to exceed three times the quantity of goods involved in the circumvention. In addition, the

United States may revoke any preferential tariff treatment provided pursuant to this Agreement to the goods involved in the circumvention, and deny such treatment, for a period not to exceed four years, to any textile or apparel goods produced by an enterprise found to have engaged in such circumvention, including any successor of the enterprise and any other entity owned or operated by a principal of the enterprise, if such entity, of which that person is a principal, produces textile or apparel goods.[5-5]

Article 5.9: Bilateral Textile and Apparel Safeguard Actions

1. Subject to paragraphs 2 through 7 and during the transition period only, if, as a result of the reduction or elimination of a customs duty provided for in this Agreement, a textile or apparel good benefiting from preferential tariff treatment under this Agreement is being imported into the territory of a Party in such increased quantities, in absolute terms or relative to the domestic market for that good, and under such conditions that imports of such good from the other Party constitute a substantial cause of serious damage or actual threat thereof, to a domestic industry producing a like or directly competitive good, the importing Party may, to the extent and for such time as may be necessary to prevent or remedy the serious damage and to facilitate adjustment by the domestic industry:
   (a) suspend the further reduction of any rate of duty provided for under this Agreement on the good; or
   (b) increase the rate of duty on the good to a level not to exceed the lesser of:
      (i) the most-favored-nation ("MFN") applied rate of duty in effect at the time the action is taken, and
      (ii) the MFN applied rate of duty in effect on the date of entry into force of this Agreement.
2. In determining serious damage, or actual threat thereof, the Party:
   (a) shall examine the effect of increased imports on the particular industry, as reflected in changes in such relevant economic variables as output, productivity, utilization of capacity, inventories, market share, exports, wages, employment, domestic prices, profits, and investment, none of which is necessarily decisive; and
   (b) shall not consider changes in technology or consumer preference as factors supporting a determination of serious damage or actual threat thereof.
3. A Party shall deliver without delay written notice of its intent to take action under this Article to the other Party, and shall enter into consultations with that Party.
4. The following conditions and limitations apply to any action taken under paragraph 1:
   (a) no action may be maintained for a period exceeding two years, except that the period may be extended by up to two years if the competent authorities of the Party applying the action determine, in conformity with the procedures set out in this Article, that the action continues to be necessary to prevent or remedy serious damage and to facilitate adjustment by the domestic industry, and that there is evidence that the industry is adjusting;
   (b) no action may be taken by a Party against any particular good of the other Party more than once during the transition period; and

(c) on termination of the action, the rate of duty shall be the rate that would have been in effect but for the action.

5. The Party taking an action under paragraph 1 shall provide to the Party against whose good the action is taken mutually agreed trade liberalizing compensation in the form of concessions having substantially equivalent trade effects or equivalent to the value of the additional duties expected to result from the emergency action. Such concessions shall be limited to textile and apparel goods, unless the Parties otherwise agree. If the Parties concerned are unable to agree on compensation within 30 days in the consultations under paragraph 3, the exporting Party may take action with respect to textile and apparel goods of the other Party that has trade effects substantially equivalent to the action taken under paragraph 1. The Party taking such action shall apply the action only for the minimum period necessary to achieve the substantially equivalent effects. However, the right to take such action shall not be exercised for the first 24 months that the action pursuant to paragraph 1 is in effect, provided that the action pursuant to paragraph 1 has been applied as a result of an absolute increase in imports and that such emergency action conforms to the provisions of this Article.

6. Nothing in this Article shall be construed to affect a Party's rights and obligations under Chapter 7, except that an action under this Article shall be considered a "safeguard measure" for purposes of Article 7.2.7 (Conditions and Limitations). Nothing in Chapter 7 shall be construed to affect a Party's rights and obligations under this Article.

7. Nothing in this Article shall be construed to limit the ability of a Party to restrain imports of textile and apparel goods in a manner consistent with the WTO Agreement on Textiles and Clothing or the WTO Agreement on Safeguards.

8. For purposes of this Article:
   (a) **substantial cause** means a cause that is important and not less than any other cause;
   (b) **transition period** means the 10-year period following entry into force of the terms of this Agreement relating to textile and apparel goods under Article 5.10.

Article 5.10: Effective Date

The terms of this Agreement regarding textile and apparel goods shall take effect on the date on which:

(a) the Parties have consulted with regard to their adoption or maintenance of laws necessary to implement this Chapter and have agreed that such laws are in place, and

(b) the Parties have exchanged written notifications that their respective internal requirements for this Chapter to take effect have been fulfilled,

or on such other date as the Parties may agree.

Article 5.11: Definitions

For purposes of this Chapter:

1. **circumvention** means providing a false declaration or false information for the purpose of, or with the effect of, violating or evading existing customs, country of origin labeling, or trade laws of the respective Party relating to imports of textile and apparel goods, if such action results in the avoidance of tariffs, quotas, embargoes, prohibitions, restrictions, trade remedies, including antidumping or countervailing duties, or safeguard measures, or in obtaining preferential tariff treatment. Examples of circumvention include illegal transshipment; rerouting; fraud; false declarations concerning country of origin, fiber content, quantities, description, or classification; falsification of documents; and smuggling;

2. **free trade zone** means any area, designated under Singapore's Free Trade Zone Act or any successor act, used to store, assemble, mix, or otherwise manipulate any goods or to carry out such manufacture, in accordance with such act;

3. **host Party** means the Party in whose territory a site visit requested under Article 5.4.2 is conducted;

4. **Outward Processing Arrangement** means the arrangement whereby a registered Singapore textile or apparel goods producer is permitted to process outside Singapore subsidiary or minor processes of its textile or apparel goods without affecting the Singapore country of origin status of the textile or apparel goods;

5. **preferential tariff treatment** means the customs duty rate that is applicable to an originating good pursuant to Chapter 2;

6. **registered enterprise** means an enterprise that is a producer or exporter of textile or apparel goods and that is registered by Singapore under the system described in Article 5.3.2;

7. **requesting Party** means the Party seeking to conduct a site visit under Article 5.4.2;

8. **textile or apparel good** means a product listed in the Annex to the WTO Agreement on Textiles and Clothing; and

9. **transshipment or transshipped** means the removal of a good from the conveyance on which it was brought into the territory of a Party and the placement of such good on the same or another conveyance for the purpose of taking it out of the territory of the Party, including when such good undergoes processing or manipulation in a free trade zone.

6. TECHNICAL BARRIERS TO TRADE

Article 6.1: Scope

This Chapter applies to technical regulations, standards, and conformity assessment procedures as defined in the WTO TBT Agreement.

Article 6.2: Enhanced Cooperation and Chapter 6 Coordinator

1. With a view to facilitating trade in goods between them, the Parties should to the maximum extent possible seek to enhance their cooperation with each other in the area of technical regulations, standards, and conformity assessment procedures and to

deepen the mutual understanding and awareness of each other's systems, including through:

(a) exchanging information on technical regulations, standards and conformity assessment procedures;

(b) holding consultations to address and resolve any matters that may arise from the application of specific technical regulations, standards and conformity assessment procedures;

(c) promoting the use of international standards by each Party in its technical regulations, standards and conformity assessment procedures; and

(d) facilitating and promoting mechanisms relating to technical regulations, standards and conformity assessment procedures that would enhance and promote trade between the Parties, including mechanisms established at APEC and other plurilateral fora.

2. In order to facilitate the cooperation described in paragraph 1, each Party shall designate a Chapter 6 Coordinator, which shall:

(a) be responsible for coordinating with interested parties in the Party's territory in all matters pertaining to enhanced cooperation under this Chapter, including with respect to proposals for enhanced cooperation and responses to such proposals; and

(b) normally carry out its functions through agreed communication channels and meet with the other Party's Chapter 6 Coordinator as and when they agree is necessary for the efficient and effective discharge of their functions.

Article 6.3: Conformity Assessment and Other Areas of Mutual Interest

1. Each Party shall take steps to implement Phase I and Phase II of the APEC Mutual Recognition Arrangement for Conformity Assessment of Telecommunications Equipment with respect to the other Party.

2. The Parties should to the maximum extent possible also work towards enhancing the momentum of cooperation in line with their respective bilateral, regional and plurilateral agreements, including the APEC work program on Standards and Conformance. To achieve this objective the Parties should to the maximum extent possible examine the feasibility of cooperating with each other on conformity assessment procedures and other areas of mutual interest, including agreements where the relevant authorities from both Parties are willing to do so.

3. Each Party should to the maximum extent possible consider progress made on achieving the objectives of this Chapter during meetings of the Joint Committee established under Article 20.1 (Joint Committee).

4. The Parties establish the Medical Products Working Group referred to in Article 20.1.2(b) (Joint Committee), as set out in Annex 6A to this Chapter.

Article 6.4: Definitions

For purposes of this Chapter:

1. **WTO TBT Agreement** means the WTO Agreement on Technical Barriers to Trade; and

2. **APEC** means the Asia Pacific Economic Cooperation Forum.

Annex 6A. Working Group on Medical Products

1. The Parties establish a Medical Products Working Group to promote the protection of public health through expeditious, science-based regulatory procedures for new medical products. The purpose of the Working Group is to provide a forum for cooperation on product regulation issues of mutual interest, to the extent permitted by resources, through means other than mutual recognition agreements or other binding commitments.

2. The Working Group shall:
   (a) seek to ensure that regulatory procedures for the review of applications for marketing authorization with respect to new medical products are
      (i) expeditious, transparent, without conflict of interest, and nondiscriminatory,
      (ii) based on generally-accepted international scientific standards, such as the International Conference on Harmonization, and
      (iii) based only on the assessment of product quality, safety, and efficacy;
   (b) seek to ensure that the measures of each Party that promote and protect public health through regulatory procedures for medical products are transparent and are developed through a process that
      (i) provides for effective notice to and comment by interested persons, and
      (ii) provides a meaningful opportunity for interested persons of the other Party to consult with FDA or HSA, as appropriate; and
   (c) provide a forum for consultation between the health authorities of each Party regarding matters of interest, including general scientific and regulatory policy and specific measures pertaining to the promotion and protection of public health through expeditious, science-based regulatory procedures.

3. FDA and HSA shall chair the Working Group. The chairs shall be responsible for establishing the time and place for meetings of the Working Group and for developing the procedures for such meetings and other activities of the Working Group. Such procedures shall include that:
   (a) FDA shall report on the activities of the Working Group to the U.S. Secretary of Health and Human Services;
   (b) HSA shall report on the activities of the Working Group to the Singapore Minister for Health; and
   (c) the Working Group shall issue periodic reports to the Joint Committee established under Article 20.1 (Joint Committee).

4. The Parties shall ensure that the activities of the Working Group do not preclude or interfere with other opportunities for meetings and cooperation between FDA and HSA.

5. For purposes of this Annex:
   (a) **FDA** means the United States Food and Drug Administration;

(b) **HSA** means the Health Sciences Authority of Singapore; and

(c) **Working Group** means the Medical Products Working Group comprising representatives of FDA and HSA.

7. SAFEGUARDS

Article 7.1: Application of a Bilateral Safeguard Measure

Subject to Articles 7.2 through 7.5, if as a result of the reduction or elimination of a customs duty under this Agreement, an originating good of the other Party is being imported into the territory of a Party in such increased quantities, in absolute terms or relative to domestic production, and under such conditions that the imports of such originating good from the other Party constitute a substantial cause of serious injury or threat thereof, to a domestic industry producing a like or directly competitive good, such Party may:

(a) suspend the further reduction of any rate of customs duty provided for under this Agreement for the good;

(b) increase the rate of customs duty on the good to a level not to exceed the lesser of

(i) the most-favored-nation (MFN) applied rate of duty on the good in effect at the time the action is taken, and

(ii) the MFN applied rate of duty on the good in effect on the day immediately preceding the date of entry into force of this Agreement; or

(c) in the case of a customs duty applied to a good on a seasonal basis, increase the rate of duty to a level not to exceed the lesser of the MFN applied rate of duty that was in effect on the good for the immediately preceding corresponding season or the date of entry into force of this Agreement.

Article 7.2: Conditions and Limitations

The following conditions and limitations shall apply with regard to a measure described in Article 7.1:

1. A Party shall notify the other Party in writing upon initiation of an investigation described in paragraph 2 and shall consult with the other Party as far in advance of taking any such measure as practicable, with a view to reviewing the information arising from the investigation, exchanging views on the measure and reaching an agreement on compensation as set out in Article 7.4. If a Party takes a provisional measure pursuant to Article 7.3, the Party shall also notify the other Party prior to taking such measure, and shall initiate consultations with the other Party immediately after such measure is taken.

2. A Party shall take a measure only following an investigation by that Party's competent authorities in accordance with Articles 3 and 4.2(c) of the WTO Agreement on Safeguards; and to this end, Articles 3 and 4.2(c) of the WTO Agreement on Safeguards are incorporated into and made a part of this Agreement, *mutatis mutandis*.

3. In the investigation described in paragraph 2, a Party shall comply with the requirements of Article 4.2(a) and (b) of the WTO Agreement on Safeguards; and to this end, Article 4.2(a) and (b) are incorporated into and made a part of this Agreement, *mutatis mutandis*.

4. Negative injury determinations shall not be subject to modification, except pursuant to reviews by judicial or administrative tribunals, to the extent provided under domestic legislation.

5. The investigation shall in all cases be completed within one year following its date of institution.

6. No measure may be maintained:

    (a) except to the extent and for such time as may be necessary to prevent or remedy serious injury and to facilitate adjustment;

    (b) for a period exceeding two years; except that the period may be extended by up to two years if the competent authorities determine, in conformity with the procedures set out in paragraphs 1 through 5, that the measure continues to be necessary to prevent or remedy serious injury and to facilitate adjustment and that there is evidence that the industry is adjusting; or

    (c) beyond the expiration of the transition period, except with the consent of the Party against whose originating good the measure is taken.

7. No measure may be applied against the same originating good on which a measure has been taken or that has been subject to any other safeguard measure[7-1] since the date of entry into force of the Agreement.

8. Where the expected duration of the measure is over one year, the importing Party shall progressively liberalize it at regular intervals during the period of application.

9. Upon the termination of the measure, the rate of customs duty shall be the rate which would have been in effect but for the measure.

Article 7.3: Provisional Measures

In critical circumstances where delay would cause damage which it would be difficult to repair, a Party may take a measure described in Article 7.1(a), (b) or (c) on a provisional basis pursuant to a preliminary determination that there is clear evidence that imports from the other Party have increased as the result of the reduction or elimination of a customs duty under this Agreement, and such imports constitute a substantial cause of serious injury, or threat thereof, to the domestic industry. The duration of such provisional measure shall not exceed 200 days, during which time the requirements of Articles 7.2.2 and 7.2.3 shall be met. Any tariff increases shall be promptly refunded if the investigation described in Article 7.2.2 does not result in a finding that the requirements of Article 7.1 are met. The duration of any provisional measure shall be counted as part of the period described in Article 7.2.6(b).

Article 7.4: Compensation

The Party applying a measure described in Article 7.1 shall provide to the other Party mutually agreed trade liberalizing compensation in the form of concessions having substantially equivalent trade effects or equivalent to the value of the additional duties expected to result from the measure. If the Parties are unable to agree on compensation within 30 days in the consultations under Article 7.2, the Party against whose originating good the measure is applied may take action with respect to originating goods of the other Party that has trade effects substantially equivalent to the measure described in Article 7.1. The Party taking such action shall apply the action only for the minimum period necessary to achieve the substantially equivalent effects, and in any event, only while the measure under Article 7.1 is being applied.

Article 7.5: Global Safeguard Measures

Each Party retains its rights and obligations under Article XIX of GATT 1994 and the WTO Agreement on Safeguards. This Agreement does not confer any additional rights or obligations on the Parties with regard to global safeguard measures, except that a Party taking a global safeguard measure may exclude imports of an originating good from the other Party if such imports are not a substantial cause of serious injury or threat thereof.

Article 7.6: Definitions

For purposes of this Chapter:

1. **domestic industry** means the producers as a whole of the like or directly competitive product operating in the territory of a Party, or those whose collective output of the like or directly competitive products constitutes a major proportion of the total domestic production of those products;
2. **global safeguard measure** means a measure applied under Article XIX of GATT 1994 and the WTO Agreement on Safeguards;
3. **serious injury** means a significant overall impairment in the position of a domestic industry;
4. **substantial cause** means a cause which is important and not less than any other cause;
5. **threat of serious injury** means serious injury that, on the basis of facts and not merely on allegation, conjecture or remote possibility, is clearly imminent; and
6. **transition period** means the ten-year period following entry into force of this Agreement.

8. CROSS-BORDER TRADE IN SERVICES

Article 8.1: Definitions

For purposes of this Chapter:

1. **central level of government** means
   (a) for the United States, the federal level of government; and
   (b) for Singapore, the national level of government;
2. **cross-border trade in services or cross-border supply of services** means the supply of a service
   (a) from the territory of one Party into the territory of the other Party;
   (b) in the territory of one Party by a person of that Party to a person of the other Party; or

(c) by a national of a Party in the territory of the other Party;

but does not include the supply of a service in the territory of a Party by an investor of the other Party or a covered investment as defined in Article 15.1 (Definitions);

3. **enterprise** means an entity constituted or organized under applicable law, whether or not for profit, and whether privately or governmentally owned or controlled, including a corporation, trust, partnership, sole proprietorship, joint venture, association, or similar organization and a branch of an enterprise;

4. **enterprise of a Party** means an enterprise organized or constituted under the laws of a Party and a branch located in the territory of a Party and carrying out business activities there;

5. **local level of government** means, for Singapore, entities with sub-national legislative or executive powers under domestic law, including Town Councils and Community Development Councils;

6. **professional services** means services, the provision of which requires specialized post-secondary education, or equivalent training or experience, and for which the right to practice is granted or restricted by a Party, but does not include services provided by trades-persons or vessel and aircraft crew members;

7. **regional level of government** means, for the United States, a state of the United States, the District of Columbia, or Puerto Rico; for Singapore, "regional level of government" is not applicable, as Singapore has no government at the regional level;

8. **service supplier** means a person of a Party that seeks to supply or supplies a service;[8-1] and

9. **specialty air services** means any non-transportation air services, such as aerial fire-fighting, sightseeing, spraying, surveying, mapping, photography, parachute jumping, glider towing and helicopter-lift for logging and construction, and other airborne agricultural, industrial, and inspection services.

Article 8.2: Scope and Coverage

1.
   (a) This Chapter applies to measures by a Party affecting cross-border trade in services by service suppliers of the other Party.
   (b) Measures covered by subparagraph (a) include measures affecting:
      (i) the production, distribution, marketing, sale and delivery of a service;
      (ii) the purchase or use of, or payment for, a service;
      (iii) the access to and use of distribution, transport, or telecommunications networks and services in connection with the supply of a service; and
      (iv) the provision of a bond or other form of financial security as a condition for the supply of a service.
   (c) For purposes of this Chapter, **measures by a Party** means measures taken by:
      (i) central, regional or local governments and authorities; and
      (ii) non-governmental bodies in the exercise of powers delegated by central, regional or local governments or authorities.

2. Articles 8.5, 8.8 and 8.12 also apply to measures by a Party affecting the supply of a service in its territory by an investor of the other Party or a covered investment as defined in Article 15.1 (Definitions).[8-2]

3. This Chapter does not apply to:
   (a) financial services as defined in Article 10.20 (Definitions), except that paragraph 2 shall apply where the service is supplied by an investor or investment of the other Party that is not an investor or an investment in a financial institution (as defined in Article 10.20.4) in the Party's territory;
   (b) government procurement;
   (c) air services, including domestic and international air transportation services, whether scheduled or non-scheduled, and related services in support of air services, other than:
      (i) aircraft repair and maintenance services during which an aircraft is withdrawn from service; and
      (ii) specialty air services; or
   (d) subsidies or grants provided by a Party, including government-supported loans, guarantees and insurance.
4. This Chapter does not impose any obligation on a Party with respect to a national of the other Party seeking access to its employment market, or employed on a permanent basis in its territory, and does not confer any right on that national with respect to that access or employment.
5.
   (a) This Chapter does not apply to services supplied in the exercise of governmental authority within the territory of each respective Party.
   (b) For purposes of this Chapter, a **service supplied in the exercise of governmental authority** means any service which is supplied neither on a commercial basis, nor in competition with one or more service suppliers.

Article 8.3: National Treatment

1. Each Party shall accord to service suppliers of the other Party treatment no less favorable than that it accords, in like circumstances, to its own service suppliers.
2. The treatment to be accorded by a Party under paragraph 1 means, with respect to a regional level of government, treatment no less favorable than the most favorable treatment accorded, in like circumstances, by that regional level of government to service suppliers of the Party of which it forms a part.

Article 8.4: Most-Favored-Nation Treatment

Each Party shall accord to service suppliers of the other Party treatment no less favorable than that it accords, in like circumstances, to service suppliers of a non-Party.

Article 8.5: Market Access

A Party shall not adopt or maintain, either on the basis of a regional subdivision or on the basis of its entire territory, measures that:

   (a) limit

(i)   the number of service suppliers whether in the form of numerical quotas, monopolies, exclusive service suppliers or the requirement of an economic needs test;

(ii) the total value of service transactions or assets in the form of numerical quotas or the requirement of an economic needs test;

(iii) the total number of service operations or the total quantity of services output expressed in terms of designated numerical units in the form of quotas or the requirement of an economic needs test;[8-3]

(iv) the total number of natural persons that may be employed in a particular service sector or that a service supplier may employ and who are necessary for, and directly related to, the supply of a specific service in the form of numerical quotas or the requirement of an economic needs test; and

(b) restrict or require specific types of legal entity or joint venture through which a service supplier may supply a service.

Article 8.6: Local Presence

A Party shall not require a service supplier of the other Party to establish or maintain a representative office or any form of enterprise, or to be resident, in its territory as a condition for the cross-border supply of a service.

Article 8.7: Non-Conforming Measures

1. Articles 8.3, 8.4, 8.5, and 8.6 do not apply to:
    (a) any existing non-conforming measure that is maintained by a Party at
        (i)   the central level of government, as set out by that Party in its Schedule to Annex 8A;
        (ii) a regional level of government, as set out by that Party in its Schedule to Annex 8A; or
        (iii) a local government level of government;
    (b) the continuation or prompt renewal of any non-conforming measure referred to in subparagraph (a); or
    (c) an amendment to any non-conforming measure referred to in subparagraph (a) to the extent that the amendment does not decrease the conformity of the measure, as it existed immediately before the amendment, with Articles 8.3, 8.4, 8.5, and 8.6.

2. Articles 8.3, 8.4, 8.5, and 8.6 do not apply to any measure that a Party adopts or maintains with respect to sectors, sub-sectors or activities as set out in its Schedule to Annex 8B.

Article 8.8: Domestic Regulation

1. Where a Party requires authorization for the supply of a service, the Party's competent authorities shall, within a reasonable period of time after the submission of an application considered complete under domestic laws and regulations, inform the applicant of the decision concerning the application. At the request of the

applicant, the competent authorities of the Party shall provide, without undue delay, information concerning the status of the application. This obligation shall not apply to authorization requirements that are within the scope of Article 8.7.2.

2. With a view to ensuring that measures relating to qualification requirements and procedures, technical standards and licensing requirements do not constitute unnecessary barriers to trade in services, each Party shall endeavor to ensure, as appropriate for individual sectors, that such measures are:

   (a) based on objective and transparent criteria, such as competence and the ability to supply the service;

   (b) not more burdensome than necessary to ensure the quality of the service; and

   (c) in the case of licensing procedures, not in themselves a restriction on the supply of the service.

3. If the results of the negotiations related to Article VI:4 of GATS (or the results of any similar negotiations undertaken in other multilateral fora in which both Parties participate) enter into effect, this Article shall be amended, as appropriate, after consultations between the Parties, to bring those results into effect under this Agreement. The Parties agree to coordinate on such negotiations, as appropriate.

Article 8.9: Recognition

1. For the purposes of the fulfillment, in whole or in part, of its standards or criteria for the authorization, licensing or certification of services suppliers, and subject to the requirements of paragraph 4, a Party may recognize the education or experience obtained, requirements met, or licenses or certifications granted in a particular country, including the other Party and non-Parties. Such recognition, which may be achieved through harmonization or otherwise, may be based upon an agreement or arrangement with the country concerned or may be accorded autonomously.

2. Where a Party recognizes, autonomously or by agreement or arrangement, the education or experience obtained, requirements met or licenses or certifications granted in the territory of a non-Party, nothing in Article 8.4 shall be construed to require the Party to accord such recognition to the education or experience obtained, requirements met or licenses or certifications granted in the territory of the other Party.

3. A Party that is a party to an agreement or arrangement of the type referred to in paragraph 1, whether existing or future, shall afford adequate opportunity for the other Party, if the other Party is interested, to negotiate its accession to such an agreement or arrangement or to negotiate comparable ones with it. Where a Party accords recognition autonomously, it shall afford adequate opportunity for the other Party to demonstrate that education, experience, licenses, or certifications obtained or requirements met in that other Party's territory should be recognized.

4. A Party shall not accord recognition in a manner which would constitute a means of discrimination between countries in the application of its standards or criteria for the authorization, licensing or certification of services suppliers, or a disguised restriction on trade in services.

5. Annex 8C applies to measures by a Party relating to the licensing or certification of professional service suppliers as set out in the provisions of that Annex.

Article 8.10: Transfers and Payments

1. Each Party shall permit all transfers and payments relating to the cross-border supply of services to be made freely and without delay into and out of its territory.[8-4] Such transfers and payments include:
   (a) payments for services;
   (b) funds taken abroad to consume a service;
   (c) interest, royalty payments, management fees, licensing fees, and technical assistance and other fees;
   (d) payments made under a contract; and
   (e) inflows of funds necessary to perform a service.
2. Each Party shall permit such transfers and payments relating to the cross-border supply of services to be made in a freely usable currency at the market rate of exchange prevailing on the date of transfer.
3. Notwithstanding paragraphs 1 and 2, a Party may prevent a transfer or payment through the equitable, non-discriminatory and good faith application of its laws relating to:
   (a) bankruptcy, insolvency or the protection of the rights of creditors;
   (b) issuing, trading or dealing in securities, futures, options, or derivatives;
   (c) financial reporting or record keeping of transfers when necessary to assist law enforcement or financial regulatory authorities;
   (d) criminal or penal offenses; or
   (e) ensuring compliance with orders or judgments in judicial or administrative proceedings.

Article 8.11: Denial of Benefits

A Party may deny the benefits of this Chapter to a service supplier of the other Party if:

(a) the service is being supplied by an enterprise owned or controlled by nationals of a non-Party and the denying Party:
   (i) does not maintain diplomatic relations with the non-Party; or
   (ii) adopts or maintains measures with respect to the non-Party that prohibit transactions with the enterprise or that would be violated or circumvented if the benefits of this Chapter were accorded to the enterprise; or
(b) the service is being supplied by an enterprise that has no substantial business activities in the territory of the other Party and it is owned or controlled by persons of a non-Party or the denying Party.

Article 8.12: Transparency in Development and Application of Regulations

In addition to the obligations in Chapter 19 (Transparency):

(a) Each Party shall maintain or establish appropriate mechanisms for responding to inquiries from interested persons regarding regulations[8-5] relating to the subject matter of this Chapter and their requirements.

(b) If a Party does not provide advance notice and comment pursuant to Article 19.3, it shall, to the extent possible, provide by publicly available means the reasons therefor.

(c) At the time it adopts final regulations relating to the subject matter of this Chapter, each Party shall, to the extent possible, including upon request, address by publicly available means substantive comments received from interested persons with respect to the proposed regulations.

(d) To the extent possible, each Party shall allow reasonable time between publication of final regulations and their effective date.

Article 8.13: Implementation

The Parties will meet annually, or as otherwise agreed, on issues related to implementation of this Chapter and any issues of mutual interest.

Annex 8A

1. A Party's Schedule to this Annex sets out, pursuant to Articles 8.7.1 and 15.12.1 (NonConforming Measures), a Party's existing measures that are not subject to some or all of the obligations imposed by:

   (a) Article 8.3 (National Treatment) or 15.4.1 (National Treatment and Most-Favored-Nation Treatment);

   (b) Article 8.4 (Most-Favored-Nation Treatment) or 15.4.3 (National Treatment and Most-Favored-Nation Treatment);

   (c) Article 8.5 (Market Access);

   (d) Article 8.6 (Local Presence);

   (e) Article 15.8 (Performance Requirements); or

   (f) Article 15.9 (Senior Management and Boards of Directors).

2. Each Schedule entry sets out the following elements:

   (a) **sector** refers to the sector for which the entry is made;

   (b) **sub-sector**, for Singapore, refers to the subsector for which the entry is made;

   (c) **industry classification** refers, for Singapore, where applicable, to the activity covered by the non-conforming measure, according to the provisional CPC codes as used in the Provisional Central Product Classification (Statistical Papers Series M No. 77, Department of International Economic and Social Affairs, Statistical Office of the United Nations, New York, 1991);

   (d) **obligations concerned** specifies the obligation(s) referred to in paragraph 1 that, pursuant to Article 8.7.1(a) (Non-Conforming Measures) or 15.12.1(a) (NonConforming Measures), as the case may be, do not apply to the listed measure(s);

   (e) **level of government** indicates the level of government maintaining the listed measure(s);

   (f) **measures** identifies the laws, regulations or other measures for which the entry is made. A measure cited in the **measures** element:

      (i) means the measure as amended, continued or renewed as of the date of entry into force of this Agreement, and

      (ii) includes any subordinate measure adopted or maintained under the authority of and consistent with the measure;

    (g) **description**, for Singapore, sets out the non-conforming aspects of the measure for which the entry is made; and **description**, for the United States, provides a general, non-binding, description of the **measures**; and

    (h) **phase-out** sets out commitments, if any, for liberalization after the date of entry into force of this Agreement.

3.   In accordance with Article 8.7.1(a) (Non-Conforming Measures) and 15.12.1(a) (NonConforming Measures), the articles of this Agreement specified in the "obligations concerned" element of an entry do not apply to the law, regulation or other measure identified in the "measures" or "description" element of that entry.

4.   Where a Party maintains a measure that requires that a service provider be a citizen, permanent resident, or resident of its territory as a condition to the provision of a service in its territory, a Schedule entry for that measure taken in the Schedule to Annex 8A or 8B with respect to Articles 8.3, 8.4 or 8.6 shall operate as a Schedule entry with respect to Articles 15.4 (National Treatment and Most-Favored-Nation Treatment) or15.8 (Performance Requirements) to the extent of that measure.

Annex 8B

1.   A Party's Schedule to this Annex sets out, pursuant to Articles 8.7.2 (Non-Conforming Measures) and 15.12.2 (Non-Conforming Measures), the specific sectors, sub-sectors or activities for which that Party may maintain existing, or adopt new or more restrictive, measures that do not conform with obligations imposed by:

    (a) Article 8.3 (National Treatment) or 15.4.1 (National Treatment and Most-Favored-Nation Treatment);

    (b) Article 8.4 (Most-Favored-Nation Treatment) or 15.4.3 (National Treatment and Most-Favored-Nation Treatment);

    (c) Article 8.5 (Market Access);

    (d) Article 8.6 (Local Presence);

    (e) Article 15.8 (Performance Requirements); or

    (f) Article 15.9 (Senior Management and Boards of Directors).

2.   Each Schedule entry sets out the following elements:

    (a) **sector** refers to the sector for which the entry is made;

    (b) **sub-sector**, for Singapore, refers to the subsector for which the entry is made;

    (c) **industry classification** refers, for Singapore, where applicable, to the activity covered by the non-conforming measure, according to the provisional CPC codes as used in the Provisional Central Product Classification (Statistical Papers Series M No. 77, Department of International Economic and Social Affairs, Statistical Office of the United Nations, New York, 1991);

    (d) **obligations concerned** specifies the obligation(s) referred to in paragraph 1 that, pursuant to Articles 8.7.2 (Non-Conforming Measures) and Article 15.12.2 (NonConforming Measures), do not apply to the sectors, sub-sectors or activities listed in the entry;

(e) **description** sets out the scope of the sector, sub-sector or activities covered by the entry; and

(f) **existing measures** identifies, for transparency purposes, existing measures that apply to the sector, sub-sector or activities covered by the entry.

3. In accordance with Articles 8.7.2 (Non-Conforming Measures) and 15.12.2 (NonConforming Measures), the articles of this Agreement specified in the "obligations concerned" element of an entry do not apply to the sectors, sub-sectors and activities identified in the description element of that entry.

Annex 8C. Professional Services

Development of Professional Standards

1. The Parties shall encourage the relevant bodies in their respective territories to develop mutually acceptable standards and criteria for licensing and certification of professional service providers and to provide recommendations on mutual recognition to the Joint Committee.

2. The standards and criteria referred to in paragraph 1 may be developed with regard to the following matters:

   (a) education - accreditation of schools or academic programs;

   (b) examinations - qualifying examinations for licensing, including alternative methods of assessment such as oral examinations and interviews;

   (c) experience - length and nature of experience required for licensing;

   (d) conduct and ethics - standards of professional conduct and the nature of disciplinary action for non-conformity with those standards;

   (e) professional development and re-certification - continuing education and ongoing requirements to maintain professional certification;

   (f) scope of practice - extent of, or limitations on, permissible activities;

   (g) local knowledge - requirements for knowledge of such matters as local laws, regulations, language, geography or climate; and

   (h) consumer protection - alternatives to residency requirements, including bonding, professional liability insurance and client restitution funds, to provide for the protection of consumers.

3. On receipt of a recommendation referred to in paragraph 1, the Joint Committee shall review the recommendation within a reasonable time to determine whether it is consistent with this Agreement. Based on the Joint Committee's review, each Party shall encourage its respective competent authorities, where appropriate, to implement the recommendation within a mutually agreed time.

Temporary Licensing

4. Where the Parties agree, each Party shall encourage the relevant bodies in its territory to develop procedures for the temporary licensing of professional service providers of another Party.

Review

5. The Joint Committee shall, at least once every three years, review the implementation of this Section.

9. TELECOMMUNICATIONS

Article 9.1: Scope and Coverage

1. This Chapter applies to measures affecting trade in telecommunications services.
2. This Chapter does not apply to any measure adopted or maintained by a Party relating to cable or broadcast distribution of radio or television programming.[9-1]
3. Nothing in this Chapter shall be construed to:
    (a) require a Party (or require a Party to compel any enterprise) to establish, construct, acquire, lease, operate, or provide telecommunications transport networks or telecommunications services where such networks or services are not offered to the public generally; or
    (b) require a Party to compel any enterprise engaged in the cable or broadcast distribution of radio or television programming to make available its cable or broadcast facilities as a public telecommunications transport network, unless a Party specifically designates such facilities as such.

Article 9.2: Access to and Use of Public Telecommunications Transport Networks and Services[9-2]

1. Each Party shall ensure that enterprises of the other Party have access to and use of any public telecommunications transport network and service, including leased circuits, offered in its territory or across its borders on reasonable, non-discriminatory (including with respect to timeliness), and transparent terms and conditions, including as set out in paragraphs 2 through 4.
2. Each Party shall ensure that such enterprises are permitted to:
    (a) purchase or lease, and attach terminal or other equipment that interfaces with the public telecommunications network;
    (b) provide services to individual or multiple end-users over any leased or owned circuit(s);
    (c) connect leased or owned circuits with public telecommunications transport networks and services in the territory, or across the borders, of that Party, or with circuits leased or owned by another enterprise;
    (d) perform switching, signaling, processing, and conversion functions; and
    (e) use operating protocols of their choice.
3. Each Party shall ensure that enterprises of the other Party may use public telecommunications transport networks and services for the movement of information in its territory or across its borders and for access to information

contained in data bases or otherwise stored in machine-readable form in the territory of either Party.

4. Notwithstanding paragraph 3, a Party may take such measures as are necessary to

   (a) ensure the security and confidentiality of messages; or

   (b) protect the privacy of customer proprietary network information; subject to the requirement that such measures are not applied in a manner that would constitute a means of arbitrary or unjustifiable discrimination or a disguised restriction on trade in services.

Article 9.3: Interconnection with Suppliers of Public Telecommunications Services

1. Each Party shall ensure that suppliers of public telecommunications services in its territory provide, directly or indirectly, interconnection with the facilities and equipment of suppliers of public telecommunications services of the other Party.

2. In carrying out paragraph 1, each Party shall ensure that suppliers of public telecommunications services in its territory take reasonable steps to protect the confidentiality of proprietary information of, or relating to, suppliers and end-users of public telecommunications services and only use such information for the purpose of providing public telecommunications services.

Article 9.4: Conduct of Major Suppliers[9-3][9-4]

Treatment by Major Suppliers

1. Each Party shall ensure that any major supplier in its territory accords suppliers of public telecommunications services of the other Party treatment no less favorable than such major supplier accords to itself, its subsidiaries, its affiliates, or any non-affiliated service supplier regarding:

   (a) the availability, provisioning, rates, or quality of like public telecommunications services; and

   (b) the availability of technical interfaces necessary for interconnection.

   A Party shall assess such treatment on the basis of whether such suppliers of public telecommunications services, subsidiaries, affiliates, and non-affiliated service suppliers are in like circumstances.

Competitive Safeguards

2.

   (a) Each Party shall maintain appropriate measures for the purpose of preventing suppliers of public telecommunications services who, alone or together, are a major supplier in its territory from engaging in or continuing anti-competitive practices.

   (b) For purposes of subparagraph (a), anti-competitive practices include:

      (i) engaging in anti-competitive cross-subsidization;

> (ii) using information obtained from competitors with anti-competitive results; and
>
> (iii) not making available, on a timely basis, to suppliers of public telecommunications services, technical information about essential facilities and commercially relevant information that is necessary for them to provide public telecommunications services.

Unbundling of Network Elements

3.

    (a) Recognizing that both Parties currently provide for access to unbundled network elements, each Party shall provide its telecommunications regulatory body the authority to require that major suppliers in its territory provide suppliers of public telecommunications services of the other Party access to network elements on an unbundled basis at terms, conditions, and cost-oriented rates, that are reasonable, non-discriminatory (including with respect to timeliness), and transparent for the supply of public telecommunications services.

    (b) Which network elements will be required to be made available in the territory of a Party, and which suppliers may obtain such elements, shall be determined in accordance with national law and regulation.

    (c) In determining the network elements to be made available, a Party's telecommunications regulatory body shall consider, at a minimum, in accordance with national law and regulation:

        (i) whether access to such network elements as are proprietary in nature are necessary; and whether the failure to provide access to such network elements would impair the ability of suppliers of public telecommunications services of the other Party to provide the services it seeks to offer; or

        (ii) whether the network elements can be replicated or obtained from other sources at reasonable rates, such that the unavailability of these network elements from the major supplier will not impair the ability of other suppliers of public telecommunications services to provide a competing service; or

        (iii) whether the network elements are technically or operationally required for the provision of a competing service; or

        (iv) other factors as established in national law;

    as that body construes these factors.

Co-Location

4.

    (a) Each Party shall ensure that major suppliers in its territory provide to suppliers of public telecommunications services of the other Party physical co-location, at premises owned or controlled by the major supplier, of equipment necessary for interconnection or access to unbundled network elements on terms and conditions, and at cost-oriented rates, that are reasonable, non-discriminatory (including with respect to timeliness), and transparent.

(b) Where physical co-location is not practical for technical reasons or because of space limitations, each Party shall ensure that major suppliers in its territory provide or facilitate virtual co-location on terms and conditions, and at cost-oriented rates, that are reasonable, non-discriminatory (including with respect to timeliness), and transparent.

(c) Each Party may determine, in accordance with national law and regulation, which premises in its territory shall be subject to subparagraphs (a) and (b)

Resale

5. Each Party shall ensure that major suppliers in its territory:

(a) offer for resale, at reasonable[9-5] rates, to suppliers of public telecommunications services of the other Party, public telecommunications services that such major supplier provides at retail to end-users; and

(b) do not impose unreasonable or discriminatory conditions or limitations on the resale of such public telecommunications services.[9-6]

Poles, Ducts, and Conduits

6.

(a) Each Party shall ensure that major suppliers in its territory provide access to poles, ducts, and conduits, owned or controlled by such major suppliers to suppliers of public telecommunications services of the other Party, under terms, conditions, and cost-oriented[9-7] rates, that are reasonable, non-discriminatory (including with respect to timeliness), and transparent.

(b) Nothing shall prevent a Party from determining, under its domestic law and regulation, which particular structures owned or controlled by the major suppliers in its territory, are required to be made available in accordance with paragraph (a) provided that this is based on a determination that such structures cannot feasibly be economically or technically substituted in order to provide a competing service.

Number Portability

7. Each Party shall ensure that major suppliers in its territory provide number portability to the extent technically feasible, on a timely basis and on reasonable terms and conditions.

Interconnection

8.

(a) General Terms and Conditions

Each Party shall ensure that any major supplier in its territory provides interconnection for the facilities and equipment of suppliers of public telecommunications services of the other Party:

(i) at any technically feasible point in the major supplier's network;

(ii) under non-discriminatory terms, conditions (including technical standards and specifications), and rates;

(iii) of a quality no less favorable than that provided by such major supplier for its own like services or for like services of non-affiliated suppliers of public telecommunications services or for its subsidiaries or other affiliates;

(iv) in a timely fashion, on terms, conditions, (including technical standards and specifications), and cost-oriented rates, that are transparent, reasonable, having regard to economic feasibility, and sufficiently unbundled so that the supplier need not pay for network components or facilities that it does not require for the service to be provided; and

(v) upon request, at points in addition to the network termination points offered to the majority of suppliers of public telecommunications services, subject to charges that reflect the cost of construction of necessary additional facilities.[9-8]

(b) Options for Interconnecting with Major Suppliers

Each Party shall ensure that suppliers of public telecommunications services of the other Party may interconnect their facilities and equipment with those of major suppliers in its territory pursuant to at least one of the following options:

(i) a reference interconnection offer or another standard interconnection offer containing the rates, terms, and conditions that the major supplier offers generally to suppliers of public telecommunications services; or

(ii) the terms and conditions of an existing interconnection agreement or through negotiation of a new interconnection agreement.

(c) Public Availability of Interconnection Offers

Each Party shall require each major supplier in its territory to make publicly available either a reference interconnection offer or another standard interconnection offer containing the rates, terms, and conditions that the major supplier offers generally to suppliers of public telecommunications services.

(d) Public Availability of the Procedures for Interconnection Negotiations

Each Party shall make publicly available the applicable procedures for interconnection negotiations with major suppliers in its territory.

(e) Public Availability of Interconnection Agreements Concluded with Major Suppliers

(i) Each Party shall require major suppliers in its territory to file all interconnection agreements to which they are party with its telecommunications regulatory body.

(ii) Each Party shall make available for inspection to suppliers of public telecommunications services which are seeking interconnection,

interconnection agreements in force between a major supplier in its territory and any other supplier of public telecommunications services in such territory, including interconnection agreements concluded between a major supplier and its affiliates and subsidiaries.

(f) Resolution of Interconnection Disputes

Each Party shall ensure that suppliers of public telecommunications services of the other Party, that have requested interconnection with a major supplier in the Party's territory have recourse to a telecommunications regulatory body to resolve disputes regarding the terms, conditions, and rates for interconnection within a reasonable and publicly available period of time.

Provisioning and Pricing of Leased Circuits Services[9-9]

9.

(a) Each Party shall ensure that major suppliers of leased circuits services in its territory provide enterprises of the other Party leased circuits services that are public telecommunications services, on terms and conditions under pricing structures, and at rates that are reasonable, non-discriminatory (including with respect to timeliness), and transparent.

(b) Each Party may determine whether rates for leased circuits services in its territory are reasonable by taking into account the rates of like leased circuits services in comparable markets in other countries.

Article 9.5: Submarine Cable Landing Stations

1. Where under national law and regulation, a Party has authorized a supplier of public telecommunications services in its territory to operate a submarine cable system (including the landing facilities and services) as a public telecommunications service, that Party shall ensure that such supplier provides that public telecommunications service[9-10] to suppliers of public telecommunications services of the other Party on reasonable terms, conditions, and rates that are no less favorable than such supplier offers to any other supplier of public telecommunications services in like circumstances.

2. Where submarine cable landing facilities and services cannot be economically or technically substituted, and a major supplier of public international telecommunication services that controls such cable landing facilities and services has the ability to materially affect the price and supply for those facilities and services for the provision of public telecommunications services in a Party's territory, the Party shall ensure that such major supplier:

    (a) permits suppliers of public telecommunications services of the other Party to:

        (i) use the major supplier's cross-connect links in the submarine cable landing station to connect their equipment to backhaul links and submarine cable capacity of any supplier of telecommunications; and

        (ii) co-locate their transmission and routing equipment used for accessing submarine cable capacity and backhaul links at the submarine cable landing station at terms, conditions, and cost-oriented rates, that are reasonable and non-discriminatory; and

(b) provides suppliers of telecommunications of the other Party submarine cable capacity, backhaul links, and cross-connect links in the submarine cable landing station at terms, conditions, and rates that are reasonable and non-discriminatory.

Article 9.6: Independent Regulation and Privatization

1. Each Party shall ensure that its telecommunications regulatory body is separate from, and not accountable to, any supplier of public telecommunications services. To this end, each Party shall ensure that its telecommunications regulatory body does not hold any financial interest or maintain an operating role in such a supplier.

2. Each Party shall ensure that the decisions of, and procedures used by its telecommunications regulatory body are impartial with respect to all interested persons. To this end, each Party shall ensure that any financial interest that it holds in a supplier of public telecommunications services does not influence the decisions of and procedures of its telecommunications regulatory body.

3. Where a Party has an ownership interest in a supplier of public telecommunications services, it shall notify the other Party of any intention to eliminate such interest as soon as feasible.

Article 9.7: Universal Service

Each Party shall administer any universal service obligation that it maintains in a transparent, nondiscriminatory, and competitively neutral manner and shall ensure that its universal service obligation is not more burdensome than necessary for the kind of universal service that it has defined.

Article 9.8: Licensing Process

1. When a Party requires a supplier of public telecommunications services to have a license, the Party shall make publicly available:
   (a) all the licensing criteria and procedures it applies;
   (b) the period of time normally required to reach a decision concerning an application for a license; and
   (c) the terms and conditions of all licenses it has issued.

2. Each Party shall ensure that an applicant receives, upon request, the reasons for the denial of a license.

Article 9.9: Allocation and Use of Scarce Resources[9-11]

1. Each Party shall administer its procedures for the allocation and use of scarce resources, including frequencies, numbers, and rights of way, in an objective, timely, transparent, and nondiscriminatory fashion.

2. Each Party shall make publicly available the current state of allocated frequency bands but shall not be required to provide detailed identification of frequencies assigned or allocated by each government for specific government uses.

Article 9.10: Enforcement

Each Party shall ensure that its telecommunications regulatory body maintains appropriate procedures and authority to enforce domestic measures relating to the obligations under Articles 9.2 through 9.5. Such procedures and authority shall include the ability to impose effective sanctions, which may include financial penalties, injunctive relief (on an interim or final basis), or modification, suspension, and revocation of licenses.

Article 9.11: Resolution of Domestic Telecommunications Disputes

Further to Articles 19.5 (Administrative Proceedings) and 19.6 (Review and Appeal), each Party shall ensure the following:

Recourse to Telecommunications Regulatory Bodies

1. Each Party shall ensure that enterprises of the other Party have recourse (within a reasonable period of time) to a telecommunications regulatory body or other relevant body to resolve disputes arising under domestic measures addressing a matter set out in Articles 9.2 through 9.5.

Reconsideration

2. Each Party shall ensure that any enterprise aggrieved or whose interests are adversely affected by a determination or decision of the telecommunications regulatory body may petition that body for reconsideration of that determination or decision. Neither Party may permit such a petition to constitute grounds for non-compliance with such determination or decision of the telecommunications regulatory body unless an appropriate authority stays such determination or decision.

Judicial Review

3. Each Party shall ensure that any enterprise aggrieved by a determination or decision of the telecommunications regulatory body may obtain judicial review of such determination or decision by an impartial and independent judicial authority.

Article 9.12: Transparency

Further to Chapter 19 (Transparency), each Party shall ensure that:

1. rulemakings, including the basis for such rulemakings, of its telecommunications regulatory body and end-user tariffs filed with its telecommunications regulatory body are promptly published or otherwise made available to all interested persons;

2. interested persons are provided with adequate advance public notice of and the opportunity to comment on any rulemaking proposed by the telecommunications regulatory body;

3. its measures relating to public telecommunications services are made publicly available, including:

    (a) tariffs and other terms and conditions of service;

    (b) specifications of technical interfaces;

    (c) conditions applying to attachment of terminal or other equipment to the public telecommunications transport network; and

    (d) notification, permit, registration, or licensing requirements, if any; and

4. information on bodies responsible for preparing, amending, and adopting standards-related measures is made publicly available.

Article 9.13: Flexibility in the Choice of Technologies

A Party shall endeavor not to prevent suppliers of public telecommunications services from having the flexibility to choose the technologies that they use to supply their services, including commercial mobile services, subject to the ability of each Party to take measures to ensure that end-users of different networks are able to communicate with each other.

Article 9.14: Forbearance and Minimal Regulatory Environment

The Parties recognize the importance of relying on market forces to achieve wide choice and efficient supply of telecommunications services. To this end, each Party may forbear from applying regulation to a telecommunications service that such Party classifies, under its laws and regulations, as a public telecommunications service upon a determination by its telecommunications regulatory body that:

(a) enforcement of such regulation is not necessary to prevent unreasonable or discriminatory practices;

(b) enforcement of such regulation is not necessary for the protection of consumers; and

(c) forbearance is consistent with the public interest, including promoting and enhancing competition among suppliers of public telecommunications services.

Article 9.15: Relationship to Other Chapters

In the event of any inconsistency between this Chapter and another Chapter, this Chapter shall prevail to the extent of such inconsistency.

Article 9.16: Definitions

For purposes of this Chapter:

1. **backhaul links** means end-to-end transmission links from a submarine cable landing station to another primary point of access to the Party's public telecommunications transport network;

2. **physical co-location** means physical access to and control over space in order to install, maintain, or repair equipment used to provide public telecommunications services;

3. **cost-oriented** means based on cost, and may include a reasonable profit, and may involve different cost methodologies for different facilities or services;

4. **commercial mobile services** means public telecommunications services supplied through mobile wireless means;

5. **cross-connect links** means the links in a submarine cable landing station used to connect submarine cable capacity to the transmission, switching and routing equipment of different suppliers of public telecommunications services co-located in that submarine cable landing station;

6. **customer proprietary network information** means information made available to the supplier of public telecommunications services by the end-user solely by virtue of the end-user-telecommunications service supplier relationship. This includes information regarding the end-user's calling patterns (including the quantity, technical configuration, type, destination, location, and amount of use of the service) and other information that appears on or may pertain to an end-user's telephone bill;

7. **end-user** means a final consumer of or subscriber to a public telecommunications service, including a service supplier but excluding a supplier of public telecommunications services;

8. **enterprise** means an entity constituted or organized under applicable law, whether or not for profit, and whether privately or government owned or controlled. Forms that an enterprise may take include a corporation, trust, partnership, sole proprietorship, branch, joint venture, association, or similar organization;

9. **essential facilities** means facilities of a public telecommunications transport network or service that:

    (a) are exclusively or predominantly provided by a single or limited number of suppliers; and

    (b) cannot feasibly be economically or technically substituted in order to provide a service;

10. **interconnection** means linking with suppliers providing public telecommunications transport networks or services in order to allow the users of one supplier to communicate with users of another supplier and to access services provided by another supplier;

11. **leased circuits** means telecommunications facilities between two or more designated points which are set aside for the dedicated use of or availability to a particular customer or other users of the customer's choosing;

12. **major supplier** means a supplier of public telecommunications services that has the ability to materially affect the terms of participation (having regard to price and supply) in the relevant market for public telecommunications services as a result of:

    (a) control over essential facilities; or

    (b) use of its position in the market;

13. **network element** means a facility or equipment used in the provision of a public telecommunications service, including features, functions, and capabilities that are provided by means of such facility or equipment;

14. **non-discriminatory** means treatment no less favorable than that accorded to any other user of like public telecommunications transport networks or services in like circumstances;

15. **number portability** means the ability of end-users of public telecommunications services to retain, at the same location, existing telephone numbers without impairment of quality, reliability, or convenience when switching between like suppliers of public telecommunications services;

16. **person** means either a natural person or an enterprise;

17. **public telecommunications transport network** means telecommunications infrastructure which a Party requires to provide public telecommunications services between defined network termination points;

18. **public telecommunications service** means any telecommunications service (which a Party may define to include certain facilities used to deliver these telecommunications services) that a Party requires, explicitly or in effect, to be offered to the public generally. Such services may include inter alia, telephone and data transmission typically involving customer-supplied information between two or more points without any end-to-end change in the form or content of the customer's information;[9-12]

19. **reference interconnection offer** means an interconnection offer extended by a major supplier and filed with or approved by a telecommunications regulatory body that is sufficiently detailed to enable a supplier of public telecommunications services that is willing to accept its rates, terms, and conditions to obtain interconnection without having to engage in negotiations with the major supplier concerned;

20. **service supplier** means any person that supplies a service;

21. **submarine cable landing station** means the premises and buildings where international submarine cables arrive and terminate and are connected to backhaul links;

22. **supplier of public telecommunications services** means any provider of public telecommunications services, including those who provide such services to other suppliers of public telecommunications services;[9-13]

23. **telecommunications** means the transmission and reception of signals by any electromagnetic means;[9-14]

24. **telecommunications regulatory body** means a national body responsible for the regulation of telecommunications; and

25. **user** means an end-user or a supplier of public telecommunications services.

10. FINANCIAL SERVICES

Article 10.1: Scope and Coverage

1. This Chapter applies to measures adopted or maintained by a Party relating to:
   (a) financial institutions of the other Party;
   (b) investors of the other Party, and investments of such investors, in financial institutions in the Party's territory; and
   (c) cross-border trade in financial services.

2. Chapters 8 (Cross-Border Trade in Services) and 15 (Investment) apply to measures described in paragraph 1 only to the extent that such Chapters or Articles of such Chapters are incorporated into this Chapter.

   (a) Articles 8.11 (Denial of Benefits), 15.6 (Expropriation),[10-1] 15.7 (Transfers), 15.10 (Investment and Environment), 15.11 (Denial of Benefits), and 15.13 (Special Formalities and Information Requirements) are hereby incorporated into and made a part of this Chapter.

   (b) Section C of Chapter 15 (Investor-State Dispute Settlement) is hereby incorporated into and made a part of this Chapter solely for claims that a Party has breached Articles 15.6 (Expropriation), 15.7 (Transfers), 15.11 (Denial of Benefits), and 15.13 (Special Formalities and Information Requirements), as incorporated into this Chapter.

   (c) Article 8.10 (Transfers and Payments), is incorporated into and made a part of this Chapter to the extent that cross-border trade in financial services is subject to obligations pursuant to Article 10.5.

3. This Chapter does not apply to measures adopted or maintained by a Party relating to:

   (a) activities or services forming part of a public retirement plan or statutory system of social security; or

   (b) activities or services conducted for the account or with the guarantee or using the financial resources of the Party, including its public entities, except that this Chapter shall apply if a Party allows any of the activities or services referred to in subparagraphs (a) or (b) to be conducted by its financial institutions in competition with a public entity or a financial institution.

4. This Chapter does not apply to laws, regulations or requirements governing the procurement by government agencies of financial services purchased for governmental purposes and not with a view to commercial resale or use in the supply of services for commercial sale.

Article 10.2: National Treatment

1. Each Party shall accord to investors of the other Party treatment no less favorable than that it accords to its own investors, in like circumstances, with respect to the establishment, acquisition, expansion, management, conduct, operation, and sale or other disposition of financial institutions and investments in financial institutions in its territory.

2. Each Party shall accord to financial institutions of the other Party and to investments of investors of the other Party in financial institutions treatment no less favorable than that it accords to its own financial institutions, and to investments of its own investors in financial institutions, in like circumstances, with respect to the establishment, acquisition, expansion, management, conduct, operation, and sale or other disposition of financial institutions and investments.

3. For purposes of the national treatment obligations in Article 10.5.1, a Party shall accord to cross-border financial service suppliers of the other Party treatment no less favorable than that it accords to its own financial service suppliers, in like circumstances, with respect to the supply of the relevant service.

Article 10.3: Most-Favored-Nation Treatment

1. Each Party shall accord to investors of the other Party, financial institutions of the other Party, investments of investors in financial institutions, and cross-border financial service suppliers of the other Party treatment no less favorable than that it accords to the investors, financial institutions, investments of investors in financial institutions and cross-border financial service suppliers of a non-Party, in like circumstances.

2. A Party may recognize prudential measures of the other Party or of a non-Party in the application of measures covered by this Chapter. Such recognition may be:
   (a) accorded unilaterally;
   (b) achieved through harmonization or other means; or
   (c) based upon an agreement or arrangement with the non-Party.

3. A Party according recognition of prudential measures under paragraph 2 shall provide adequate opportunity to the other Party to demonstrate that circumstances exist in which there are or would be equivalent regulation, oversight, implementation of regulation, and, if appropriate, procedures concerning the sharing of information between the Parties.

4. Where a Party accords recognition of prudential measures under paragraph 2(c) and the circumstances set out in paragraph 3 exist, the Party shall provide adequate opportunity to the other Party to negotiate accession to the agreement or arrangement, or to negotiate a comparable agreement or arrangement.

Article 10.4: Market Access for Financial Institutions

A Party shall not adopt or maintain, with respect to financial institutions of the other Party,[10-2] either on the basis of a regional subdivision or on the basis of its entire territory, measures that:

(a) impose limitations on
   (i) the number of financial institutions whether in the form of numerical quotas, monopolies, exclusive service suppliers or the requirements of an economic needs test;
   (ii) the total value of financial service transactions or assets in the form of numerical quotas or the requirement of an economic needs test;
   (iii) the total number of financial service operations or the total quantity of financial services output expressed in terms of designated numerical units in the form of quotas or the requirement of an economic needs test; or
   (iv) the total number of natural persons that may be employed in a particular financial service sector or that a financial institution may employ and who are necessary for, and directly related to, the supply of a specific financial service in the form of a numerical quota or the requirement of an economic needs test; or
(b) restrict or require specific types of legal entity or joint venture through which a financial institution may supply a service.

Article 10.5: Cross-Border Trade in Financial Services

1. Each Party shall permit, under terms and conditions that accord national treatment, cross-border financial service suppliers of the other Party to supply the services it has specified in Annex 10A.
2. Each Party shall permit persons located in its territory, and its nationals wherever located, to purchase financial services from cross-border financial service suppliers of the other Party located in the territory of the other Party. This obligation does not require a Party to permit such suppliers to do business or solicit in its territory. Each Party may define "doing business" and "solicitation" for purposes of this obligation, as long as such definitions are not inconsistent with paragraph 1.

Article 10.6: New Financial Services

Each Party shall permit a financial institution of the other Party to supply any new financial service that the first Party would permit its own financial institutions, in like circumstances, to supply without additional legislative action by the first Party. Notwithstanding Article 10.4(b), a Party may determine the institutional and juridical form through which the new financial service may be supplied and may require authorization for the supply of the service. Where a Party requires such authorization of the new financial service, a decision shall be made within a reasonable time and the authorization may only be refused for prudential reasons.[10-3]

Article 10.7: Treatment of Certain Information

Nothing in this Chapter requires a Party to furnish or allow access to:

(a) information related to the financial affairs and accounts of individual customers of financial institutions or cross-border financial service suppliers; or
(b) any confidential information, the disclosure of which would impede law enforcement or otherwise be contrary to the public interest or prejudice legitimate commercial interests of particular enterprises.

Article 10.8: Senior Management and Boards of Directors

1. A Party may not require financial institutions of the other Party[10-4] to engage individuals of any particular nationality as senior managerial or other essential personnel.
2. A Party may not require that more than a simple majority of the board of directors of a financial institution of the other Party be composed of nationals of the Party, persons residing in the territory of the Party, or a combination thereof.

Article 10.9: Non-Conforming Measures

1. Articles 10.2 through 10.5 and 10.8 do not apply to:
   (a) any existing non-conforming measure that is maintained by a Party at

> (i)   the central level of government, as set out by that Party in its Schedule to Annex 10B,
>
> (ii) a regional level of government, as set out by that Party in its Schedule to Annex 10B, or
>
> (iii) a local level of government;

(b) the continuation or prompt renewal of any non-conforming measure referred to in subparagraph (a); or

(c) an amendment to any non-conforming measure referred to in subparagraph (a) to the extent that the amendment does not decrease the conformity of the measure, as it existed immediately before the amendment, with Articles 10.2 through 10.4 and 10.8.

2. Annex 10C sets out certain specific commitments by each Party.

3. A non-conforming measure set out in a Party's Schedule to Annex 8A or 8B as a measure to which Article 8.3 (National Treatment), 8.4 (Most-Favored-Nation Treatment), 8.5 (Market Access), or 15.4 (National Treatment and Most-Favored-Nation Treatment) does not apply shall be treated as a non-conforming measure described in paragraph 1(a) to which Article 10.2, 10.3, or 10.4, as the case may be, does not apply, to the extent that the measure, sector, sub-sector or activity set out in the schedule of non-conforming measures is covered by this Chapter.

Article 10.10: Exceptions

1. Notwithstanding any other provision of this Chapter or Chapters 9 (Telecommunications), 14 (Electronic Commerce), or 15 (Investment), including specifically Article 9.15 (Relationship to Other Chapters), and in addition Article 8.2.2 (Scope and Coverage) with respect to the supply of financial services in the territory of a Party by an investor of the other Party or a covered investment, a Party shall not be prevented from adopting or maintaining measures for prudential reasons,[10-5] including for the protection of investors, depositors, policy holders or persons to whom a fiduciary duty is owed by a financial institution or cross-border financial service supplier, or to ensure the integrity and stability of the financial system. Where such measures do not conform with the provisions of this Agreement referred to in this paragraph, they shall not be used as a means of avoiding the Party's commitments or obligations under such provisions.

2. Nothing in this Chapter or Chapters 9 (Telecommunications), 14 (Electronic Commerce), or 15 (Investment), including specifically Article 9.15 (Relationship to Other Chapters), and in addition Article 8.2.2 (Scope and Coverage) with respect to the supply of financial services in the territory of a Party by an investor of the other Party or a covered investment, applies to nondiscriminatory measures of general application taken by any public entity in pursuit of monetary and related credit policies or exchange rate policies. This paragraph shall not affect a Party's obligations under Article 8.10 (Transfers and Payments), Article 15.7 (Transfers), or Article 15.8 (Performance Requirements).

3. Notwithstanding Articles 8.10 (Transfers and Payments) and 15.7 (Transfers), as incorporated into this Chapter, a Party may prevent or limit transfers by a financial institution or cross-border financial service supplier to, or for the benefit of, an

affiliate of or person related to such institution or supplier, through the equitable, non-discriminatory and good faith application of measures relating to maintenance of the safety, soundness, integrity or financial responsibility of financial institutions or cross-border financial service suppliers. This paragraph does not prejudice any other provision of this Agreement that permits a Party to restrict transfers.

4. For greater certainty, nothing in this Chapter shall be construed to prevent the adoption or enforcement by a Party of measures necessary to secure compliance with laws or regulations that are not inconsistent with this Chapter including those relating to the prevention of deceptive and fraudulent practices or to deal with the effects of a default on financial services contracts, subject to the requirement that such measures are not applied in a manner which would constitute a means of arbitrary or unjustifiable discrimination between countries where like conditions prevail, or a disguised restriction on investment in financial institutions or cross-border trade in financial services.

Article 10.11: Transparency

1. The Parties recognize that transparent regulations and policies governing the activities of financial institutions and cross-border financial service suppliers are important in facilitating the ability of financial institutions located outside the territory of the Party, financial institutions of the other Party, and cross-border financial service suppliers to gain access to and operate in each other's markets. Each Party commits to promote regulatory transparency in financial services. Accordingly, the Financial Services Committee established under Article 10.16 shall consult with the goal of promoting objective and transparent regulatory processes in each Party, taking into account (1) the work undertaken by the Parties in the General Agreement on Trade in Services and the Parties' work in other fora relating to trade in financial services and (2) the importance for regulatory transparency of identifiable policy objectives and clear and consistently applied regulatory processes that are communicated or otherwise made available to the public.

2. In lieu of Article 19.3.2 (Publication), each Party shall, to the extent practicable,
   (a) publish in advance any regulations of general application relating to the subject matter of this Chapter that it proposes to adopt; and
   (b) provide interested persons and the other Party a reasonable opportunity to comment on such proposed regulations.

3. Each Party's regulatory authorities shall make available to interested persons their requirements, including any documentation required, for completing applications relating to the supply of financial services.

4. On the request of an applicant, the regulatory authority shall inform the applicant of the status of its application. If such authority requires additional information from the applicant, it shall notify the applicant without undue delay.

5. A regulatory authority shall make an administrative decision on a completed application of an investor in a financial institution, a financial institution or a cross-border financial service supplier of the other Party relating to the supply of a financial service within 120 days, and shall promptly notify the applicant of the decision. An application shall not be considered complete until all relevant hearings

are held and all necessary information is received. Where it is not practicable for a decision to be made within 120 days, the regulatory authority shall notify the applicant without undue delay and shall endeavor to make the decision within a reasonable time thereafter.

6. Each Party shall maintain or establish appropriate mechanisms that will respond to inquiries from interested persons regarding measures of general application covered by this Chapter.

7. Each Party shall ensure that the rules of general application adopted or maintained by self-regulatory organizations of the Party are promptly published or otherwise made available in such a manner as to enable interested persons to become acquainted with them.

8. To the extent practicable, each Party should allow reasonable time between publication of final regulations and their effective date.

9. At the time it adopts final regulations, a Party should, to the extent practicable, address in writing substantive comments received from interested persons with respect to the proposed regulations.

Article 10.12: Self-Regulatory Organizations

Where a Party requires a financial institution or a cross-border financial service supplier of the other Party to be a member of, participate in, or have access to, a self-regulatory organization to provide a financial service in or into the territory of that Party, the Party shall ensure observance of the obligations of Articles 10.2 and 10.3 by such self-regulatory organization.

Article 10.13: Payment and Clearing Systems

Under terms and conditions that accord national treatment, each Party shall grant to financial institutions of the other Party established in its territory access to payment and clearing systems operated by public entities, and to official funding and refinancing facilities available in the normal course of ordinary business. This paragraph is not intended to confer access to the Party's lender of last resort facilities.

Article 10.14: Domestic Regulation

Except with respect to non-conforming measures listed in its schedule to Annex 10B, each Party shall ensure that all measures of general application to which this Chapter applies are administered in a reasonable, objective and impartial manner.

Article 10.15: Expedited Availability of Insurance Services

The Parties recognize the importance of maintaining and developing regulatory procedures to expedite the offering of insurance services by licensed suppliers. The Parties recognize the importance of consulting, as necessary, regarding any such initiatives.

Article 10.16: Financial Services Committee

1. The Parties hereby establish a Financial Services Committee. The principal representative of each Party shall be an official of the Party's authority responsible for financial services set out in Annex 10D.

2. The Committee shall:
   (a) supervise the implementation of this Chapter and its further elaboration;
   (b) consider issues regarding financial services that are referred to it by a Party; and
   (c) participate in the dispute settlement procedures in accordance with Article 10.19.

3. The Committee shall meet annually, or as otherwise agreed, to assess the functioning of this Agreement as it applies to financial services. The Committee shall inform the Joint Committee established under Article 20.1 (Joint Committee) of the results of each meeting.

Article 10.17: Consultations

1. A Party may request consultations with the other Party regarding any matter arising under this Agreement that affects financial services. The other Party shall give sympathetic consideration to the request. The Parties shall report the results of their consultations to the Financial Services Committee.

2. Consultations under this Article shall include officials of the authorities specified in Annex 10D.

Article 10.18: Dispute Settlement

1. Article 20.4 (Additional Dispute Settlement Procedures) applies as modified by this Article to the settlement of disputes arising under this Chapter.

2. When a Party claims that a dispute arises under this Chapter, Article 20.4.4(a) (Additional Dispute Settlement Procedures) shall apply, except that:
   (a) where the Parties so agree, the panel shall be composed entirely of panelists meeting the qualifications in paragraph 3;
   (b) in any other case,
      (i) each Party may select panelists meeting the qualifications set out in paragraph 3 or Article 20.4.4(c) (Additional Dispute Settlement Procedures), and
      (ii) if the Party complained against invokes Article 10.10 (Exceptions), the chair of the panel shall meet the qualifications set out in paragraph 3, unless the Parties agree otherwise.

3. Financial services panelists shall:
   (a) have expertise or experience in financial services law or practice, which may include the regulation of financial institutions;
   (b) be chosen strictly on the basis of objectivity, reliability and sound judgment; and
   (c) meet the qualifications set out in Article 20.4.4(b)(ii) and 20.4.4(b)(iii) (Additional Dispute Settlement Procedures).

4. Notwithstanding Article 20.6 (Non-Implementation), where a Panel finds a measure to be inconsistent with this Agreement and the measure under dispute affects:
    (a) only the financial services sector, the complaining Party may suspend benefits only in the financial services sector;
    (b) the financial services sector and any other sector, the complaining Party may suspend benefits in the financial services sector that have an effect equivalent to the effect of the measure in the Party's financial services sector; or
    (c) only a sector other than the financial services sector, the complaining Party may not suspend benefits in the financial services sector.

Article 10.19: Investment Disputes in Financial Services

1. Where an investor of a Party submits a claim under Section C of Chapter 15 (Investor-State Dispute Settlement) against the other Party and the respondent invokes Article 10.10, on request of the respondent, the tribunal shall refer the matter in writing to the Financial Services Committee for a decision. The tribunal may not proceed pending receipt of a decision or report under this Article.
2. In a referral pursuant to paragraph 1, the Financial Services Committee shall decide the issue of whether and to what extent Article 10.10 is a valid defense to the claim of the investor. The Committee shall transmit a copy of its decision to the tribunal and to the Joint Committee. The decision shall be binding on the tribunal.
3. Where the Financial Services Committee has not decided the issue within 60 days of the receipt of the referral under paragraph 1, the respondent or the Party of the claimant may request the establishment of a panel under Article 20.4.4 (Additional Dispute Settlement Procedures). The panel shall be constituted in accordance with Article 10.18. The panel shall transmit its final report to the Committee and to the tribunal. The report shall be binding on the tribunal.
4. Where no request for the establishment of a panel pursuant to paragraph 3 has been made within 10 days of the expiration of the 60-day period referred to in paragraph 3, a tribunal may proceed to decide the matter.
5. For purposes of this Article, **tribunal** means a tribunal established pursuant to Section C of Chapter 15 (Investor-State Dispute Settlement).

Article 10.20: Definitions
For purposes of this Chapter:

1. **central level** means
    (a) for the United States, the federal level, and
    (b) for Singapore, the national level;
2. **cross-border financial service supplier of a Party** means a person of a Party that is engaged in the business of supplying a financial service within the territory of the Party and that seeks to supply or supplies financial services through the cross-border supply of such services;
3. **cross-border supply of a financial service or cross-border trade in financial services** means the supply of a financial service:

   (a) from the territory of one Party into the territory of the other Party,

   (b) in the territory of one Party by a person of that Party to a person of the other Party, or

   (c) by a national of one Party in the territory of the other Party, but does not include the supply of a financial service in the territory of one Party by an investor of the other Party, or investments of such investors, in financial institutions in the Party's territory.

4. **financial institution** means any financial intermediary or other institution that is authorized to do business and regulated or supervised as a financial institution under the law of the Party in whose territory it is located;

5. **financial institution of the other Party** means a financial institution, including a branch, located in the territory of a Party that is controlled by persons of the other Party;

6. **financial service** means any service of a financial nature. Financial services include all insurance and insurance-related services, and all banking and other financial services (excluding insurance), as well as services incidental or auxiliary to a service of a financial nature. Financial services include the following activities:

Insurance and insurance-related services

   (a) Direct insurance (including co-insurance):
      (i)   life
      (ii) non-life
   (b) Reinsurance and retrocession;
   (c) Insurance intermediation, such as brokerage and agency;
   (d) Service auxiliary to insurance, such as consultancy, actuarial, risk assessment and claim settlement services.

Banking and other financial services (excluding insurance)

   (e) Acceptance of deposits and other repayable funds from the public;
   (f) Lending of all types, including consumer credit, mortgage credit, factoring and financing of commercial transactions;
   (g) Financial leasing;
   (h) All payment and money transmission services, including credit, charge and debit cards, travelers checks and bankers drafts;
   (i) Guarantees and commitments;
   (j) Trading for own account or for account of customers, whether on an exchange, in an over-the-counter market or otherwise, the following:
      (i)   money market instruments (including checks, bills, certificates of deposits);
      (ii) foreign exchange;
      (iii) derivative products including, but not limited to, futures and options;
      (iv) exchange rate and interest rate instruments, including products such as swaps, forward rate agreements;
      (v)   transferable securities;

(vi) other negotiable instruments and financial assets, including bullion;

(k) Participation in issues of all kinds of securities, including underwriting and placement as agent (whether publicly or privately) and supply of services related to such issues;

(l) Money broking;

(m) Asset management, such as cash or portfolio management, all forms of collective investment management, pension fund management, custodial, depository and trust services;

(n) Settlement and clearing services for financial assets, including securities, derivative products, and other negotiable instruments;

(o) Provision and transfer of financial information, and financial data processing and related software by suppliers of other financial services;

(p) Advisory, intermediation and other auxiliary financial services on all the activities listed in subparagraphs (e) through (o), including credit reference and analysis, investment and portfolio research and advice, advice on acquisitions and on corporate restructuring and strategy.

7. **financial service supplier of a Party** means a person of a Party that is engaged in the business of supplying a financial service within the territory of that Party;

8. **investment** means "investment" as defined in Article 15.1.13 (Definitions), except that, with respect to "loans" and "debt instruments" referred to in that Article:

(a) a loan to or debt instrument issued by a financial institution is an investment only where it is treated as regulatory capital by the Party in whose territory the institution is located; and

(b) a loan granted by or debt instrument owned by a financial institution, other than a loan to or debt instrument of a financial institution referred to in subparagraph (a), is not an investment.

For greater certainty, a loan granted by or debt instrument owned by a cross-border financial service supplier, other than a loan to or debt instrument issued by a financial institution, is an investment if such loan or debt instrument meets the criteria for investments set out in Article 15.1.13 (Definitions).

9. **investor of a Party** means a Party or state enterprise thereof, or a person of that Party, that attempts to make, is making, or has made an investment in the territory of the other Party; provided, however, that a natural person who is a dual national shall be deemed to be exclusively a national of the State of his/her dominant and effective nationality;

10. **new financial service** means, for purposes of Article 10.6, a financial service not supplied in the territory of the first Party that is supplied within the territory of the other Party, and includes any new form of delivery of a financial service or the sale of a financial product that is not sold in the first Party's territory.

11. **person of a Party** means "person of a Party" as defined in Article 1.2 (General Definitions) and, for greater certainty, does not include a branch of an institution of a non-party;

12. **public entity** means a central bank or monetary authority of a Party, or any financial institution owned or controlled by a Party that is principally engaged in carrying out governmental functions or activities for governmental purposes, not including an entity principally engaged in supplying financial services on commercial terms; for

greater certainty, a public entity[10-6] shall not be considered a designated monopoly or a government enterprise for purposes of Chapter 12 (Anticompetitive Business Conduct, Designated Monopolies and Government Enterprises);

13. **regional level** means
    (a) for the United States, the 50 states, the District of Columbia and Puerto Rico, and
    (b) Singapore has no government at the regional level; for Singapore, "local government level" means entities with sub-national legislative or executive powers under domestic law, including Town Councils and Community Development Councils.

14. **self-regulatory organization** means any non-governmental body, including any securities or futures exchange or market, clearing agency, other organization or association, that exercises regulatory or supervisory authority over financial service suppliers or financial institutions, by statute or delegation from central, regional or local governments or authorities; for greater certainty, a self-regulatory organization shall not be considered a designated monopoly for purposes of Chapter 12 (Anticompetitive Business Conduct, Designated Monopolies and Government Enterprises).

Annex 10A. Application of Article 10.5

United States

Insurance and insurance-related services

1. For the United States, Article 10.5 applies to the cross-border supply of or trade in financial services as defined in subparagraph (a) of the definition of cross-border supply of financial services in Article 10.20 with respect to
    (a) insurance of risks relating to:
        (i) maritime shipping and commercial aviation and space launching and freight (including satellites), with such insurance to cover any or all of the following: the goods being transported, the vehicle transporting the goods and any liability arising therefrom; and
        (ii) goods in international transit;
    (b) reinsurance and retrocession, services auxiliary to insurance as referred to in subparagraph (d) of the definition of financial service, and insurance intermediation such as brokerage and agency as referred to in subparagraph (c) of the definition of financial service.

2. For the United States, Article 10.5 applies to the cross-border supply of or trade in financial services as defined in paragraph (c) of the definition of cross-border supply of financial services in Article 10.20 with respect to insurance services.

Banking and other financial services (excluding insurance)

3. For the United States, Article 10.5 applies with respect to the provision and transfer of financial information and financial data processing and related software as referred to in subparagraph (o) of the definition of financial service, and advisory and other auxiliary services, excluding intermediation, relating to banking and other financial services as referred to in subparagraph (p) of the definition of financial service.

Singapore

Insurance and insurance-related services

1. For Singapore, Article 10.5 applies to the cross-border supply of or trade in financial services as defined in sub paragraph (a) of the definition of cross-border supply of a financial service or cross-border trade in financial services in Article 10.20 with respect to:
   (a) reinsurance and retrocession;
   (b) services auxiliary to insurance comprising actuarial, loss adjustors, average adjustors and consultancy services;
   (c) insurance of "MAT" risks comprising
      (i) maritime shipping and commercial aviation and space launching and freight (including satellites), with such insurance to cover any or all of the following: the goods being transported, the vehicle transporting the goods and any liability arising therefrom; and
      (ii) goods in international transit;
   (d) reinsurance intermediation by brokerages; and
   (e) MAT intermediation by brokerages.
2. For Singapore, Article 10.5 applies to the cross-border supply of or trade in financial services as defined in subparagraph (c) of the definition of cross-border supply of a financial service or cross-border trade in financial services in Article 10.20 with respect to services auxiliary to insurance comprising actuarial, loss adjustors, average adjustors and consultancy services.

Banking and other financial services (excluding insurance)

3. For Singapore, Article 10.5 applies with respect to
   (a) financial leasing, provided that access to customer information of banks in Singapore is limited to financial institutions licensed in Singapore;
   (b) provision and transfer of financial information;
   (c) provision of financial data processing and related software;
   (d) trading in money market instruments, foreign exchange, exchange rate and interest rate instruments with financial institutions in Singapore;
   (e) corporate finance advisory services, offered:

(i) to a related corporation or accredited investors only, provided that clients do not engage in public offerings of securities on the basis of such advice, and that such advice is not disclosed to clients' shareholders who are not accredited investors or to the public; or

(ii) through a related corporation that is holding (or exempted from holding) a capital markets services license to advise on corporate finance under the Securities and Futures Act (Cap. 289); and

(f) advisory and other auxiliary services, excluding intermediation and services described in subparagraph (e), relating to banking and other financial services referred to in subparagraph (p) in the definition of "financial service" in Article 10.20 to the extent that such services are permitted in the future by Singapore.

Annex 10B. Introductory Note for the Schedule of Singapore to Annex 10b

1. The Schedule of Singapore to Annex 10B sets out:
   (a) in Section A, the headnotes that limit or clarify the commitments of Singapore with respect to the obligations described in subparagraphs (i) – (v) of paragraph (b), and
   (b) in Section B, pursuant to Article 10.9 (Non-Conforming Measures), the existing measures of Singapore that are not subject to some or all of the obligations imposed by:
      (i) Article 10.2 (National Treatment);
      (ii) Article 10.3 (Most-Favored-Nation Treatment);
      (iii) Article 10.4 (Market Access for Financial Institutions);
      (iv) Article 10.5 (Cross-Border Trade);
      (v) Article 10.8 (Senior Management and Boards of Directors).

2. Each entry in Section B as described in paragraph 1(b) sets out the following elements:
   (a) **Type of reservation** sets out the obligations referred to in paragraph 1(b) with respect to which the entry is made;
   (b) **Level of government** indicates the level of government maintaining the listed measure(s);
   (c) **Measure** identifies the laws, regulations or other measures for which the entry is made. A measure cited in the **measure** element:
      (i) means the measure as amended, continued or renewed as of the date of entry into force of this Agreement;
      (ii) includes any subordinate measure adopted or maintained under the authority of and consistent with the measure;
   (d) **Description** sets out the non-conforming aspects of the entry.

3. In accordance with Article 10.9.1(a), the articles of this Agreement referred to by their titles in the **Type of reservation** element of an entry do not apply to the law, regulation or other measures identified in the **Measures** element or described in the **Description** element of that entry.

4. Both Parties agree that references in the Schedule of a Party to the Annex to any enterprise or entity apply as well to any successor enterprise or entity, which shall be entitled to benefit from any listing of a non-conforming measure with respect to that enterprise or entity.

Introductory Note for the United States Schedule to Annex 10b

Relating to Banking and Other Non-Insurance Financial Services

1. The Schedule of the United States to Annex 10B with respect to banking and other non-insurance financial services sets out:
   (a) in Section A, the headnotes that limit or clarify the commitments of the United States with respect to the obligations described in subparagraphs (i)-(iv) of paragraph (b), and
   (b) in Section B, pursuant to Article 10.9 (Non-Conforming Measures), the existing measures of the United States that are not subject to some or all of the obligations imposed by:
      (i) Article 10.2 (National Treatment);
      (ii) Article 10.3 (Most-Favored-Nation Treatment);
      (iii) Article 10.4 (Market Access for Financial Institutions); or
      (iv) Article 10.8 (Senior Management and Boards of Directors).
2. Each entry in Section B as described in paragraph 1(b) sets out the following elements:
   (a) **Description of Non-Conforming Measures** sets out the non-conforming aspects of the entry and the subsector, financial institution, or activities covered by the entry;
   (b) **Measures** identifies the laws, regulations or other measures for which the entry is made. A measure cited in the Measures element:
      (i) means the measure as amended, continued or renewed as of the date of entry into force of this Agreement, and
      (ii) includes any subordinate measure adopted or maintained under the authority of and consistent with the measure;
   (c) **Obligations Concerned** indicates the obligations referred to in paragraph 1(b) with respect to which the entry is made.

Relating to Insurance

3. The Schedule of the United States to Annex 10B with respect to insurance sets out:
   (a) headnotes that limit or clarify the commitments of the United States with respect to the obligations described in subparagraphs (i)-(v) of paragraph (b), and
   (b) pursuant to Article 10.9 (Non-Conforming Measures), a schedule of existing measures of the United States that do not conform to some or all of the obligations imposed by:
      (i) Article 10.2 (National Treatment);

    (ii) Article 10.3 (Most-Favored-Nation Treatment);

    (iii) Article 10.4 (Market Access for Financial Enterprises);

    (iv) Article 10.5 (Cross-Border Trade); or

    (v) Article 10.8 (Senior Management and Boards of Directors).

4. Each entry in the schedule of non-conforming measures described in paragraph 3(b) sets out the following elements:

    (a) **Obligations Concerned** specifies the obligation(s) referred to in paragraph 3(b) that, pursuant to Article 10.9, do not apply to the listed measure(s);

    (b) **Level of Government** indicates the level of government maintaining the listed measure(s);

    (c) **Measures** identifies the laws, regulations or other measures for which the entry is made. A measure cited in the Measures element:

        (i) means the measure as amended, continued or renewed as of the date of entry into force of this Agreement, and

        (ii) includes any subordinate measure adopted or maintained under the authority of and consistent with the measure;

    (d) **Description** provides a general, nonbinding description of the Measures.

Common Provisions

5. In accordance with Article 10.9.1 (a), the articles of this Agreement specified in the Obligations Concerned element of an entry do not apply to the law, regulation or other measure identified in the Measures element or in the Description of Non-Conforming Measures element of that entry.

6. Where the United States maintains a measure that requires that a service supplier be a citizen, permanent resident or resident of its territory as a condition to the provision of a service in its territory, a listing for that measure taken in Annex 10B with respect to Articles 10.2, 10.3, 10.4, or 10.5 shall operate as a reservation with respect to Articles 15.4 (National Treatment and Most-Favored-Nation Treatment) and 15.8 (Performance Requirements), to the extent of that measure.

7. Both Parties agree that references in the Schedule of a Party to Annex 10B to any enterprise or entity apply as well to any successor enterprise or entity, which shall be entitled to benefit from any listing of a non-conforming measure with respect to that enterprise or entity.

Annex 10C. Specific Commitments

Singapore

Related to Article 10.1 (Scope and Coverage)

1. This Chapter shall apply to the following services to the extent they are covered by the obligations of this Chapter through application of the exception in Article 10.1.3:
- Sale and distribution services for government debt.

Related to Article 10.4 (Market Access)

2. Notwithstanding item 1 of the non-conforming measures related to banking listed in Singapore's Schedule to Annex 10B, Singapore shall approve, by the date of entry into force of this Agreement, one new full bank license and two additional customer service locations for a financial institution of the United States.

Related to Article 10.5 (Cross Border Trade)

3. No later than January 1, 2006, the Parties shall consult on further liberalization by Singapore of cross-border trade in the services described in paragraph 3(f) of Singapore's Schedule to Annex 10A.

Related to Article 10.15 (Expedited Availability of Insurance Services)

4. Singapore shall not require product filing or approval for insurance products other than for life insurance products, Central Provident Fund-related products and investment-linked products. Where product filing or approval is required, Singapore shall allow the introduction of the product, which Singapore shall deem to be approved unless the product is disapproved within a reasonable time, endeavoring to do so within 30 days. Singapore shall not maintain limitations on the number or frequency of product introductions. This specific commitment does not apply where a financial institution of the United States seeks to supply a new financial service pursuant to Article 10.6 (New Financial Services).

Related to Article 10.17 (Consultations)

5. No later than January 1, 2007, and every three years thereafter, the Parties shall consult concerning any existing limitations on acquisitions of control by United States financial institutions of Singapore-incorporated banks that are controlled by persons of Singapore.

Related to Portfolio Management

6.

(a) Singapore shall allow, in a manner consistent with Article 10.1, a financial institution (other than a trust company or insurance company), organized outside its territory, to provide investment advice and portfolio management services, excluding (1) custodial services, (2) trustee services, and (3) execution services that are not related to managing a collective investment scheme, to the manager of a collective investment scheme, where the manager is

(i) located in the territory of Singapore, and

(ii) related to the financial institution.

(b) For purposes of this paragraph,

     (i) **collective investment scheme** has the meaning given to it under Section 2 of the Securities and Futures Act (Cap. 289); and

     (ii) **related** means a related corporation as defined under Section 6 of the Companies Act (Cap. 50).

7. Singapore shall accord most-favored-nation treatment to financial institutions of the United States in the award of asset management mandates by the Government of Singapore Investment Corporation.

Related to Credit and Charge Cards

8. Singapore shall consider applications for access to automated teller machine networks operated by local banks in the territory of Singapore for credit and charge cards of non-bank issuers that are controlled by persons of the United States.

United States

Related to Article 10.1 (Scope and Coverage)

1. For the United States, this chapter shall apply to the following services to the extent they are covered by the obligations of this chapter through application of the exception in Article 10.1.3:
    (a) fiscal agency or depository services,
    (b) liquidation and management services for regulated financial institutions; and
    (c) sale and distribution services for government debt.

Related to Article 10.15 (Expedited Availability of Insurance Services)

2. Recognizing the principles of federalism under the U.S. Constitution, the history of state regulation of insurance in the United States, and the McCarran-Ferguson Act, the United States welcomes the efforts of the National Association of Insurance Commissioners ("NAIC") relating to the availability of insurance services as expressed in the NAIC's "Statement of Intent: The Future of Insurance Regulation.", including the initiatives on speed-to-market intentions and regulatory re-engineering (under Part II of the Statement of Intent). This specific commitment does not apply where a financial institution of Singapore seeks to supply a new financial service pursuant to Article 10.6.

Related to Portfolio Management

3.
    (a) The United States shall allow, in a manner consistent with Article 10.1, a financial institution (other than a trust company or insurance company), organized outside its territory, to provide investment advice and portfolio management services, excluding (1) custodial services, (2) trustee services, and (3) execution services that are not related to managing a collective investment

scheme, to a collective investment scheme located in the territory of the United States.

(b) For purposes of this paragraph, **collective investment scheme** means an investment company registered with the Securities and Exchange Commission under the Investment Company Act of 1940.

Annex 10D. The Financial Services Committee

1. On request by either Party, the Financial Services Committee shall consider any matter relating to:

    (a) the transfer of information in electronic or other form, into and out of a Party's territory, by a financial institution for data processing where such processing is required in the ordinary course of business;

    (b) the protection of the privacy of individuals in relation to the processing and dissemination of personal data and the protection of confidentiality of individual records and accounts.

Authorities Responsible for Financial Services

2. The authority of each Party responsible for financial services is:

    (a) for Singapore, the Monetary Authority of Singapore;

    (b) for the United States, the Department of the Treasury for banking and other financial services and the Office of the United States Trade Representative, in coordination with the Department of Commerce and other agencies, for insurance services.

11. TEMPORARY ENTRY OF BUSINESS PERSONS

Article 11.1: Definitions

For purposes of this Chapter:

business person means a national of a Party who is engaged in trade in goods, the provision of services or the conduct of investment activities;

immigration measure means any law, regulation, or procedure affecting the entry and sojourn of aliens, including the issuance of immigration documents authorizing employment to an alien; and

temporary entry means entry into the territory of a Party by a business person of the other Party without the intent to establish permanent residence.

Article 11.2: General Principles

1. This Chapter reflects the preferential trading relationship between the Parties, the Parties' mutual desire to facilitate temporary entry on a comparable basis and of establishing transparent criteria and procedures for temporary entry, and the need to ensure border security and to protect the domestic labor force and permanent employment in their respective territories.
2. This Chapter shall not apply to measures regarding citizenship, permanent residence, or employment on a permanent basis.

Article 11.3: General Obligations

1. Each Party shall apply its measures relating to the provisions of this Chapter in accordance with Article 11.2 and, in particular, shall apply expeditiously those measures so as to avoid unduly impairing or delaying trade in goods or services or conduct of investment activities under this Agreement.
2. For greater certainty, nothing in this Chapter shall prevent a Party from applying measures to regulate the entry of natural persons into, or their temporary stay in, its territory, including those measures necessary to protect the integrity of, and to ensure the orderly movement of natural persons across its borders, provided that such measures are not applied in such a manner as to unduly impair or delay trade in goods or services or conduct of investment activities under this Agreement. The sole fact of requiring a visa, or other document authorizing employment to a business person, for natural persons shall not be regarded as unduly impairing or delaying trade in goods or services or conduct of investment activities under this Agreement.

Article 11.4: Grant of Temporary Entry

1. Each Party shall grant temporary entry to business persons listed in Annex 11A who are otherwise qualified for entry under applicable measures relating to public health and safety and national security, in accordance with this Chapter.
2. A Party may refuse to issue an immigration document authorizing employment to a business person where the temporary entry of that person might affect adversely:
   (a) the settlement of any labor dispute that is in progress at the place or intended place of employment; or
   (b) the employment of any person who is involved in such dispute.
3. When a Party refuses pursuant to paragraph 2 to issue an immigration document authorizing employment, it shall:
   (a) take measures to allow the business person to be informed in writing; and
   (b) promptly notify the other Party in writing of the reasons for the refusal.
4. Each Party shall set any fees for processing applications for temporary entry of business persons in a manner consistent with Article 11.3.1.

Article 11.5: Regulatory Transparency

1. Each Party shall maintain or establish contact points or other mechanisms to respond to inquiries from interested persons regarding regulations affecting the temporary entry of business persons.
2. If a Party receives comments regarding a proposed regulation from interested persons, it should publish a concise statement addressing those comments at the time that it adopts the final regulations.
3. To the extent possible, each Party shall allow reasonable time between publication of final regulations affecting the temporary entry of business persons and their effective date.
4. Each Party shall, within a reasonable period of time after an application requesting temporary entry is considered complete under its domestic laws and regulations, inform the applicant of the decision concerning the application. At the request of the applicant, the Party shall provide, without undue delay, information concerning the status of the application.
5. Prior to the entry into force of this Agreement, the Parties shall exchange information on current procedures relating to the processing of applications for temporary entry, including processing goals that apply to business persons of the other Party. Each Party shall endeavor to achieve these goals and make available upon request to the other Party, in accordance with its domestic law, data respecting the attainment of these processing goals.
6. For purposes of this Article, **regulation** means a measure of general application other than a law, and includes a measure that establishes or applies to licensing authorization or criteria.

Article 11.6: Provision of Information
Further to Article 19.3 (Publication), each Party shall:

(a) provide to the other Party such materials as will enable it to become acquainted with its measures relating to this Chapter; and
(b) no later than six months after the date of entry into force of this Agreement, prepare, publish, and make available in its own territory, and in the territory of the other Party, explanatory material in a consolidated document regarding the requirements for temporary entry under this Chapter in such a manner as will enable business persons of the other Party to become acquainted with them.

Article 11.7: Temporary Entry Coordinators

1. Each Party shall establish a Temporary Entry Coordinator, which shall include officials responsible for immigration measures.
2. The Temporary Entry Coordinators of the Parties shall:
    (a) establish their own schedule of meetings;
    (b) exchange information on measures that affect the temporary entry of business persons under this Chapter;

(c) consider the development of measures to facilitate the temporary entry of business persons on a comparable basis;

(d) consider the implementation and administration of this Chapter; and

(e) make available, upon request, to the other Party in accordance with its domestic law, data respecting the granting of temporary entry under this Chapter to business persons of the other Party who have been issued immigration documents.

Article 11.8: Dispute Settlement

1. A Party may not initiate proceedings under Article 20.4 (Additional Dispute Settlement Procedures) regarding a refusal to grant temporary entry under this Chapter or a particular case arising under Article 11.3.1 unless:

    (a) the matter involves a pattern of practice; and

    (b) the business person has exhausted the available administrative remedies regarding the particular matter.

2. The remedies referred to in paragraph (1)(b) shall be deemed to be exhausted if a final determination in the matter has not been issued by the competent authority within one year of the institution of an administrative proceeding, and the failure to issue a determination is not attributable to delay caused by the business person.

Article 11.9: Relation to Other Chapters

Except for this Chapter, Chapters 1 (Establishment of a Free Trade Area and Definitions), 20 (Administration and Dispute Settlement), and 21 (General Provisions), and Articles 19.2 (Contact Points), 19.3 (Publication), 19.4 (Notification and Provision of Information), and 19.5 (Administrative Proceedings) of Chapter 19 (Transparency), no provision of this Agreement shall impose any obligation on a Party regarding its immigration measures.

Annex 11A

Section I: Business Visitors

1. Each Party shall grant temporary entry for up to 90 days to a business person seeking to engage in a business activity set out in Appendix 11A.1, without requiring that person to obtain an employment authorization, provided that the business person otherwise complies with immigration measures applicable to temporary entry, and on presentation of:

    (a) proof of nationality of a Party;

    (b) documentation demonstrating that the business person will be so engaged and describing the purpose of entry; and

    (c) evidence demonstrating that the proposed business activity is international in scope and that the business person is not seeking to enter the local labor market.

2. Each Party may provide that a business person satisfy the requirements of paragraph 1 by demonstrating that:

(a) the primary source of remuneration for the proposed business activity is outside the territory of the Party granting temporary entry; and

(b) the business person's principal place of business and the actual place of accrual of profits, at least predominantly, remain outside such territory.

3. A Party shall normally accept an oral declaration as to the principal place of business and the actual place of accrual of profits. Where the Party requires further proof, it shall normally consider a letter from the employer attesting to these matters as sufficient proof.

4. Neither Party may:

(a) as a condition for temporary entry under paragraph 1, require prior approval procedures, petitions, labor certification tests, or other procedures of similar effect; or

(b) impose or maintain any numerical restriction relating to temporary entry under paragraph 1.

Section II: Traders and Investors

1. Each Party shall grant temporary entry and provide confirming documentation to a business person seeking to:

(a) carry on substantial trade in goods or services principally between the territory of the Party of which the business person is a national and the territory of the other Party into which entry is sought, or

(b) establish, develop, administer, or provide advice or key technical services to the operation of an investment to which the business person or the business person's enterprise has committed, or is in the process of committing, a substantial amount of capital, in a capacity that is supervisory, executive, or involves essential skills, provided that the business person otherwise complies with immigration measures applicable to temporary entry.

2. Neither Party may:

(a) as a condition for temporary entry under paragraph 1, require labor certification tests or other procedures of similar effect; or

(b) impose or maintain any numerical restriction relating to temporary entry under paragraph 1.

Section III: Intra-Company Transferees

1. Each Party shall grant temporary entry and provide confirming documentation to a business person employed by an enterprise who seeks to render services to that enterprise or a subsidiary or affiliate thereof, in a capacity that is managerial, executive, or involves specialized knowledge, provided that the business person otherwise complies with existing immigration measures applicable to temporary entry. A Party may require the business person to have been employed continuously by the enterprise for one year within the three-year period immediately preceding the date of the application for admission. The Parties understand that, as used in this paragraph, "a business person employed by an enterprise who seeks to render

services to that enterprise or a subsidiary or affiliate thereof, in a capacity that is managerial, executive or involves special knowledge" has the same meaning as "managers, executives and specialists" as defined in relation to intra-corporate transferees in a Party's Schedule of Specific Commitments to the GATS.

2. A Party shall not:
   (a) as a condition for temporary entry under paragraph 1, require labor certification tests or other procedures of similar effect; or
   (b) impose or maintain any numerical restriction relating to temporary entry under paragraph 1.

Section IV: Professionals

1. Each Party shall grant temporary entry and provide confirming documentation to a business person seeking to engage in a business activity as a professional, or to perform training functions related to a particular profession, including conducting seminars, if the business person otherwise complies with immigration measures applicable to temporary entry, on presentation of:
   (a) proof of nationality of a Party;
   (b) documentation demonstrating that the business person will be so engaged and describing the purpose of entry; and
   (c) documentation demonstrating the attainment of the relevant minimum educational requirements or alternative credentials.

2. For purposes of this Chapter, **professional** means a national of a Party who is engaged in a specialty occupation requiring:
   (a) theoretical and practical application of a body of specialized knowledge; and
   (b) attainment of a post-secondary degree in the specialty requiring four or more years of study (or the equivalent of such a degree) as a minimum for entry into the occupation. Such degrees include the Bachelor's Degree, Master's Degree, and the Doctoral Degree conferred by institutions in the United States and Singapore.

3. Notwithstanding paragraph 2, each Party shall grant temporary entry to business persons seeking to engage in a business activity as a professional in one of the professions listed in Appendix 11A.2, provided that the business person possesses the credentials specified and otherwise complies with the requirements in paragraph 1 of this Section.

4. To assist in the implementation of this Chapter, the Parties shall exchange illustrative lists of professions that meet the definition of professional by the date of entry into force of this Agreement. The Parties shall also exchange information on post-secondary education, in order to facilitate the evaluation of applications for temporary entry.

5. A Party shall not:
   (a) as a condition for temporary entry under paragraph 1, require prior approval procedures, petitions, labor certification tests, or other procedures of similar effect; or
   (b) impose or maintain any numerical restriction relating to temporary entry under paragraph 1.

6. Notwithstanding paragraph 5(a), a Party may require a business person seeking temporary entry under this Section to comply with procedures applicable to temporary entry of professionals, such as an attestation of compliance with the Party's labor and immigration laws or a requirement that the business person meet certain salary criteria.

7. Notwithstanding paragraphs 1 and 5, a Party may establish an annual numerical limit, which shall be set out in Appendix 11A.3, regarding temporary entry of business persons of the other Party seeking to engage in business activities as a professional.

8. A Party establishing a numerical limit pursuant to paragraph 7, unless the Parties agree otherwise, may, in consultation with the other Party, grant temporary entry under paragraph 1 to a business person who practices in a profession where accreditation, licensing, and certification requirements are mutually recognized by the Parties.

9. Nothing in paragraph 7 or 8 shall be construed to limit the ability of a business person to seek temporary entry under a Party's applicable immigration measures relating to the entry of professionals other than those adopted or maintained pursuant to paragraph 1.

APPENDIX 11A.1. BUSINESS VISITORS

Definitions

For purposes of this Appendix, **territory of the other Party** means the territory of the Party other than the territory of the Party into which temporary entry is sought.

The Parties agree that the business visitors referred to below are not seeking to establish a direct employer-employee relationship in the territory of the Party into which temporary entry is sought.

Research and Design

- Technical, scientific, and statistical researchers conducting independent research or research for an enterprise located in the territory of the other Party.

Growth, Manufacture, and Production

- Purchasing and production management personnel conducting commercial transactions for an enterprise located in the territory of the other Party.

Marketing

- Market researchers and analysts conducting independent research or analysis or research or analysis for an enterprise located in the territory of the other Party.
- Trade fair and promotional personnel attending a trade convention.

Sales

- Sales representatives and agents negotiating contracts for, but not delivering or providing, goods or services for an enterprise located in the territory of the other Party that do not involve direct transactions with the general public.
- Buyers purchasing for an enterprise located in the territory of the other Party.

Distribution

- With respect to temporary entry into the United States, Singaporean customs brokers performing brokerage duties relating to the export of goods from the territory of the United States to or through the territory of Singapore. With respect to temporary entry into the territory of Singapore, United States customs brokers performing brokerage duties relating to the export of goods from the territory of Singapore to or through the territory of the United States.
- Customs brokers providing consulting services regarding the facilitation of the import or export of goods.

After-sales Service

- Installers, repair and maintenance personnel, and supervisors, possessing highly specialized knowledge essential to a seller's contractual obligation, performing services or training workers to perform services, pursuant to a warranty or other directly-related service contract included as part of the sale of commercial or industrial equipment or machinery, including computer software, purchased from an enterprise located outside the territory of the Party into which temporary entry is sought, during the life of the warranty or directly-related service agreement.

General Service

- Managers, executives, and specialists[1] entering to negotiate specified or defined commercial transactions for an enterprise located in the territory of the other Party.
- Managers, executives, and specialists[1] in the financial services sector (insurers, bankers, or investment brokers) entering to negotiate specified or defined commercial transactions for an enterprise located in the territory of the other Party.
- Public relations and advertising managers, executives, and specialists[1] attending or participating in conventions, or consulting with business associates regarding specified or defined commercial transactions for an enterprise located in the territory of the other Party.
- Tourism personnel (tour and travel agents, tour guides, or tour operators) attending or participating in conventions or conducting a tour that has begun in the territory of the other Party.
- Translators or interpreters performing services as employees of an enterprise located in the territory of the other Party, and for a defined commercial transaction for that enterprise.

APPENDIX 11A.2

PROFESSION	MINIMUM EDUCATION REQUIREMENTS AND ALTERNATIVE CREDENTIALS
Disaster Relief Claims Adjuster	Baccalaureate Degree, and successful completion of training in the appropriate areas of insurance adjustment pertaining to disaster relief claims; or three years experience in claims adjustment and successful completion of training in the appropriate areas of insurance adjustment pertaining to disaster relief claims.
Management Consultant	Baccalaureate Degree. If the degree is in a discipline not related to the area of the consulting agreement, then equivalent professional experience as established by statement or professional credential attesting to three years experience in a field or specialty related to the consulting agreement is required.

APPENDIX 11A.3

United States

1. Beginning on the date of entry into force of this Agreement, the United States shall annually approve as many as 5,400 initial applications of business persons of Singapore seeking temporary entry under Section IV of Annex 11A to engage in a business activity at a professional level.

2. For purposes of paragraph 1, the United States shall not take into account:
   (a) the renewal of a period of temporary entry;
   (b) the entry of a spouse or children accompanying or following to join the principal business person;
   (c) an admission under section 101(a)(15)(H)(i)(b) of the Immigration and Nationality Act, 1952, as it may be amended, including the worldwide numerical limit established by section 214(g)(1)(A) of that Act; or
   (d) an admission under any other provision of section 101(a)(15) of that Act relating to the entry of professionals.

12. ANTICOMPETITIVE BUSINESS CONDUCT, DESIGNATED MONOPOLIES, AND GOVERNMENT ENTERPRISES

Article 12.1: Objectives

Recognizing that the conduct subject to this Chapter has the potential to restrict bilateral trade and investment, the Parties believe proscribing such conduct, implementing economically sound competition policies, and engaging in cooperation will help secure the benefits of this Agreement.

Article 12.2: Anticompetitive Business Conduct

1. Each Party shall adopt or maintain measures to proscribe anticompetitive business conduct[12-1] with the objective of promoting economic efficiency and consumer welfare, and shall take appropriate action with respect to such conduct.

2. Each Party shall establish or maintain an authority responsible for the enforcement of its measures to proscribe anticompetitive business conduct. The enforcement policy of the Parties' national authorities responsible for the enforcement of such measures includes not discriminating on the basis of the nationality of the subjects of their proceedings. Each Party shall ensure that a person subject to the imposition of a sanction or remedy for violation of such measures is provided with the opportunity to be heard and to present evidence, and to seek review of such sanction or remedy in a domestic court or independent tribunal.

Article 12.3: Designated Monopolies and Government Enterprises

1. Designated Monopolies
   (a) Nothing in this Chapter shall be construed to prevent a Party from designating a monopoly.
   (b) Where a Party designates a monopoly and the designation may affect the interests of persons of the other Party, the Party shall:
      (i) at the time of the designation endeavor to introduce such conditions on the operation of the monopoly as will minimize or eliminate any nullification or impairment of benefits in the sense of Article 20.4.1(c) (Additional Dispute Settlement Procedures); and
      (ii) provide written notification, in advance wherever possible, to the other Party of the designation and any such conditions.
   (c) Each Party shall ensure that any privately-owned monopoly that it designates after the date of entry into force of this Agreement and any government monopoly that it designates or has designated:
      (i) acts in a manner that is not inconsistent with the Party's obligations under this Agreement wherever such a monopoly exercises any regulatory, administrative, or other governmental authority that the Party has delegated to it in connection with the monopoly good or service, such as the power to grant import or export licenses, approve commercial transactions, or impose quotas, fees or other charges;
      (ii) acts solely in accordance with commercial considerations in its purchase or sale of the monopoly good or service in the relevant market, including with regard to price, quality, availability, marketability, transportation, and other terms and conditions of purchase or sale, except to comply with any terms of its designation that are not inconsistent with subparagraph (iii) or (iv);
      (iii) provides non-discriminatory treatment to covered investments, to goods of the other Party, and to service suppliers of the other Party in its purchase or sale of the monopoly good or service in the relevant market; and

        (iv) does not use its monopoly position to engage, either directly or indirectly, including through its dealings with its parent, subsidiaries, or other enterprises with common ownership, in anticompetitive practices in a non-monopolized market in its territory that adversely affect covered investments.

2. Government Enterprises

   (a) Nothing in this Agreement shall be construed to prevent a Party from establishing or maintaining a government enterprise.

   (b) Each Party shall ensure that any government enterprise that it establishes or maintains acts in a manner that is not inconsistent with the Party's obligations under this Agreement wherever such enterprise exercises any regulatory, administrative, or other governmental authority that the Party has delegated to it, such as the power to expropriate, grant licenses, approve commercial transactions, or impose quotas, fees, or other charges.

   (c) The United States shall ensure that any government enterprise that it establishes or maintains accords non-discriminatory treatment in the sale of its goods or services to covered investments.

   (d) Singapore shall ensure that any government enterprise:

      (i) acts solely in accordance with commercial considerations in its purchase or sale of goods or services, such as with regard to price, quality, availability, marketability, transportation, and other terms and conditions of purchase or sale, and provides non-discriminatory treatment to covered investments, to goods of the United States, and to service suppliers of the United States, including with respect to its purchases or sales;[12-2] and

      (ii) does not, either directly or indirectly, including through its dealings with its parent, subsidiaries, or other enterprises with common ownership:

         (A) enter into agreements among competitors that restrain competition on price or output or allocate customers for which there is no plausible efficiency justification, or

         (B) engage in exclusionary practices that substantially lessen competition in a market in Singapore to the detriment of consumers.

   (e) Singapore shall take no action or attempt in any way, directly or indirectly, to influence or direct decisions of its government enterprises, including through the exercise of any rights or interests conferring effective influence over such enterprises, except in a manner consistent with this Agreement. However, Singapore may exercise its voting rights in government enterprises in a manner that is not inconsistent with this Agreement.

   (f) Singapore shall continue reducing, with a goal of substantially eliminating, its aggregate ownership and other interests that confer effective influence in entities organized under the laws of Singapore, taking into account, in the timing of individual divestments, the state of relevant capital markets.

   (g) Singapore shall:

      (i) at least annually, make public a consolidated report that details for each covered entity:

         (A) the percentage of shares and the percentage of voting rights that Singapore and its government enterprises cumulatively own;

(B) a description of any special shares or special voting or other rights that Singapore or its government enterprises hold, to the extent different from the rights attached to the general common shares of such entity;

(C) the name and government title(s) of any government official serving as an officer or member of the board of directors; and

(D) its annual revenue or total assets, or both, depending on the basis on which the enterprise qualifies as a covered entity.

(ii) on receipt from the United States of a request regarding a specific enterprise, provide to the United States the information listed in clause (i), for any enterprise that is not a covered entity or an enterprise excluded under Article 12.8.1 (d) and 12.8.1(e), with the understanding that the information may be made public.

3. The charging of different prices in different markets, or within the same market, where such differences are based on normal commercial considerations, such as taking account of supply and demand conditions, is not in itself inconsistent with this Article.

4. This Article does not apply to government procurement.

Article 12.4: Cooperation

The Parties recognize the importance of cooperation and coordination to further effective competition law and policy development in the free trade area and agree to cooperate on these matters.

Article 12.5: Transparency and Information Requests

1. The Parties recognize the value of transparency of their competition policies.

2. Each Party, at the request of the other Party, shall make available public information concerning the enforcement of its measures proscribing anticompetitive business conduct.

3. Each Party, at the request of the other Party, shall make available public information concerning government enterprises, and designated monopolies, public or private. Requests for such information shall indicate the entities involved, specify the particular products and markets concerned, and include some indicia that these entities may be engaging in practices that may hinder trade or investment between the Parties.

4. Each Party, at the request of the other Party, shall make available public information concerning exemptions to its measures proscribing anticompetitive business conduct. Requests for such information shall specify the particular products and markets of concern and include some indicia that the exemption might hinder trade or investment between the Parties.

Article 12.6: Consultations

1. To foster understanding between the Parties, or to address specific matters that arise under this Chapter, each Party shall, at the request of the other Party, enter into

consultations regarding representations made by the other Party. In its request, the Party shall indicate, if relevant, how the matter affects trade or investment between the Parties. The Party addressed shall accord full and sympathetic consideration to the concerns of the other Party.

2. Where consultations under paragraph 1 concern conduct covered by Article 12.3.2(d)(ii), Singapore shall inform the United States of the steps it has taken or plans to take to examine the conduct at issue, shall apprise the United States when Singapore's responsible authorities decide to initiate or not to initiate enforcement proceedings regarding the conduct, and shall keep the United States regularly apprised of developments in, and the results of, any enforcement proceedings it initiates.

Article 12.7: Disputes

A Party shall not have recourse to dispute settlement under this Agreement for any matter arising under Article 12.2, 12.4, or 12.6.

Article 12.8: Definitions

For purposes of this Chapter:

1. **covered entity** means:
    (a) an enterprise organized under the laws of Singapore in which effective influence exists, or is rebuttably presumed to exist, whose annual revenue is greater than SGD 50 million;
    (b) an enterprise organized under the laws of Singapore in which effective influence exists, or is rebuttably presumed to exist, whose total assets are greater than SGD 50 million; and
    (c) any entity organized under the laws of Singapore in which the Government of Singapore owns a special voting share with veto rights relating to such matters as the disposal of the undertaking, the acquisition by any person of a specified percentage of the enterprise's share capital, appointments to the board of directors or of management, winding up or dissolution of the enterprise, or any change to the constituent documents concerning the aforementioned matters; but excludes:
    (d) government enterprises organized and operating solely for the purpose of:
        (i)   investing the reserves of the Government of Singapore in foreign markets; or
        (ii) holding investments referred to in clause (i); and (e) Temasek Holdings (Pte) Ltd.
    The revenue and total asset thresholds above shall be adjusted for inflation (or deflation) every five years. The Parties may otherwise revise the thresholds by mutual agreement;

2. **covered investment** means, with respect to a Party, an investment in its territory of an investor of the other Party. Covered investments shall include those existing at the date of entry into force of this Agreement as well as those established, acquired, or expanded thereafter;

3. **a delegation** includes a legislative grant, and a government order, directive, or other act, transferring to the monopoly or government enterprise, or authorizing the exercise by the monopoly or government enterprise of, government authority;

4. **designate means** to establish, designate, or authorize a monopoly, or to expand the scope of a monopoly, to cover an additional good or service, whether formally or in effect;

5. **effective influence** exists where the government and its government enterprises, alone or in combination:

    (a) own more that 50 percent of the voting rights of an entity; or

    (b) have the ability to exercise substantial influence over the composition of the board of directors or any other managing body of an entity, to determine the outcome of decisions on the strategic, financial, or operating policies or plans of an entity, or otherwise to exercise substantial influence over the management or operation of an entity. Where the government and its government enterprises, alone or in combination, own 50 percent or less, but more than 20 percent, of the voting securities of the entity and own the largest block of voting rights of such entity, there is a rebuttable presumption that effective influence exists. Annex 12A provides an illustration of how the analysis of effective influence should proceed;

6. **government enterprise** means:

    (a) for the United States, an enterprise owned, or controlled through ownership interests, by that Party; and

    (b) for Singapore, an enterprise in which that Party has effective influence;

7. **government monopoly** means a monopoly that is owned, or controlled through ownership interests, by the national government of a Party or by another such monopoly;

8. **in accordance with commercial considerations** means consistent with normal business practices of privately-held enterprises in the relevant business or industry;

9. **market** means the geographical and commercial market for a good or service;

10. **monopoly** means an entity, including a consortium or government agency, that in any relevant market in the territory of a Party is designated as the sole provider or purchaser of a good or service, but does not include an entity that has been granted an exclusive intellectual property right solely by reason of such grant; and

11. **non-discriminatory treatment** means the better of national treatment and most-favored-nation treatment, as set out in the relevant provisions of this Agreement and subject to the terms and conditions set out in the relevant Annexes thereto.

Annex 12A

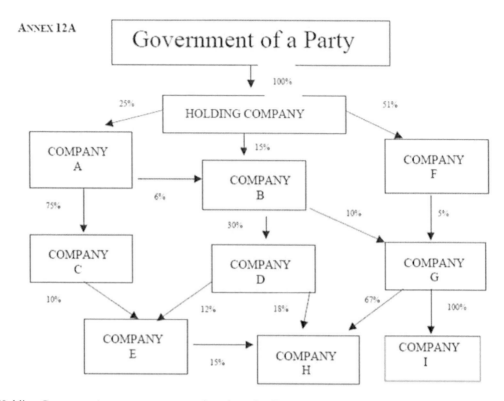

Holding Company: A government enterprise, since the Government owns more than 50% of it (100%).

Company A: Presumed to be a government enterprise, since Holding Company, a government enterprise, owns more than 20% of its shares (assuming Holding Company is largest shareholder).

Company B: Presumed to be a government enterprise, since Holding Company and Company A, a government enterprise, together own more than 20% of its shares (21%) (assuming that the block of 21% owned by Holding Company and Company A is the largest block of shares).

Company C: Presumed to be a government enterprise, since Company A, a government enterprise, owns more than 50% of its shares (75%).

Company D: Presumed to be a government enterprise, since Company B, a government enterprise, owns more than 20% of its shares (30%) (assuming Company B owns the largest block of shares).

Company E: Presumed to be a government enterprise, since Company C, a government enterprise, and Company D, a government enterprise, together own more than 20% of its shares (22%) (assuming the block of 22% owned by Companies C and D constitutes the largest block of shares).

Company F: A government enterprise, since Holding Company owns more than 50% of its shares.

Company G: Not a government enterprise, since Company B, a government enterprise, and Company F, a government enterprise, together do not own more than 20% of its shares (15%).

Company H: Not a government enterprise, although Company D, a government enterprise, and Company E, together owns more than 20% of its shares (33%), Companies D and E do not, together, own the largest block of shares, since Company G, not a government enterprise, owns 67% of its shares.

Company I: Not a government enterprise, since Company G is not a government enterprise.

13. GOVERNMENT PROCUREMENT

Article 13.1: General

1. The Parties reaffirm their rights and obligations under the GPA and their interest in further expanding bilateral trading opportunities in each Party's government procurement market.

2. The Parties recognize their shared interest in promoting international liberalization of government procurement markets in the context of the rules-based international trading system. The Parties shall continue to cooperate in the review under Article XXIV:7 of the GPA and on procurement matters in APEC and other appropriate international fora. The Parties shall also actively cooperate to implement the WTO Doha Ministerial mandate related to the negotiation of a multilateral agreement on transparency in government procurement.

3. Nothing in this Chapter shall be construed to derogate from either Party's rights or obligations under the GPA.

4. The Parties confirm their desire and determination to apply the APEC Non-Binding Principles on Government Procurement, as appropriate, to all their government procurement that is outside the scope of the GPA and this Chapter.

Article 13.2: Scope and Coverage

1. This Chapter applies to measures adopted or maintained by a Party regarding government procurement.

2. For purposes of this Chapter, **government procurement** means a procurement:
   (a) by an entity specified in a Party's Schedule 1 to Annex 13A;
   (b) of any combination of goods and services specified in a Party's Schedule 2 to Annex 13A;
   (c) by any contractual means, including those listed in Article I:2 of the GPA and any build-operate-transfer contract; and
   (d) in which the contract has a value not less than the relevant threshold set out in Schedule 1 to Annex 13A.

3. Except as otherwise specified in Annexes 13A and 13B, this Chapter does not cover non-contractual agreements or any form of governmental assistance, including:
   (a) cooperative agreements;
   (b) grants;
   (c) loans;
   (d) equity infusions;
   (e) guarantees;
   (f) fiscal incentives; and
   (g) governmental provision of goods and services to persons or governmental authorities not specifically covered under the Schedules to Annexes 13A and 13B of this Chapter.

4. Singapore shall not exercise any control or influence, including through any shares that it owns or controls or its personnel selections to corporate boards or positions, in

procurement conducted by government enterprises, as defined in Article 12.8 (Definitions).

5.   In accordance with Article III:3 of the GPA, the provisions of this Chapter do not affect the rights and obligations provided for in Chapters 2 (National Treatment and Market Access for Goods), 8 (Cross-Border Trade in Services), 10 (Financial Services), and 15 (Investment).

6.

   (a)   To ensure comprehensive coverage, this Chapter covers government procurement of digital products, as defined in Article 14.4 (Definitions), that are transmitted electronically and are created, produced, contracted for, commissioned, or first made available on commercial terms in the territory of the other Party.

   (b)   For greater certainty, digital products do not include digitized representations of financial instruments. In addition, the obligations on digital products under this Chapter shall not apply to the procurement of broadcasting services.

   (c)   For greater certainty, a Party's obligations relating to the government procurement of digital products are addressed only in this Chapter.

Article 13.3: Incorporation of GPA Provisions

1.   The Parties shall apply the provisions of Articles II, III, IV:1, VI-XV, XVI:1, XVIII, XIX:1-4, XX, the Agreement Notes, and Appendices II-IV of the GPA to all government procurement. To that end, these GPA Articles and Appendices, the notes to the Appendices, Notes to Annexes 1 to 5 of Appendix I, [13-1] Singapore's General Note, and U.S. General Notes 1-4 are incorporated into and made a part of this Chapter, *mutatis mutandis*. For greater certainty, Article VI is not intended to preclude a Party from preparing, adopting, or applying technical specifications to promote the conservation of natural resources.

2.   For purposes of the incorporation of the GPA under paragraph 1, the term:

   (a)   "Agreement" in the GPA means "Chapter;" except that "countries not Parties to this Agreement" means "non-Parties" and "Party to the Agreement@ in GPA Article III:2(b) means "Party";

   (b)   "Appendix I" in the GPA means "Annex 13A";

   (c)   "Annex 1" in the GPA means "Schedule 1.A";

   (d)   "Annex 2" in the GPA means "Schedule 1.B";

   (e)   "Annex 3" in the GPA means "Schedule 1.C";

   (f)   "Annex 4" in the GPA means "Schedule 2.B";

   (g)   "Annex 5" in the GPA means "Schedule 2.C";

   (h)   "from other Parties" in GPA Article IV:1 means "from the other Party";

   (i)   "any other Party" in GPA Article III:1(b) means "a non-Party"; and

   (j)   "among suppliers of other Parties or" in GPA Article VIII shall not be incorporated.

3.   If the GPA is amended or is superseded by another agreement, the Parties shall amend this Chapter, as appropriate, after consultations.

Article 13.4: Exceptions

1. Nothing in this Chapter shall be construed to prevent either Party from imposing or enforcing measures:
   (a) necessary to protect public morals, order, or safety;
   (b) necessary to protect human, animal, or plant life or health;
   (c) necessary to protect intellectual property; or
   (d) relating to products or services of handicapped persons, of philanthropic institutions, or of prison labor, provided that such measures are not applied in a manner that would constitute a means of arbitrary or unjustifiable discrimination between countries where the same conditions prevail or a disguised restriction on international trade.

2. The Parties understand that paragraph 1(b) includes environmental measures necessary to protect human, animal, or plant life or health.

Article 13.5: Modifications and Rectifications to Coverage

1. Where a Party proposes to modify or make minor amendments or technical rectifications of a purely formal nature to its Schedules to Annex 13A, it shall notify the other Party. If the other Party does not object to the proposed modification, minor amendment, or technical rectification within 30 days of the notification, the modification, minor amendment, or technical rectification shall enter into force immediately.

2. If a Party objects to the proposed removal of an entity from Annex 13A on the grounds that government control or influence over that entity has not been effectively eliminated, that Party may request further information or consultations with a view to clarifying the nature of such government control or influence, if any, and reaching agreement with the other Party on the entity's status under this Chapter. If the Party removing an entity from Annex 13A reaches agreement with the other Party that government control or influence over the entity has been effectively eliminated, the other Party shall not be entitled to compensatory adjustments.

3. A Party may modify its Schedules to Annex 13A for reasons other than the elimination of government control or influence only in exceptional circumstances. In such cases, it shall propose to the other Party appropriate compensatory adjustments in order to maintain a level of coverage comparable to that existing prior to the modification. In considering proposed modifications and any consequential compensatory adjustment, allowance shall be made for the market-opening effects of the removal of government control or influence. The modification shall take effect on agreement by the Parties that the proposed adjustments will maintain a comparable level of coverage.

Article 13.6: Definitions

For purposes of this Chapter:

1. **APEC** means Asia Pacific Economic Cooperation;

2. **broadcasting services** means a series of text, video, images, sound recordings and other products scheduled by a content provider for audio and/or visual reception, and for which the content provider has no choice over the scheduling of the series;

3. **build-operate-transfer contract** means any contractual arrangement the primary purpose of which is to provide for the construction or rehabilitation of physical infrastructure, plant, buildings, facilities, or other government-owned works and under which, as consideration for a supplier=s execution of a contractual arrangement, an entity grants to the supplier, for a specified period of time, temporary ownership or a right to control and operate, and demand payment for, the use of such works for the duration of the contract; and

4. **GPA** means WTO Agreement on Government Procurement.

Annex 13A.Schedule 1

Covered Entities

For the United States

A. Central Government Entities
All entities included in United States Appendix I, Annex 1 of the GPA, for procurement covered by that Annex.
Thresholds:
for all goods and services (except construction services): US$ 56,190, to be adjusted every two years in accordance with the formula specified in Annex 13B; and
for construction services: US$ 6,481,000, to be adjusted in accordance with the United States' Appendix I, Annex 1 of the GPA and the procedures set forth in that Agreement, converted into U.S. dollars.

B. Sub-Central Government Entities
All entities included in United States Appendix I, Annex 2 of the GPA, for procurement covered by that Annex.
Thresholds:
for all goods and services (except construction services): US$ 460,000; and
for construction services: US$ 6,481,000.
These thresholds are to be adjusted in accordance with the United States= Appendix I, Annex 2 of the GPA and the procedures set forth in that Agreement, converted into U.S. dollars.

C. All Other Entities
All entities included in the United States' Appendix I, Annex 3 of the GPA, for procurement covered by that Annex.
Thresholds:
for all goods and services (except construction services): the SDR equivalent of US$ 250,000 or US$ 518,000 (400,000 SDRs) in accordance with the respective lists in U.S. Appendix I, Annex 3; and

for construction services: US$ 6,481,000.

These thresholds are to be adjusted in accordance with the United States' Appendix I, Annex 3 of the GPA and the procedures set forth in that Agreement, converted into U.S. dollars.

For Singapore:

A. Central Government Entities
   All entities included in Singapore Appendix I, Annex 1 of the GPA, for procurement covered by that Annex.
   Thresholds:
   > for all goods and services (except construction services): S$ 102,710, to be adjusted in accordance with the formula specified in Annex 13B; and
   > for construction services: S$ 11,376,000, to be adjusted in accordance with adjustment of thresholds under Singapore Appendix I, Annex 1 of the GPA and the procedures set forth in that Agreement, converted into Singapore dollars.

B. Sub-Central Government Entities
   Not applicable for Singapore.

C. All Other Entities:
   All entities included in Singapore Appendix I, Annex 3 of the GPA, for procurement covered by that Annex.
   Thresholds:
   > for all goods and services (except construction services): S$ 910,000; and
   > for construction services: S$ 11,376,000.

These thresholds are to be adjusted in accordance with adjustment of thresholds under Singapore Appendix I, Annex 3 of the GPA and the procedures set forth in that Agreement, converted into Singapore dollars.

Schedule 2

Covered Goods and Services

For the United States

A. Goods
   This Chapter applies to all goods covered under the United States Appendix I of the GPA, as well as the products covered by Federal Supply Code 58 (Communications, Detection & Coherent Radiation Equipment), except for the Department of Defense, and subject to the exclusions set out in United States Appendix I for specific entities.

B. Services (Other than construction services)
   This Chapter applies to all services in the Universal List of Services, as contained in document MTN.GNS/W/120 of the WTO, procured by the entities specified in Schedule 1, excluding the following services:

(1) all transportation services, including Launching Services (CPC Categories 71, 72, 73, 74, 8859, 8868);
Note: Transportation services, where incidental to a contract for the procurement of supplies, are not subject to this Chapter.
(2) dredging;
(3) all services purchased in support of military forces overseas;
(4) management and operation contracts of certain government or privately owned facilities used for government purposes, including federally funded research and development centers (FFRDCs);
(5) public utilities services;
(6) basic telecommunications network and services listed in paragraph 2C(a) to (g) of document MTN.GNS/W/120 of the WTO, such as public voice and data services. This exclusion does not include information services, as defined in 47 U.S.C. 153 (20).
(7) research and Development; and
(8) printing Services (for GPA Annex 2 entities only).
C. Construction Services
This Chapter applies to government procurement of all services covered under Appendix I, Annex 5 of the GPA.

For Singapore

A. Goods
This Chapter applies to all goods covered under Singapore=s Appendix I, Annex I of the GPA.
B. Services (Other than construction services)
This Chapter applies to all services in the Universal List of Services, as contained in document MTN.GNS/W/120 of the WTO, excluding the following services:
(1) research and development services;
(2) police, public order, public safety and security services and compulsory social security services;
(3) radio and television services, including transmission services;
(4) exam Services;
(5) asset management and other financial services procured by MOF (Ministry of Finance) and MAS (Monetary Authority of Singapore) for the purpose of managing official foreign reserves and other foreign assets of the Government of Singapore;
(6) urban planning and landscape architectural services;
(7) real estate services (excluding consultancy services, agency services, auction and valuation services);
(8) supply of potable water for human consumption;
(9) social services;
(10)printing of Government legislation and gazette; and
(11)sale and distribution services for government debt.
C. Construction Services

This Chapter applies to government procurement of all services covered under Singapore=s Appendix I, Annex 5 of the GPA.

Annex 13B. Indexation and Conversion of Thresholds

1. The calculations referenced in Annex 13A of this Agreement shall be adjusted in accordance with the following formula:

$$T_0 (1 + \delta_i) = T_1$$

in which:

T_0 = threshold value on January 1, 2002

δ_i = accumulated inflation rate for the ith two-year period

T_1 = new threshold value

and the accumulated inflation rate (δ_i) is measured by:

for the United States, the producer price index for finished products published by the U.S. Bureau of Labor Statistics; and

for Singapore, the consumer price index published by the Singapore Department of Statistics.

2. The first adjustment for inflation, to take effect on January 1, 2004, shall be calculated using the period from November 1, 2001 to October 31, 2003. All subsequent adjustments shall be calculated using two-year periods, each period beginning November 1. The adjustments shall take effect on January 1 of the year immediately following the end of the two-year period.

14. ELECTRONIC COMMERCE

Article 14.1: General

The Parties recognize the economic growth and opportunity provided by electronic commerce and the importance of avoiding barriers to its use and development and the applicability of WTO rules to electronic commerce.

Article 14.2: Electronic Supply of Services

For greater certainty, the Parties affirm that measures related to the supply of a service using electronic means falls within the scope of the obligations contained in the relevant provisions of Chapters 8 (Cross-Border Trade in Services), 10 (Financial Services), and 15 (Investment), subject to any exceptions applicable to such obligations and except where an obligation does not apply to any such measure pursuant to Articles 8.7 (Non-Conforming Measures), 10.9 (Non-Conforming Measures), or 15.12 (Non-Conforming Measures).

Article 14.3: Digital Products

1. A Party shall not apply customs duties or other duties, fees, or charges on or in connection with the importation or exportation of digital products by electronic transmission.[14-1]

2. Each Party shall determine the customs value of an imported carrier medium bearing a digital product according to the cost or value of the carrier medium alone, without regard to the cost or value of the digital product stored on the carrier medium.

3. A Party shall not accord less favorable treatment to some digital products than it accords to other like digital products:
   (a) on the basis that
       (i) the digital products receiving less favorable treatment are created, produced, published, stored, transmitted, contracted for, commissioned, or first made available on commercial terms, outside its territory; or
       (ii) the author, performer, producer, developer, or distributor of such digital products is a person of the other Party or a non-Party,
       or
   (b) so as otherwise to afford protection to the other like digital products that are created, produced, published, stored, transmitted, contracted for, commissioned, or first made available on commercial terms, in its territory.

4.
   (a) A Party shall not accord less favorable treatment to digital products created, produced, published, stored, transmitted, contracted for, commissioned, or first made available on commercial terms in the territory of the other Party than it accords to like digital products created, produced, published, stored, transmitted, contracted for, commissioned, or first made available on commercial terms, in the territory of a non-Party.
   (b) A Party shall not accord less favorable treatment to digital products whose author, performer, producer, developer, or distributor is a person of the other Party than it accords to like digital products whose author, performer, producer, developer, or distributor is a person of a non-Party.

5. Paragraphs 3 and 4 do not apply to any non-conforming measure described in Article 8.7 (Non-Conforming Measures), 10.9 (Non-Conforming Measures), or 15.12 (Non-Conforming Measures).

6. This Article does not apply to measures affecting the electronic transmission of a series of text, video, images, sound recordings, and other products scheduled by a content provider for aural and/or visual reception, and for which the content consumer has no choice over the scheduling of the series.

Article 14.4: Definitions

For purposes of this Chapter:

1. **carrier medium** means any physical object capable of storing a digital product by any method now known or later developed, and from which a digital product can be

perceived, reproduced, or communicated, directly or indirectly, and includes, but is not limited to, an optical medium, a floppy disk, or a magnetic tape;

2. **digital products** means computer programs, text, video, images, sound recordings and other products that are digitally encoded, regardless of whether they are fixed on a carrier medium or transmitted electronically;[14-2]

3. **electronic transmission** or **transmitted electronically** means the transfer of digital products using any electromagnetic or photonic means; and

4. **using electronic means** means employing computer processing.

15. INVESTMENT

Section A – Definitions

Article 15.1: Definitions

For purposes of this Chapter, it is understood that:

1. **central level of government** means:
   (a) for the United States, the federal level of government; and
   (b) for Singapore, the national level of government;

2. **Centre** means the International Centre for Settlement of Investment Disputes ("ICSID") established by the ICSID Convention;

3. **claimant** means an investor of a Party that is a party to an investment dispute with the other Party;

4. **covered investment** means, with respect to a Party, an investment in its territory of an investor of the other Party in existence as of the date of entry into force of this Agreement or established, acquired, or expanded thereafter;

5. **disputing parties** means the claimant and the respondent;

6. **disputing party** means either the claimant or the respondent;

7. **enterprise** means any entity constituted or organized under applicable law, whether or not for profit, and whether privately or governmentally owned or controlled, including a corporation, trust, partnership, sole proprietorship, joint venture, association, or similar organization; and a branch of an enterprise;

8. **enterprise of a Party** means an enterprise constituted or organized under the law of a Party, and a branch located in the territory of a Party and carrying out business activities there;

9. **freely usable currency** means "freely usable currency" as determined by the International Monetary Fund under its *Articles of Agreement*;

10. **government enterprise** means "government enterprise" as defined in Chapter 12 (Anticompetitive Business Conduct, Designated Monopolies, and Government Enterprises);

11. **ICSID Additional Facility Rules** means the *Rules Governing the Additional Facility for the Administration of Proceedings by the Secretariat of the International Centre for Settlement of Investment Disputes*;

12. **ICSID Convention** means the *Convention on the Settlement of Investment Disputes between States and Nationals of Other States*, done at Washington, March 18, 1965;

13. **investment** means every asset owned or controlled, directly or indirectly, by an investor, that has the characteristics of an investment.[15-1] Forms that an investment may take include:

   (a) an enterprise;

   (b) shares, stock, and other forms of equity participation in an enterprise;

   (c) bonds, debentures, other debt instruments, and loans;[15-2]

   (d) futures, options, and other derivatives;

   (e) turnkey, construction, management, production, concession, revenue-sharing, and other similar contracts;

   (f) intellectual property rights;

   (g) licenses, authorizations, permits, and similar rights conferred pursuant to applicable domestic law;[15-3][15-4] and

   (h) other tangible or intangible, movable or immovable property, and related property rights, such as leases, mortgages, liens, and pledges.

14. **investment agreement**[15-5] means a written agreement that takes effect on or after the date of entry into force of this Agreement between a national authority[15-6] of a Party and a covered investment or an investor of the other Party (i) that grants rights with respect to natural resources or other assets that a national authority controls, and (ii) that the covered investment or the investor relies on in establishing or acquiring the covered investment;

15. **investment authorization**[15-7] means an authorization that the foreign investment authority of a Party grants to a covered investment or an investor of the other Party;

16. **investor of a non-Party** means, with respect to a Party, an investor that is seeking to make, is making, or has made an investment in the territory of that Party, that is not an investor of either Party;

17. **investor of a Party** means a Party or a national or an enterprise of a Party that is seeking to make, is making, or has made an investment in the territory of the other Party; provided, however, that a natural person who is a dual national shall be deemed to be exclusively a national of the State of his/her dominant and effective nationality;

18. **monopoly** means "monopoly" as defined in Chapter 12 (Anticompetitive Business Conduct, Designated Monopolies, and Government Enterprises);

19. **New York Convention** means the *United Nations Convention on the Recognition and Enforcement of Foreign Arbitral Awards*, done at New York, June 10, 1958;

20. **non-disputing Party** means the Party that is not a party to an investment dispute;

21. **protected information** means confidential business information or information that is privileged or otherwise protected from disclosure under a Party's law;

22. **regional level of government** means, for the United States, a state of the United States, the District of Columbia, or Puerto Rico. For Singapore, "regional level of government" is not applicable, as Singapore has no government at the regional level;

23. **respondent** means the Party that is a party to an investment dispute;

24. **Secretary-General** means the Secretary-General of ICSID;

25. **tribunal** means an arbitration tribunal established under Article 15.18 or 15.24; and

26. **UNCITRAL Arbitration Rules** means the arbitration rules of the United Nations Commission on International Trade Law.

Section B – Investment

Article 15.2: Scope and Coverage

This Chapter applies to measures adopted or maintained by a Party relating to:

(a) investors of the other Party;
(b) covered investments; and
(c) with respect to Articles 15.8 and 15.10, all investments in the territory of the Party.

Article 15.3: Relation to Other Chapters

1. In the event of any inconsistency between this Chapter and another Chapter, the other Chapter shall prevail to the extent of the inconsistency.
2. A requirement by a Party that a service provider of the other Party post a bond or other form of financial security as a condition of providing a service into its territory does not of itself make this Chapter applicable to the provision of that cross-border service. This Chapter applies to that Party's treatment of the posted bond or financial security.
3. This Chapter does not apply to measures adopted or maintained by a Party to the extent that they are covered by Chapter 10 (Financial Services).

Article 15.4: National Treatment and Most-Favored-Nation Treatment

1. Each Party shall accord to investors of the other Party treatment no less favorable than that it accords, in like circumstances, to its own investors with respect to the establishment, acquisition, expansion, management, conduct, operation, and sale or other disposition of investments in its territory. Each Party shall accord to covered investments treatment no less favorable than that it accords, in like circumstances, to investments in its territory of its own investors with respect to the establishment, acquisition, expansion, management, conduct, operation, and sale or other disposition of investments. The treatment each Party shall accord under this paragraph is "national treatment."
2. The treatment to be accorded by a Party under paragraph 1 means, with respect to a state, territory or possession, treatment no less favorable than the most favorable treatment accorded, in like circumstances, by that state, territory, or possession, to investors, and to investments of investors, of the Party of which it forms a part.
3. Each Party shall accord to investors of the other Party treatment no less favorable than that it accords, in like circumstances, to investors of any non-Party with respect to the establishment, acquisition, expansion, management, conduct, operation, and sale or other disposition of investments in its territory. Each Party shall accord to covered investments treatment no less favorable than that it accords, in like

circumstances, to investments in its territory of investors of any non-Party with respect to the establishment, acquisition, expansion, management, conduct, operation, and sale or other disposition of investments. The treatment each Party shall accord under this paragraph is "most-favored-nation treatment."

4. Each Party shall accord to investors of the other Party and to their covered investments the better of national treatment or most-favored-nation treatment.

Article 15.5: Minimum Standard of Treatment[15-8]

1. Each Party shall accord to covered investments treatment in accordance with customary international law, including fair and equitable treatment and full protection and security.

2. For greater certainty, paragraph 1 prescribes the customary international law minimum standard of treatment of aliens as the minimum standard of treatment to be afforded to covered investments. The concepts of "fair and equitable treatment" and "full protection and security" do not require treatment in addition to or beyond that which is required by that standard, and do not create additional substantive rights.

    (a) The obligation in paragraph 1 to provide "fair and equitable treatment" includes the obligation not to deny justice in criminal, civil, or administrative adjudicatory proceedings in accordance with the principle of due process embodied in the principal legal systems of the world; and

    (b) The obligation in paragraph 1 to provide "full protection and security" requires each Party to provide the level of police protection required under customary international law.

3. A determination that there has been a breach of another provision of this Agreement, or of a separate international agreement, does not establish that there has been a breach of this Article.

4. Without prejudice to paragraph 1 and notwithstanding Article 15.12.5(b), each Party shall accord to investors of the other Party, and to covered investments, non-discriminatory treatment with respect to measures it adopts or maintains relating to losses suffered by investments in its territory owing to armed conflict or civil strife.

5. Paragraph 4 does not apply to existing measures relating to subsidies or grants that would be inconsistent with Article 15.4.1 and 15.4.2 but for Article 15.12.5(b).

Article 15.6: Expropriation[15-9]

1. Neither Party may expropriate or nationalize a covered investment either directly or indirectly through measures equivalent to expropriation or nationalization ("expropriation"), except:

    (a) for a public purpose;

    (b) in a non-discriminatory manner;

    (c) on payment of prompt, adequate, and effective compensation in accordance with paragraphs 2, 3, and 4; and

    (d) in accordance with due process of law and Article 15.5.1, 15.5.2, and 15.5.3.

2. Compensation shall:

(a) be paid without delay;

(b) be equivalent to the fair market value of the expropriated investment immediately before the expropriatory action was taken ("the date of expropriation");

(c) be fully realizable and freely transferable; and

(d) not reflect any change in value occurring because the expropriatory action had become known before the date of expropriation.

3. If the fair market value is denominated in a freely usable currency, the compensation paid shall be no less than the fair market value on the date of expropriation, plus interest at a commercially reasonable rate for that currency, accrued from the date of expropriation until the date of payment.

4. If the fair market value is denominated in a currency that is not freely usable, the compensation paid – converted into the currency of payment at the market rate of exchange prevailing on the date of payment – shall be no less than:

(a) the fair market value on the date of expropriation, converted into a freely usable currency at the market rate of exchange prevailing on that date, plus

(b) interest, at a commercially reasonable rate for that freely usable currency, accrued from the date of expropriation until the date of payment.

5. This Article does not apply to the issuance of compulsory licenses granted in relation to intellectual property rights in accordance with the Agreement on Trade-Related Aspects of Intellectual Property Rights ("TRIPS Agreement"), or to the revocation, limitation, or creation of intellectual property rights, to the extent that such issuance, revocation, limitation, or creation is consistent with Chapter 16 (Intellectual Property Rights) of this Agreement.

Article 15.7: Transfers[15-10]

1. Each Party shall permit all transfers relating to a covered investment to be made freely and without delay into and out of its territory. Such transfers include:

(a) contributions to capital;

(b) profits, dividends, capital gains, and proceeds from the sale of all or any part of the covered investment or from the partial or complete liquidation of the covered investment;

(c) interest, royalty payments, management fees, and technical assistance and other fees;

(d) payments made under a contract entered into by the investor, or the covered investment, including payments made pursuant to a loan agreement;

(e) payments made pursuant to Article 15.6 and Article 15.5.4; and

(f) payments arising under Section C.

2. Each Party shall permit transfers relating to a covered investment to be made in a freely usable currency at the market rate of exchange prevailing at the time of transfer.

3. Each Party shall permit returns in kind relating to a covered investment to be made as authorized or specified in an investment authorization or other written agreement between the Party and a covered investment or an investor of the other Party.

4. Notwithstanding paragraphs 1, 2, and 3, a Party may prevent a transfer through the equitable, non-discriminatory, and good faith application of its law relating to:

    (a) bankruptcy, insolvency, or the protection of the rights of creditors;

    (b) issuing, trading, or dealing in securities, futures, options, or derivatives;

    (c) financial reporting or record keeping of transfers when necessary to assist law enforcement or financial regulatory authorities;

    (d) criminal or penal offenses; or

    (e) ensuring compliance with orders or judgments in judicial or administrative proceedings.

Article 15.8: Performance Requirements[15-11]

1. Neither Party may impose or enforce any of the following requirements, or enforce any commitment or undertaking, in connection with the establishment, acquisition, expansion, management, conduct, operation, or sale or other disposition of an investment of an investor of a Party or of a non-Party in its territory:

    (a) to export a given level or percentage of goods or services;

    (b) to achieve a given level or percentage of domestic content;

    (c) to purchase, use, or accord a preference to goods produced in its territory, or to purchase goods from persons in its territory;

    (d) to relate in any way the volume or value of imports to the volume or value of exports or to the amount of foreign exchange inflows associated with such investment;

    (e) to restrict sales of goods or services in its territory that such investment produces or supplies by relating such sales in any way to the volume or value of its exports or foreign exchange earnings;

    (f) to transfer a particular technology, production process, or other proprietary knowledge to a person in its territory; or

    (g) to supply exclusively from the territory of the Party the goods that it produces or the services that it supplies to a specific regional market or to the world market.

2. Neither Party may condition the receipt or continued receipt of an advantage, in connection with the establishment, acquisition, expansion, management, conduct, operation, or sale or other disposition of an investment in its territory of an investor of a Party or of a non-Party, on compliance with any of the following requirements:

    (a) to achieve a given level or percentage of domestic content;

    (b) to purchase, use, or accord a preference to goods produced in its territory, or to purchase goods from persons in its territory;

    (c) to relate in any way the volume or value of imports to the volume or value of exports or to the amount of foreign exchange inflows associated with such investment; or

    (d) to restrict sales of goods or services in its territory that such investment produces or supplies by relating such sales in any way to the volume or value of its exports or foreign exchange earnings.

3.

    (a) Nothing in paragraph 2 shall be construed to prevent a Party from conditioning the receipt or continued receipt of an advantage, in connection with an investment in its territory of an investor of a Party or of a non-Party, on compliance with a requirement to locate production, supply a service, train or employ workers, construct or expand particular facilities, or carry out research and development, in its territory.

(b) Paragraph 1(f) does not apply:

    (i) when a Party authorizes use of an intellectual property right in accordance with Article 16.7.6 (Patents), and to measures requiring the disclosure of proprietary information that fall within the scope of, and are consistent with, Article 39 of the TRIPS Agreement; or

    (ii) when the requirement is imposed or the commitment or undertaking is enforced by a court, administrative tribunal, or competition authority to remedy a practice determined after judicial or administrative process to be anticompetitive under the Party's competition laws.

(c) Paragraphs 1(b), (c), and (f), and 2(a) and (b), shall not be construed to prevent a Party from adopting or maintaining measures, including environmental measures:

    (i) necessary to secure compliance with laws and regulations that are not inconsistent with this Agreement;

    (ii) necessary to protect human, animal, or plant life or health; or

    (iii) related to the conservation of living or non-living exhaustible natural resources; provided that such measures are not applied in an arbitrary or unjustifiable manner, and provided that such measures do not constitute a disguised restriction on investment or international trade.

(d) Paragraphs 1(a), (b), and (c), and 2(a) and (b), do not apply to qualification requirements for goods or services with respect to export promotion and foreign aid programs.

(e) Paragraphs 1(b), (c), (f), and (g), and 2(a) and (b), do not apply to government procurement.

(f) Paragraphs 2(a) and (b) do not apply to requirements imposed by an importing Party relating to the content of goods necessary to qualify for preferential tariffs or preferential quotas.

4. For greater certainty, paragraphs 1 and 2 do not apply to any requirement other than the requirements set out in those paragraphs.

Article 15.9: Senior Management and Boards of Directors

1. Neither Party may require that an enterprise of that Party that is a covered investment appoint to senior management positions individuals of any particular nationality.

2. A Party may require that a majority of the board of directors, or any committee thereof, of an enterprise of that Party that is a covered investment, be of a particular nationality, or resident in the territory of the Party, provided that the requirement does not materially impair the ability of the investor of the other Party to exercise control over its investment.

Article 15.10: Investment and Environment

Nothing in this Chapter shall be construed to prevent a Party from adopting, maintaining, or enforcing any measure otherwise consistent with this Chapter that it considers appropriate to ensure that investment activity in its territory is undertaken in a manner sensitive to environmental concerns.

Article 15.11: Denial of Benefits

A Party may deny the benefits of this Chapter to an investor of the other Party that is an enterprise of such other Party and to investments of that investor if:

(a) investors of a non-Party own or control the enterprise and the denying Party:
   (i) does not maintain diplomatic relations with the non-Party; or
   (ii) adopts or maintains measures with respect to the non-Party or an investor of the non-Party that prohibit transactions with the enterprise or that would be violated or circumvented if the benefits of this Chapter were accorded to the enterprise or to its investments; or
(b) the enterprise has no substantial business activities in the territory of the other Party, and investors of a non-Party, or of the denying Party, own or control the enterprise.

Article 15.12: Non-Conforming Measures

1. Articles 15.4, 15.8, and 15.9 do not apply to:
   (a) any existing non-conforming measure that is maintained by a Party at:
      (i) the central level of government, as set out by that Party in its Schedule to Annex 8A,
      (ii) a regional level of government, as set out by that Party in its Schedule to Annex 8A, or
      (iii) a local level of government;
   (b) the continuation or prompt renewal of any non-conforming measure referred to in subparagraph (a); or
   (c) an amendment to any non-conforming measure referred to in subparagraph (a) to the extent that the amendment does not decrease the conformity of the measure, as it existed immediately before the amendment, with Articles 15.4, 15.8, or 15.9.

2. Articles 15.4, 15.8, and 15.9 do not apply to any measure that a Party adopts or maintains with respect to sectors, sub-sectors, or activities, as set out in its Schedule to Annex 8B.

3. Neither Party may, under any measure adopted after the date of entry into force of this Agreement and covered by its Schedule to Annex 8B, require an investor of the other Party, by reason of its nationality, to sell or otherwise dispose of an investment existing at the time the measure becomes effective.

4. Article 15.4 does not apply to any measure that is an exception to, or derogation from, the obligations under Article 16.1.3 (General Provisions) as specifically provided for in that Article.

5. Articles 15.4 and 15.9 do not apply to:

(a) government procurement; or

(b) subsidies or grants provided by a Party, including government-supported loans, guarantees, and insurance.

Article 15.13: Special Formalities and Information Requirements

1. Nothing in Article 15.4.1 and 15.4.2 shall be construed to prevent a Party from adopting or maintaining a measure that prescribes special formalities in connection with covered investments, such as a requirement that investors be residents of the Party or that covered investments be legally constituted under the laws or regulations of the Party, provided that such formalities do not materially impair the protections afforded by a Party to investors of the other Party and covered investments pursuant to this Chapter.

2. Notwithstanding Article 15.4, a Party may require an investor of the other Party, or a covered investment, to provide information concerning that investment solely for informational or statistical purposes. The Party shall protect such business information that is confidential from any disclosure that would prejudice the competitive position of the investor or the covered investment. Nothing in this paragraph shall be construed to prevent a Party from otherwise obtaining or disclosing information in connection with the equitable and good faith application of its law.

Section C – Investor-State Dispute Settlement

Article 15.14: Consultation and Negotiation

In the event of an investment dispute, the claimant and the respondent should initially seek to resolve the dispute through consultation and negotiation, which may include the use of nonbinding, third-party procedures.

Article 15.15: Submission of a Claim to Arbitration[15-12]

1. In the event that a disputing party considers that an investment dispute cannot be settled by consultation and negotiation:

(a) the claimant, on its own behalf, may submit to arbitration under this Section a claim:

    (i) that the respondent has breached

        (A) an obligation under Section B,

        (B) an investment authorization, or

        (C) an investment agreement; and

    (ii) that the claimant has incurred loss or damage by reason of, or arising out of, that breach; and

(b) the claimant, on behalf of an enterprise of the respondent that is a juridical person that the claimant owns or controls directly or indirectly, may submit to arbitration under this Section a claim:

(i) that the respondent has breached
    (A) an obligation under Section B,
    (B) an investment authorization, or
    (C) an investment agreement; and
(ii) that the enterprise has incurred loss or damage by reason of, or arising out of, that breach.

2. For greater certainty, a claimant may submit to arbitration under this Section a claim that the respondent has breached an obligation under Section B through the actions of a designated monopoly or a government enterprise exercising delegated governmental authority as described in Article 12.3.1(c)(i) and 12.3.2(b) (Designated Monopolies and Government Enterprises), respectively.

3. Without prejudice to Article 10.1.2 (Scope and Coverage), no claim may be submitted under this Section that alleges a violation of any provision of this Agreement other than an obligation under Section B or the letter exchange on land expropriation.

4. At least 90 days before submitting any claim to arbitration under this Section, a claimant shall deliver to the respondent a written notice of its intention to submit the claim to arbitration ("notice of intent"). The notice shall specify:
    (a) the name and address of the claimant and, where a claim is submitted on behalf of an enterprise, the name, address, and place of incorporation of the enterprise;
    (b) for each claim, the provision of this Agreement, investment authorization, or investment agreement alleged to have been breached and any other relevant provisions;
    (c) the legal and factual basis for each claim; and
    (d) the relief sought and the approximate amount of damages claimed.

5. Provided that six months have elapsed since the events giving rise to the claim, a claimant may submit a claim referred to in paragraph 1:
    (a) under the ICSID Convention and the ICSID Rules of Procedure for Arbitration Proceedings, provided that both the respondent and the Party of the claimant are parties to the ICSID Convention;
    (b) under the ICSID Additional Facility Rules, provided that either the respondent or the Party of the claimant, but not both, is a party to the ICSID Convention;
    (c) under the UNCITRAL Arbitration Rules; or
    (d) if the claimant and respondent agree, to any other arbitration institution or under any other arbitration rules.

6. A claim shall be deemed submitted to arbitration under this Section when the claimant's notice of or request for arbitration ("notice of arbitration"):
    (a) referred to in paragraph 1 of Article 36 of the ICSID Convention is received by the Secretary-General;
    (b) referred to in Article 2 of Schedule C of the ICSID Additional Facility Rules is received by the Secretary-General;
    (c) referred to in Article 3 of the UNCITRAL Arbitration Rules, together with the statement of claim referred to in Article 18 of the UNCITRAL Arbitration Rules, are received by the respondent; or
    (d) referred to under any other arbitral institution or arbitral rules selected under paragraph 5(d) is received by the respondent.

7. The arbitration rules applicable under paragraph 5, and in effect on the date the claim or claims were submitted to arbitration under this Section, shall govern the arbitration except to the extent modified by this Agreement.

8. The claimant shall provide with the notice of arbitration referred to in paragraph 6:
    (a) the name of the arbitrator that the claimant appoints; or
    (b) the claimant's written consent for the Secretary-General to appoint the claimant's arbitrator.

Article 15.16: Consent of Each Party to Arbitration

1. Each Party consents to the submission of a claim to arbitration under this Section in accordance with this Agreement.

2. The consent under paragraph 1 and the submission of a claim to arbitration under this Section shall satisfy the requirements of:
    (a) Chapter II of the ICSID Convention (Jurisdiction of the Centre) and the ICSID Additional Facility Rules for written consent of the parties to the dispute; and
    (b) Article II of the New York Convention for an "agreement in writing."

Article 15.17: Conditions and Limitations on Consent of Each Party

1. No claim may be submitted to arbitration under this Section if more than three years have elapsed from the date on which the claimant first acquired, or should have first acquired, knowledge of the breach alleged under Article 15.15.1 and knowledge that the claimant (for claims brought under Article 15.15.1(a)) or the enterprise (for claims brought under Article 15.15.1(b)) has incurred loss or damage.

2. No claim may be submitted to arbitration under this Section unless:
    (a) the claimant consents in writing to arbitration in accordance with the procedures set out in this Agreement; and
    (b) the notice of arbitration referred to in Article 15.15.6 is accompanied,
        (i) for claims submitted to arbitration under Article 15.15.1(a), by the claimant's written waiver; and
        (ii) for claims submitted to arbitration under Article 15.15.1(b), by the claimant's and the enterprise's written waivers
        of any right to initiate or continue before any administrative tribunal or court under the law of either Party, or other dispute settlement procedures, any proceeding with respect to any measure alleged to constitute a breach referred to in Article 15.15.

3. Notwithstanding paragraph 2(b), the claimant (for claims brought under Article 15.15.1(a)) and the claimant or the enterprise (for claims brought under Article 15.15.1(b)) may initiate or continue an action that seeks interim injunctive relief and does not involve the payment of monetary damages before a judicial or administrative tribunal of the respondent, provided that the action is brought for the sole purpose of preserving the claimant's or the enterprise's rights and interests during the pendency of the arbitration.

Article 15.18: Selection of Arbitrators

1. Unless the disputing parties otherwise agree, the tribunal shall comprise three arbitrators, one arbitrator appointed by each of the disputing parties and the third, who shall be the presiding arbitrator, appointed by agreement of the disputing parties.

2. The Secretary-General shall serve as appointing authority for an arbitration under this Section.

3. If a tribunal has not been constituted within 75 days from the date that a claim is submitted to arbitration under this Section, the Secretary-General, on the request of a disputing party, shall appoint, in his or her discretion, the arbitrator or arbitrators not yet appointed.

4. For purposes of Article 39 of the ICSID Convention and Article 7 of Schedule C to the ICSID Additional Facility Rules, and without prejudice to an objection to an arbitrator on a ground other than nationality:

   (a) the respondent agrees to the appointment of each individual member of a tribunal established under the ICSID Convention or the ICSID Additional Facility Rules;

   (b) a claimant referred to in Article 15.15.1(a) may submit a claim to arbitration under this Section, or continue a claim, under the ICSID Convention or the ICSID Additional Facility Rules, only on condition that the claimant agrees in writing to the appointment of each individual member of the tribunal; and

   (c) a claimant referred to in Article 15.15.1(b) may submit a claim to arbitration under this Section, or continue a claim, under the ICSID Convention or the ICSID Additional Facility Rules, only on condition that the claimant and the enterprise agree in writing to the appointment of each individual member of the tribunal.

Article 15.19: Conduct of the Arbitration

1. The disputing parties may agree on the legal place of any arbitration under the arbitral rules applicable under Article 15.15.5(b), (c), or (d). If the disputing parties fail to reach agreement, the tribunal shall determine the place in accordance with the applicable arbitral rules, provided that the place shall be in the territory of either Party or of a third State that is a party to the New York Convention.

2. The non-disputing Party may make oral and written submissions to the tribunal regarding the interpretation of this Agreement.

3. The tribunal shall have the authority to accept and consider *amicus curiae* submissions from any persons and entities in the territories of the Parties and from interested persons and entities outside the territories of the Parties.

4. Without prejudice to a tribunal's authority to address other objections as a preliminary question, a tribunal shall address and decide as a preliminary question any objection by the respondent that, as a matter of law, a claim submitted is not a claim for which an award in favor of the claimant may be made under Article 15.25.

   (a) Such objection shall be submitted to the tribunal as soon as possible after the tribunal is constituted, and in no event later than the date the tribunal fixes for the respondent to submit its counter-memorial (or, in the case of an amendment to the notice of arbitration referred to in Article 15.15.6, the date the tribunal fixes for the respondent to submit its response to the amendment).

(b) On receipt of an objection under this paragraph, the tribunal shall suspend any proceedings on the merits, establish a schedule for considering the objection consistent with any schedule it has established for considering any other preliminary question, and issue a decision or award on the objection, stating the grounds therefor.

(c) In deciding an objection under this paragraph, the tribunal shall assume to be true the claimant's factual allegations in support of any claim in the notice of arbitration (or any amendment thereof) and, in disputes brought under the UNCITRAL Arbitration Rules, the statement of claim referred to in Article 18 of the UNCITRAL Arbitration Rules. The tribunal may also consider any relevant facts not in dispute.

(d) The respondent does not waive any objection as to competence or any argument on the merits merely because the respondent did or did not raise an objection under this paragraph or make use of the expedited procedure set out in the following paragraph.

5. In the event that the respondent so requests within 45 days after the tribunal is constituted, the tribunal shall decide on an expedited basis an objection under paragraph 4 or any objection that the dispute is not within the tribunal's competence. The tribunal shall suspend any proceedings on the merits and issue a decision or award on the objection(s), stating the grounds therefor, no later than 150 days after the date of the request. However, if a disputing party requests a hearing, the tribunal may take an additional 30 days to issue the decision or award. Regardless of whether a hearing is requested, a tribunal may, on a showing of extraordinary cause, delay issuing its decision or award by an additional brief period of time, which may not exceed 30 days.

6. When it decides a respondent's objection under paragraphs 4 or 5, the tribunal may, if warranted, award to the prevailing disputing party reasonable costs and attorneys' fees incurred in submitting or opposing the objection. In determining whether such an award is warranted, the tribunal shall consider whether either the claimant's claim or the respondent's objection was frivolous, and shall provide the disputing parties a reasonable opportunity to comment.

7. A respondent may not assert as a defense, counterclaim, right of set-off, or for any other reason that the claimant has received or will receive indemnification or other compensation for all or part of the alleged damages pursuant to an insurance or guarantee contract.

8. A tribunal may order an interim measure of protection to preserve the rights of a disputing party, or to ensure that the tribunal's jurisdiction is made fully effective, including an order to preserve evidence in the possession or control of a disputing party or to protect the tribunal's jurisdiction. A tribunal may not order attachment or enjoin the application of a measure alleged to constitute a breach referred to in Article 15.15. For purposes of this paragraph, an order includes a recommendation.

9.

(a) In any arbitration conducted under this Section, at the request of a disputing party, a tribunal shall, before issuing an award on liability, transmit its proposed award to the disputing parties and to the non-disputing Party. Within 60 days after the tribunal transmits its proposed award, the disputing parties may submit written comments to the tribunal concerning any aspect of its proposed award. The tribunal shall consider any such comments and issue its award not later than 45 days after the expiration of the 60-day comment period.

(b) Subparagraph (a) shall not apply in any arbitration conducted pursuant to this Section for which an appeal has been made available pursuant to paragraph 10.

10. If a separate multilateral agreement enters into force as between the Parties that establishes an appellate body for purposes of reviewing awards rendered by tribunals constituted pursuant to international trade or investment arrangements to hear investment disputes, the Parties shall strive to reach an agreement that would have such appellate body review awards rendered under Article 15.25 of this Section in arbitrations commenced after the appellate body's establishment.

Article 15.20: Transparency of Arbitral Proceedings

1. Subject to paragraphs 2 and 4, the respondent shall, after receiving the following documents, promptly transmit them to the non-disputing Party and make them available to the public:
   (a) the notice of intent referred to in Article 15.15.4;
   (b) the notice of arbitration referred to in Article 15.15.6;
   (c) pleadings, memorials, and briefs submitted to the tribunal by a disputing party and any written submissions submitted pursuant to Article 15.19.2 and 15.19.3 and Article 15.24;
   (d) minutes or transcripts of hearings of the tribunal, where available; and
   (e) orders, awards, and decisions of the tribunal.

2. The tribunal shall conduct hearings open to the public and shall determine, in consultation with the disputing parties, the appropriate logistical arrangements. However, any disputing party that intends to use information designated as protected information in a hearing shall so advise the tribunal. The tribunal shall make appropriate arrangements to protect the information from disclosure.

3. Nothing in this Section requires a respondent to disclose protected information or to furnish or allow access to information that it may withhold in accordance with Article 21.2 (Essential Security) or Article 21.4 (Disclosure of Information).

4. Protected information shall, if such information is submitted to the tribunal, be protected from disclosure in accordance with the following procedures:
   (a) Subject to paragraph 4(d), neither the disputing parties nor the tribunal shall disclose to the non-disputing Party or to the public any protected information where the disputing party that provided the information clearly designates it in accordance with paragraph 4(b).
   (b) Any disputing party claiming that certain information constitutes protected information shall clearly designate the information at the time it is submitted to the tribunal.
   (c) A disputing party shall, at the same time that it submits a document containing information claimed to be protected information, submit a redacted version of the document that does not contain the information. Only the redacted version

shall be provided to the non-disputing Party and made public in accordance with paragraph 1.

(d) The tribunal shall decide any objection regarding the designation of information claimed to be protected information. If the tribunal determines that such information was not properly designated, the disputing party that submitted the information may (i) withdraw all or part of its submission containing such information, or (ii) agree to resubmit complete and redacted documents with corrected designations in accordance with the tribunal's determination and paragraph 4(c). In either case, the other disputing party shall, whenever necessary, resubmit complete and redacted documents which either remove the information withdrawn under (i) by the disputing party that first submitted the information or redesignate the information consistent with the designation under (ii) of the disputing party that first submitted the information.

5. Nothing in this Section authorizes a respondent to withhold from the public information required to be disclosed by its laws.

Article 15.21: Governing Law

1. Subject to paragraph 2, a tribunal shall decide the issues in dispute related to an alleged breach of an obligation in Section B in accordance with this Agreement and applicable rules of international law.

2. A decision of the Joint Committee declaring its interpretation of a provision of this Agreement under Article 20.1.2 (Joint Committee) shall be binding on a tribunal established under this Section, and any award must be consistent with that decision.

Article 15.22: Interpretation of Annexes

1. Where a respondent asserts as a defense that the measure alleged to be a breach is within the scope of a reservation or exception set out in Annex 8A or Annex 8B, the tribunal shall, on request of the respondent, request the interpretation of the Joint Committee on the issue. The Joint Committee shall issue in writing any decision declaring its interpretation under Article 20.1.2 (Joint Committee) to the tribunal within 60 days of delivery of the request.

2. A decision issued by the Joint Committee under paragraph 1 shall be binding on the tribunal, and any award must be consistent with that decision. If the Joint Committee fails to issue such a decision within 60 days, the tribunal shall decide the issue.

Article 15.23: Expert Reports

Without prejudice to the appointment of other kinds of experts where authorized by the applicable arbitration rules, a tribunal, at the request of a disputing party or, unless the disputing parties disapprove, on its own initiative, may appoint one or more experts to report to it in writing on any factual issue concerning environmental, health, safety, or other scientific matters raised by a disputing party in a proceeding, subject to such terms and conditions as the disputing parties may agree.

Article 15.24: Consolidation

1. Where two or more claims have been submitted separately to arbitration under Article 15.15.1 and the claims have a question of law or fact in common and arise out of the same events or circumstances, any disputing party may seek a consolidation order in accordance with the agreement of all the disputing parties sought to be covered by the order or the terms of paragraphs 2 through 10.

2. A disputing party that seeks a consolidation order under this Article shall deliver, in writing, a request to the Secretary-General and to all the disputing parties sought to be covered by the order and shall specify in the request:
    (a) the names and addresses of all the disputing parties sought to be covered by the order;
    (b) the nature of the order sought; and
    (c) the grounds on which the order is sought.

3. Unless the Secretary-General finds within 30 days after receiving a request under paragraph 2 that the request is manifestly unfounded, a tribunal shall be established under this Article.

4. Unless all the disputing parties sought to be covered by the order otherwise agree, a tribunal established under this Article shall comprise three arbitrators:
    (a) one arbitrator appointed by agreement of the claimants;
    (b) one arbitrator appointed by the respondent; and
    (c) the presiding arbitrator appointed by the Secretary-General, provided, however, that the presiding arbitrator shall not be a national of either Party.

5. If, within 60 days after the Secretary-General receives a request made under paragraph 2, the respondent fails or the claimants fail to appoint an arbitrator in accordance with paragraph 4, the Secretary-General, on the request of any disputing party sought to be covered by the order, shall appoint the arbitrator or arbitrators not yet appointed. If the respondent fails to appoint an arbitrator, the Secretary-General shall appoint a national of the disputing Party, and if the claimants fail to appoint an arbitrator, the Secretary-General shall appoint a national of the non-disputing Party.

6. Where a tribunal established under this Article is satisfied that two or more claims that have been submitted to arbitration under Article 15.15.1 have a question of law or fact in common, and arise out of the same events or circumstances, the tribunal may, in the interest of fair and efficient resolution of the claims, and after hearing the disputing parties, by order:
    (a) assume jurisdiction over, and hear and determine together, all or part of the claims;
    (b) assume jurisdiction over, and hear and determine one or more of the claims, the determination of which it believes would assist in the resolution of the others; or
    (c) instruct a tribunal previously established under Article 15.18 to assume jurisdiction over, and hear and determine together, all or part of the claims, provided that:
        (i) that tribunal, at the request of any claimant not previously a disputing party before that tribunal, shall be reconstituted with its original members, except that the arbitrator for the claimants shall be appointed pursuant to paragraphs 4(a) and 5; and

(ii) that tribunal shall decide whether any prior hearing shall be repeated.

7. Where a tribunal has been established under this Article, a claimant that has submitted a claim to arbitration under Article 15.15.1 and that has not been named in a request made under paragraph 2 may make a written request to the tribunal that it be included in any order made under paragraph 6, and shall specify in the request:
   (a) the name and address of the claimant;
   (b) the nature of the order sought; and
   (c) the grounds on which the order is sought.
   The claimant shall deliver a copy of its request to the Secretary-General.

8. A tribunal established under this Article shall conduct its proceedings in accordance with the UNCITRAL Arbitration Rules, except as modified by this Section.

9. A tribunal established under Article 15.18 shall not have jurisdiction to decide a claim, or a part of a claim, over which a tribunal established or instructed under this Article has assumed jurisdiction.

10. On application of a disputing party, a tribunal established under this Article, pending its decision under paragraph 6, may order that the proceedings of a tribunal established under Article 15.18 be stayed, unless the latter tribunal has already adjourned its proceedings.

Article 15.25: Awards

1. Where a tribunal makes a final award against a respondent, the tribunal may award, separately or in combination, only:
   (a) monetary damages and any applicable interest; and
   (b) restitution of property, in which case the award shall provide that the respondent may pay monetary damages and any applicable interest in lieu of restitution.
   A tribunal may also award costs and attorneys' fees in accordance with this Section and the applicable arbitration rules.

2. Subject to paragraph 1, where a claim is submitted to arbitration under Article 15.15.1(b):
   (a) an award of restitution of property shall provide that restitution be made to the enterprise;
   (b) an award of monetary damages and any applicable interest shall provide that the sum be paid to the enterprise; and
   (c) the award shall provide that it is made without prejudice to any right that any person may have in the relief under applicable domestic law.

3. A tribunal may not award punitive damages.

4. An award made by a tribunal shall have no binding force except between the disputing parties and in respect of the particular case.

5. Subject to paragraph 6 and the applicable review procedure for an interim award, a disputing party shall abide by and comply with an award without delay.

6. A disputing party may not seek enforcement of a final award until:
   (a) in the case of a final award made under the ICSID Convention,
       (i) 120 days have elapsed from the date the award was rendered and no disputing party has requested revision or annulment of the award; or
       (ii) revision or annulment proceedings have been completed; and

  (b) in the case of a final award under the ICSID Additional Facility Rules, the UNCITRAL Arbitration Rules, or the rules selected pursuant to Article 15.15.5(d),

    (i) 90 days have elapsed from the date the award was rendered and no disputing party has commenced a proceeding to revise, set aside, or annul the award, or

    (ii) a court has dismissed or allowed an application to revise, set aside, or annul the award and there is no further appeal.

7. Each Party shall provide for the enforcement of an award in its territory.

8. If the respondent fails to abide by or comply with a final award, on delivery of a written notification by the non-disputing Party, a panel shall be established under Article 20.4.4(a) (Additional Dispute Settlement Procedures). The requesting Party may seek in such proceedings:

  (a) a determination that the failure to abide by or comply with the final award is inconsistent with the obligations of this Agreement; and

  (b) in accordance with the procedures set forth in Article 20.4.5(b) (Additional Dispute Settlement Procedures), a recommendation that the respondent abide by or comply with the final award.

9. A disputing party may seek enforcement of an arbitration award under the ICSID Convention or the New York Convention regardless of whether proceedings have been taken under paragraph 8.

10. A claim that is submitted to arbitration under this Section shall be considered to arise out of a commercial relationship or transaction for purposes of Article I of the New York Convention.

Article 15.26: Status of Letter Exchanges

The following letters exchanged this day on:

 (a) Customary International Law;
 (b) Expropriation;
 (c) Land Expropriation; and
 (d) Appellate Mechanism shall form an integral part of the Agreement.

Article 15.27: Service of Documents

Delivery of notices and other documents on a Party shall be made to the place named for that Party in Annex 15D.

Annex 15A. Transfers

1. Where a claimant submits a claim alleging that Singapore has breached an obligation under Section B, other than Article 15.4, that arises from its imposition of restrictive measures with regard to outward payments and transfers, Section C shall apply except as modified below:

(a) A claimant may submit the claim under Article 15.15 only after one year has elapsed since the measure was adopted.

(b) If the claim is submitted under Article 15.15.1(b), the claimant may, on behalf of the enterprise, only seek damages with respect to the shares of the enterprise for which the claimant has a beneficial interest.

(c) Paragraph 1(a) shall not apply to claims that arise from restrictions on:

    (i) payments or transfers on current transactions, including the transfer of profits and dividends of foreign direct investment by investors of the United States;

    (ii) transfers of proceeds of foreign direct investment by investors of the United States, excluding investments designed with the purpose of gaining direct or indirect access to the financial market; or

    (iii) payments pursuant to a loan or bond[15-13] regardless of where it is issued, including inter- and intra-company debt financing between affiliated enterprises, when such payments are made exclusively for the conduct, operation, management, or expansion of such affiliated enterprises, provided that these payments are made in accordance with the maturity date agreed on in the loan or bond agreement.

(d) Excluding restrictive measures referred to in paragraph 1(c), Singapore shall incur no liability, and shall not be subject to claims, for damages arising from its imposition of restrictive measures with regard to outward payments and transfers that were incurred within one year from the date on which restrictions were imposed, provided that such restrictive measures do not substantially impede transfers.

(e) Claims arising from Singapore's imposition of restrictive measures with regard to outward payments and transfers shall not be subject to Article 15.24 unless Singapore consents.

2. The United States may not request the establishment of an arbitral panel under Chapter 20 (Administration and Dispute Settlement) relating to Singapore's imposition of restrictive measures with regard to outward payments and transfers until one year has elapsed since the measure was adopted. In determining whether compensation is owed or benefits should be suspended, or the level of such compensation or suspension, pursuant to Article 20.6 (Non-Implementation), the aggrieved Party and the panel shall consider whether the restrictive measures were implemented at the request of the International Monetary Fund (IMF).

Annex 15B. Performance Requirements

Article 15.8.1 does not preclude enforcement of any commitment, undertaking, or requirement between private parties, where a Party did not impose or require the commitment, undertaking, or requirement. For purposes of this Annex, private parties may include designated monopolies or government enterprises, where such entities are not exercising delegated governmental authority as described in Articles 12.3.1(c)(i) and 12.3.2(b) (Designated Monopolies and Government Enterprises), respectively.

Annex 15C. Performance Requirements

Singapore

With respect to Singapore, Article 15.8.1(f) does not apply with respect to the sale or other disposition of an investment of an investor of a non-Party in its territory.

Annex 15D. Service of Documents on a Party under Section C

Singapore

Notices and other documents in disputes under Section C shall be served on Singapore by delivery to:

> Director (Trade)
> Ministry of Trade and Industry
> 100 High Street, #09-01
> The Treasury   Singapore 179434

United States

Notices and other documents in disputes under Section C shall be served on the United States by delivery to:

> Executive Director (L/EX)
> Office of the Legal Adviser
> Department of State
> Washington, DC 20520
> United States of America

16. INTELLECTUAL PROPERTY RIGHTS

Article 16.1: General Provisions

1. Each Party shall, at a minimum, give effect to this Chapter.
2.
    (a) Each Party shall ratify or accede to the following agreements:
        (i)   the Convention Relating to the Distribution of Programme-Carrying Signals Transmitted by Satellite (1974);
        (ii) the International Convention for the Protection of New Varieties of Plants (1991) (**A**UPOV Convention@);
        (iii) the WIPO Copyright Treaty (1996);
        (iv) the WIPO Performances and Phonograms Treaty (1996); and
        (v)   the Patent Cooperation Treaty (1984).
    (b) Each Party shall give effect to:

      (i)   Articles 1 through 6 of the Joint Recommendation Concerning Provisions on the Protection of Well-Known Marks (1999), adopted by the Assembly of the Paris Union for the Protection of Industrial Property and the General Assembly of the World Intellectual Property Organization (AWIPO@); and

      (ii) the Trademark Law Treaty.[16-1]

   (c) Each Party shall make best efforts to ratify or accede to:

      (i)   the Hague Agreement Concerning the International Registration of Industrial Designs (1999); and

      (ii) the Protocol Relating to the Madrid Agreement Concerning the International Registration of Marks (1989).

3. In respect of all categories of intellectual property covered in this Chapter, each Party shall accord to nationals[16-2] of the other Party treatment no less favorable than it accords to its own nationals with regard to the protection[16-3] and enjoyment of such intellectual property rights and any benefits derived from such rights.[16-4]

4. Each Party may derogate from paragraph 3 in relation to its judicial and administrative procedures, including the designation of an address for service or the appointment of an agent within the jurisdiction of a Party, only where such derogations are necessary to secure compliance with laws and regulations that are not inconsistent with this Chapter and where such practices are not applied in a manner that would constitute a disguised restriction on trade.

5. Paragraphs 3 and 4 do not apply to procedures provided in multilateral agreements concluded under the auspices of WIPO relating to the acquisition or maintenance of intellectual property rights.

6. Except as otherwise provided in this Chapter:

   (a) this Chapter gives rise to obligations in respect of all subject matter existing at the date of entry into force of this Agreement that is protected on that date in the Party where the protection is claimed and/or that meets or comes subsequently to meet the criteria for protection under the terms of this Chapter;

   (b) a Party shall not be required to restore protection to subject matter that on the date of entry into force of this Agreement has fallen into the public domain in the Party where the protection is claimed.

7. This Chapter does not give rise to obligations in respect of acts that occurred before the date of entry into force of this Agreement.

Article 16.2: Trademarks, Including Geographical Indications

1. Each Party shall provide that trademarks shall include service marks, collective marks, and certification marks,[16-5] and may include geographical indications.[16-6] Neither Party shall require, as a condition of registration, that signs be visually perceptible, but each Party shall make best efforts to register scent marks. Each Party shall afford an opportunity for the registration of a trademark to be opposed.

2. Each Party shall provide that the owner of a registered trademark shall have the exclusive right to prevent all third parties not having the owner's consent from using in the course of trade identical or similar signs, including geographical indications, for goods or services that are related to those in respect of which the trademark is registered, where such use would result in a likelihood of confusion.

3. Each Party may provide limited exceptions to the rights conferred by a trademark, such as fair use of descriptive terms, provided that such exceptions take account of the legitimate interests of the owner of the trademark and of third parties.

4. Article 6*bis* of the Paris Convention for the Protection of Industrial Property (1967) ("Paris Convention") shall apply, *mutatis mutandis*, to goods or services that are not similar to those identified by a well-known trademark, whether registered or not, provided that use of that trademark in relation to those goods or services would indicate a connection between those goods or services and the owner of the trademark and provided that the interests of the owner of the trademark are likely to be damaged by such use.

5. Neither Party shall require recordation of trademark licenses to establish the validity of the license or to assert any rights in a trademark.

6. Pursuant to Article 20 of the TRIPS Agreement, each Party shall ensure that its provisions mandating the use of a term customary in common language as the common name for a product including, *inter alia*, requirements concerning the relative size, placement, or style of use of the trademark in relation to the common name, do not impair the use or effectiveness of a trademark used in relation to such products.[16-7]

Article 16.3: Domain Names on the Internet

1. Each Party shall participate in the Governmental Advisory Committee of the Internet Corporation for Assigned Names and Numbers (ICANN), which serves to consider and provide advice on the activities of the ICANN as they relate to government concerns, including matters related to intellectual property and the domain name system, as well as to promote responsible country code Top Level Domain (ccTLD) administration, management, and operational practices.

2. Each Party shall require that registrants of domain names in its ccTLD are subject to a dispute resolution procedure, modeled along the same lines as the principles set forth in ICANN Uniform Domain Name Dispute Resolution Policy (ICANN UDRP), to address and resolve disputes related to the bad-faith registration of domain names in violation of trademarks. Each Party shall also ensure that its corresponding ccTLDs provide public access to a reliable and accurate AWHOIS@ database of domain name registrant contact information.

Article 16.4: Obligations Common to Copyright and Related Rights

1. Each Party shall provide that authors, performers, and producers of phonograms and their successors in interest have the right to authorize or prohibit all reproductions, in any manner or form, permanent or temporary (including temporary storage in electronic form).

2.
    (a) Without prejudice to Articles 11(1)(ii), 11*bis*(1)(i) and (ii), 11*ter*(1)(ii), 14(1)(ii), and 14*bis*(1) of the Berne Convention for the Protection of Literary and Artistic Works (1971) ("Berne Convention"), each Party shall provide to authors,

performers, producers of phonograms and their successors in interest the exclusive right to authorize or prohibit the communication to the public of their works, performances, or phonograms, by wire or wireless means, including the making available to the public of their works, performances, and phonograms in such a way that members of the public may access them from a place and at a time individually chosen by them. Notwithstanding paragraph 10, a Party may provide limitations or exceptions to this right in the case of performers and producers of phonograms for analog or digital free over-the-air terrestrial broadcasting and, further, a Party may provide limitations with respect to other non-interactive transmissions, in certain special cases provided that such limitations do not conflict with a normal exploitation of performances or phonograms and do not unreasonably prejudice the interests of such right holders.

   (b) Neither Party shall permit the retransmission of television signals (whether terrestrial, cable, or satellite) on the Internet without the authorization of the right holder in the subject matter of the signal.

3. Each Party shall provide to authors, performers, producers of phonograms, and their successors in interest the exclusive right of authorizing the making available to the public of the original and copies of their works and phonograms through sale or other transfer of ownership.

4. Each Party shall provide that where the term of protection of a work (including a photographic work), performance, or phonogram is to be calculated:

   (a) on the basis of the life of a natural person, the term shall be not less than the life of the author and 70 years after the author=s death; and

   (b) on a basis other than the life of a natural person, the term shall be not less than 70 years from the end of the calendar year of the first authorized publication of the work, performance, or phonogram or, failing such authorized publication within 50 years from the creation of the work, performance, or phonogram, not less than 70 years from the end of the calendar year of the creation of the work, performance, or phonogram.

5. Each Party shall apply the provisions of Article 18 of the Berne Convention, *mutatis mutandis*, to the subject matter, rights and obligations in Articles 16.4 and 16.5.

6. Each Party shall provide that for copyright and related rights, any person acquiring or holding any economic right:

   (a) may freely and separately transfer such right by contract; and

   (b) by virtue of a contract, including contracts of employment underlying the creation of works and phonograms, shall be able to exercise those rights in its own name and enjoy fully the benefits derived from those rights.

7.

   (a) In order to provide adequate legal protection and effective legal remedies against the circumvention of effective technological measures that authors, performers, producers of phonograms, and their successors in interest use in connection with the exercise of their rights and that restrict unauthorized acts in respect of their works, performances, and phonograms, each Party shall provide that any person who:

(i) knowingly, or having reasonable grounds to know, circumvents without authority any effective technological measure that controls access to a protected work, performance, phonogram, or other subject matter; or

(ii) manufactures, imports, distributes, offers to the public, provides, or otherwise traffics in devices, products, or components or offers to the public or provides services, which:

(A) are promoted, advertised, or marketed for the purpose of circumvention of any effective technological measure, or

(B) have only a limited commercially significant purpose or use other than to circumvent any effective technological measure, or

(C) are primarily designed, produced, or performed for the purpose of enabling or facilitating the circumvention of any effective technological measure;

shall be liable and subject to the remedies provided for in Article 16.9.5. Each Party shall provide that any person, other than a nonprofit library, archive, educational institution, or public noncommercial broadcasting entity, that is found to have engaged willfully and for purposes of commercial advantage or private financial gain in such activities shall be guilty of a criminal offense.

(b) For purposes of this paragraph, **effective technological measure** means any technology, device, or component that, in the normal course of its operation, controls access to a protected work, performance, phonogram, or other subject matter, or protects any copyright or any rights related to copyright.

(c) Paragraph 7(a) obligates each Party to prohibit circumvention of effective technological measures and does not obligate a Party to require that the design of, or the design and selection of parts and components for, a consumer electronics, telecommunications, or computing product provide for a response to any particular technological measure. The absence of a requirement to respond affirmatively shall not constitute a defense to a claim of violation of that Party's measures implementing paragraph 7(a).

(d) Each Party shall provide that a violation of the law implementing this paragraph is independent of any infringement that might occur under the Party=s law on copyright and related rights.

(e) Each Party shall confine exceptions to the prohibition referred to in paragraph 7(a)(ii) on technology, products, services, or devices that circumvent effective technological measures that control access to, and, in the case of clause (i) below, that protect any of the exclusive rights of copyright or related rights in a protected work, to the following activities, provided that they do not impair the adequacy of legal protection or the effectiveness of legal remedies that the Party provides against the circumvention of effective technological measures:

(i) noninfringing reverse engineering activities with regard to a lawfully obtained copy of a computer program, carried out in good faith with respect to particular elements of that computer program that have not been readily available to the person engaged in such activity, for the sole purpose of achieving interoperability of an independently created computer program with other programs;

      (ii) noninfringing good faith activities, carried out by an appropriately qualified researcher who has lawfully obtained a copy, performance, or display of a work, and who has made a good faith effort to obtain authorization for such activities, to the extent necessary for the sole purpose of identifying and analyzing flaws and vulnerabilities of technologies for scrambling and descrambling of information;

      (iii) the inclusion of a component or part for the sole purpose of preventing the access of minors to inappropriate online content in a technology, product, service, or device provided that such technology, product, service or device itself is not prohibited under the measures implementing paragraph 7(a)(ii); and

      (iv) noninfringing good faith activities that are authorized by the owner of a computer, computer system, or computer network for the sole purpose of testing, investigating, or correcting the security of that computer, computer system, or computer network.

(f) Each Party shall confine exceptions to the prohibited conduct referred to in paragraph 7(a)(i) to the activities listed in paragraph 7(e) and the following activities, provided that such exceptions do not impair the adequacy of legal protection or the effectiveness of legal remedies the Party provides against the circumvention of effective technological measures:

      (i) access by a nonprofit library, archive, or educational institution to a work not otherwise available to it, for the sole purpose of making acquisition decisions;

      (ii) noninfringing activities for the sole purpose of identifying and disabling a capability to carry out undisclosed collection or dissemination of personally identifying information reflecting the online activities of a natural person in a way that has no other effect on the ability of any person to gain access to any work; and

      (iii) noninfringing uses of a particular class of works when an actual or likely adverse impact on such noninfringing uses with respect to such particular class of works is credibly demonstrated in a legislative or administrative proceeding, provided that any exception adopted in reliance on this clause shall have effect for a period of not more than four years from the date of conclusion of such proceeding.

(g) Each Party may also provide exceptions to the prohibited conduct referred to in paragraph 7(a) for lawfully authorized activities carried out by government employees, agents, or contractors for the purpose of law enforcement, intelligence, national defense, essential security, or similar government activities.

8. In order to provide adequate and effective legal remedies to protect rights management information:

(a) each Party shall provide that any person who without authority, and knowingly, or, with respect to civil remedies, having reasonable grounds to know, that it will induce, enable, facilitate, or conceal an infringement of any copyright or related right,

      (i) knowingly removes or alters any rights management information;

(ii) distributes or imports for distribution rights management information knowing that the rights management information has been altered without authority; or

(iii) distributes, imports for distribution, broadcasts, communicates, or makes available to the public copies of works or phonograms, knowing that rights management information has been removed or altered without authority,

shall be liable and subject to the remedies in Article 16.9.5. Each Party shall provide that any person, other than a nonprofit library, archive, educational institution, or public noncommercial broadcasting entity, who is found to have engaged willfully and for purposes of commercial advantage or private financial gain in such activities shall be guilty of a criminal offense.

(b) For purposes of this paragraph, **rights management information** means information which identifies a work, performance, or phonogram; the author of the work, the performer of the performance, or the producer of the phonogram; or the owner of any right in the work, performance, or phonogram; information about the terms and conditions of the use of the work, performance, or phonogram; and any numbers or codes that represent such information, when any of these items is attached to a copy of the work, performance, or phonogram or appears in conjunction with the communication or making available of a work, performance, or phonogram to the public. Nothing in this paragraph obligates a Party to require the owner of any right in the work, performance, or phonogram to attach rights management information to copies of it or to cause rights management information to appear in connection with a communication of the work, performance, or phonogram to the public.

9. Each Party shall issue appropriate laws, orders, regulations, administrative, or executive decrees mandating that all government agencies use computer software only as authorized by the right holder. Such measures shall actively regulate the acquisition and management of software for such government use, which may take the form of procedures, such as preparing and maintaining inventories of software present on agency computers, and inventories of existing software licenses.

10. Each Party shall confine limitations or exceptions to exclusive rights in Articles 16.4 and 16.5 to certain special cases which do not conflict with a normal exploitation of the work, performance, or phonogram, and do not unreasonably prejudice the legitimate interests of the right holder.

Article 16.5: Obligations Pertaining to Related Rights

1. Each Party shall accord the rights provided for in this Chapter to performers and producers of phonograms who are nationals of the other Party and to performances or phonograms first published or fixed in the territory of the other Party. A performance or phonogram shall be considered first published in any Party in which it is published within 30 days of its original publication.[16-8]

2. Each Party shall provide to performers the exclusive right to authorize or prohibit:
   (a) the communication to the public of their unfixed performances, except where the performance is already a broadcast performance, and
   (b) the fixation of their unfixed performances.

3. With respect to all rights of performers and producers of phonograms, the enjoyment and exercise of the rights provided for in this Chapter shall not be subject to any formality.

4. For the purposes of this Chapter, the following definitions apply with respect to performers and producers of phonograms:

   (a) **performers** means actors, singers, musicians, dancers, and other persons who act, sing, deliver, declaim, play in, interpret, or otherwise perform literary or artistic works or expressions of folklore;

   (b) **phonogram** means the fixation of the sounds of a performance or of other sounds, or of a representation of sounds, other than in the form of a fixation incorporated in a cinematographic or other audiovisual work;[16-9]

   (c) **fixation** means the embodiment of sounds, or of the representations thereof, from which they can be perceived, reproduced, or communicated through a device;

   (d) **producer of a phonogram** means the person, or the legal entity, who or which takes the initiative and has the responsibility for the first fixation of the sounds of a performance or other sounds, or the representations of sounds;

   (e) **publication** of a fixed performance or a phonogram means the offering of copies of the fixed performance or the phonogram to the public, with the consent of the right holder, and provided that copies are offered to the public in reasonable quantity; and

   (f) **broadcasting** means the transmission by wireless means for public reception of sounds or of images and sounds or of the representations thereof; such transmission by satellite is also broadcasting; transmission of encrypted signals is broadcasting where the means for decrypting are provided to the public by the broadcasting organization or with its consent.

Article 16.6: Protection of Encrypted Program-Carrying Satellite Signals

1. Each Party shall make it:

   (a) a criminal offense to manufacture, assemble, modify, import, export, sell, lease, or otherwise distribute a tangible or intangible device or system, knowing or having reason to know that the device or system is primarily of assistance in decoding an encrypted program-carrying satellite signal without the authorization of the lawful distributor of such signal;

   (b) a criminal offense willfully to receive or further distribute an encrypted program-carrying satellite signal that has been decoded without the authorization of the lawful distributor of the signal; and

   (c) a civil offense to engage in any activity prohibited under subparagraph (a) or (b).

2. Each Party shall provide that any civil offense established under subparagraph (c) shall be actionable by any person that holds an interest in the encrypted program-carrying satellite signal or the content thereof.

Article 16.7: Patents

1. Each Party shall make patents available for any invention, whether a product or a process, in all fields of technology, provided that the invention is new, involves an inventive step, and is capable of industrial application. For purposes of this Article, a Party may treat the terms "inventive step" and "capable of industrial application" as being synonymous with the terms "non-obvious" and "useful", respectively. Each Party may exclude inventions from patentability only as defined in Articles 27.2 and 27.3(a) of the TRIPS Agreement.

2. Each Party shall provide that patent owners shall also have the right to assign, or transfer by succession, a patent and to conclude licensing contracts. Each Party shall provide a cause of action to prevent or redress the procurement of a patented pharmaceutical product, without the authorization of the patent owner, by a party who knows or has reason to know that such product is or has been distributed in breach of a contract between the right holder and a licensee, regardless of whether such breach occurs in or outside its territory.[16-10] Each Party shall provide that in such a cause of action, notice shall constitute constructive knowledge.

3. Each Party may provide limited exceptions to the exclusive rights conferred by a patent, provided that such exceptions do not unreasonably conflict with a normal exploitation of the patent and do not unreasonably prejudice the legitimate interests of the patent owner, taking account of the legitimate interests of third parties.

4. Each Party shall provide that a patent may only be revoked on grounds that would have justified a refusal to grant the patent, or that pertain to the insufficiency of or unauthorized amendments to the patent specification, non-disclosure or misrepresentation of prescribed, material particulars, fraud, and misrepresentation. Where such proceedings include opposition proceedings, a Party may not make such proceedings available prior to the grant of the patent.

5. If a Party permits the use by a third party of the subject matter of a subsisting patent to support an application for marketing approval of a pharmaceutical product, that Party shall provide that any product produced under such authority shall not be made, used, or sold in the territory of that Party other than for purposes related to meeting requirements for marketing approval, and if the Party permits exportation, the product shall only be exported outside the territory of that Party for purposes of meeting marketing approval requirements of that Party.

6. Neither Party shall permit the use[16-11] of the subject matter of a patent without the authorization of the right holder except in the following circumstances:
   (a) to remedy a practice determined after judicial or administrative process to be anti-competitive under the competition laws of the Party;[16-12]
   (b) in the case of public non-commercial use or in the case of a national emergency or other circumstances of extreme urgency, provided that:
      (i) such use is limited to use by the government or third parties authorized by the government;
      (ii) the patent owner is provided with reasonable and entire compensation for such use and manufacture; and
      (iii) the Party shall not require the patent owner to transfer undisclosed information or technical "know how" related to a patented invention that has

been authorized for use without the consent of the patent owner pursuant to this paragraph.

Where a Party's law allows for such use pursuant to subparagraphs (a) and (b), the Party shall respect the provisions of Article 31 of the TRIPS Agreement.

7. Each Party, at the request of the patent owner, shall extend the term of a patent to compensate for unreasonable delays that occur in granting the patent. For the purposes of this paragraph, an unreasonable delay shall at least include a delay in the issuance of the patent of more than four years from the date of filing of the application with the Party, or two years after a request for examination of the application has been made, whichever is later, provided that periods attributable to actions of the patent applicant need not be included in the determination of such delays.[16-13]

8. Where a Party provides for the grant of a patent on the basis of an examination of the invention conducted in another country, that Party, at the request of the patent owner, may extend the term of a patent for up to five years to compensate for the unreasonable delay that may occur in the issuance of the patent granted by such other country where that country has extended the term of the patent based on such delay.

Article 16.8: Certain Regulated Products

1. If a Party requires the submission of information concerning the safety and efficacy of a pharmaceutical or agricultural chemical product prior to permitting the marketing of such product, the Party shall not permit third parties not having the consent of the party providing the information to market the same or a similar product on the basis of the approval granted to the party submitting such information for a period of at least five years from the date of approval for a pharmaceutical product and ten years from the date of approval for an agricultural chemical product.[16-14]

2. If a Party provides a means of granting approval to market a product specified in paragraph 1 on the basis of the grant of an approval for marketing of the same or similar product in another country, the Party shall defer the date of any such approval to third parties not having the consent of the party providing the information in the other country for at least five years from the date of approval for a pharmaceutical product and ten years from the date of approval for an agricultural chemical product in the territory of the Party or in the other country, whichever is later.

3. Where a product is subject to a system of marketing approval pursuant to paragraph 1 or 2 and is also subject to a patent in the territory of that Party, the Party shall not alter the term of protection that it provides pursuant to paragraph 1 or 2 in the event that the patent protection terminates on a date earlier than the end of the term of such protection.

4. With respect to any pharmaceutical product that is subject to a patent:

    (a) each Party shall make available an extension of the patent term to compensate the patent owner for unreasonable curtailment of the patent term as a result of the marketing approval process;

(b) the Party shall provide that the patent owner shall be notified of the identity of any third party requesting marketing approval effective during the term of the patent; and

(c) the Party shall not grant marketing approval to any third party prior to the expiration of the patent term, unless by consent or with the acquiescence of the patent owner.

Article 16.9: Enforcement of Intellectual Property Rights

General Obligations

1. Each Party shall ensure that in judicial and administrative proceedings for the enforcement of intellectual property rights, decisions on the merits of a case, that under the law or practice of the Party are of general application, shall preferably be in writing and shall state the reasons on which the decisions are based.

2. Each Party shall ensure that its laws and regulations, procedures, final judicial decisions, and administrative rulings of general application pertaining to the enforcement of intellectual property rights shall be published, or where such publication is not practicable, made publicly available, in a national language, in such a manner as to enable the other Party and right holders to become acquainted with them. Nothing in this paragraph shall require a Party to disclose confidential information the disclosure of which would impede law enforcement or otherwise be contrary to the public interest or would prejudice the legitimate commercial interests of particular enterprises, public or private.

3. Each Party shall inform the public of its efforts to provide effective enforcement of intellectual property rights in its civil, administrative, and criminal system, including any statistical information that the Party may collect for such purposes.

4. The Parties understand that a decision that a Party makes on the distribution of enforcement resources shall not excuse that Party from complying with this Chapter.

5. Each Party shall provide for civil remedies against the actions described in paragraphs 7 and 8 of Article 16.4. These shall include at least:
   (a) provisional measures, including seizure of devices and products suspected of being involved in the prohibited activity;
   (b) the opportunity for the right holder to elect between actual damages it suffered (plus any profits attributable to the prohibited activity not taken into account in computing the actual damages) or pre-established damages;
   (c) payment to a prevailing right holder of court costs and fees and reasonable attorney's fees by the party engaged in the prohibited conduct at the conclusion of the civil judicial proceeding; and
   (d) destruction of devices and products found to be involved in the prohibited conduct.

6. In civil, administrative, and criminal proceedings involving copyright or related rights, each Party shall provide for a presumption that, in the absence of proof to the contrary, the natural person or legal entity whose name is indicated as the author, producer, performer, or publisher of the work, performance, or phonogram in the

usual manner, is the designated right holder in such work, performance, or phonogram. Each Party shall also provide for a presumption that, in the absence of proof to the contrary, the copyright or related right subsists in such subject matter.

Civil and Administrative Procedures and Remedies for the Enforcement of Intellectual Property Rights

7. Each Party shall make available to right holders[16-15] civil judicial procedures concerning the enforcement of any intellectual property right.

8. Each Party shall provide that in civil judicial proceedings, its judicial authorities shall have the authority, at least with respect to works, phonograms, and performances protected by copyright or related rights, and in cases of trademark infringement, to order the infringer to pay the right holder damages adequate to compensate for the injury the right holder has suffered because of an infringement of that person=s intellectual property right by an infringer engaged in infringing activity, as well as the profits of the infringer that are attributable to the infringement and are not taken into account in computing the actual damages. In addition, in determining injury to the right holder, the judicial authorities shall, *inter alia*, consider the value of the infringed-upon good or service, according to the suggested retail price of the legitimate good or service.

9. In civil judicial proceedings, each Party shall, at least with respect to works, phonograms and performances protected by copyright or related rights, and in cases of trademark counterfeiting, establish or maintain pre-established damages that shall be available on the election of the right holder. Each Party shall provide that pre-established damages shall be in an amount sufficiently high to constitute a deterrent to future infringements and with the intent to compensate the right holder for the harm caused by the infringement.

10. Each Party shall provide that its judicial authorities, except in exceptional circumstances, shall have the authority to order, at the conclusion of the civil judicial proceedings concerning copyright or related rights and trademark counterfeiting, that a prevailing right holder shall be paid court costs or fees and reasonable attorney=s fees by the infringing party.

11. In civil judicial proceedings concerning copyright or related rights infringement and trademark counterfeiting, each Party shall provide that its judicial authorities shall have the authority to order the seizure of suspected infringing goods and any related materials and implements used to accomplish the prohibited activity.

12. Each Party shall provide that:
    (a) in civil judicial proceedings, at the right holder=s request, goods that have been found to be pirated or counterfeit shall be destroyed, except in exceptional cases;
    (b) its judicial authorities have the authority to order that materials and implements which have been used in the creation of the infringing goods be, without compensation of any sort, promptly destroyed or, in exceptional cases, without compensation of any sort, disposed of outside the channels of commerce in such a manner as to minimize the risks of further infringements; and

    (c) in regard to counterfeit trademarked goods, the simple removal of the trademark unlawfully affixed shall not be sufficient to permit the release of goods into the channels of commerce.

13. Each Party shall provide that in civil judicial proceedings, its judicial authorities shall have the authority to order the infringer to identify third parties that are involved in the production and distribution of the infringing goods or services and their channels of distribution and to provide this information to the right holder. Each Party shall provide that its judicial authorities shall have the authority to fine or imprison, in appropriate cases, persons who fail to abide by valid orders issued by such authorities.

Provisional Measures Concerning the Enforcement of Intellectual Property Rights

14. Each Party shall provide that requests for relief *inaudita altera parte* shall be dealt with expeditiously in accordance with the Party's judicial rules.
15. Each Party shall provide that:
    (a) its judicial authorities have the authority to require the plaintiff to provide any reasonably available evidence in order to satisfy themselves with a sufficient degree of certainty that the plaintiff's right is being infringed or that such infringement is imminent, and to order the plaintiff to provide a reasonable security or equivalent assurance set at a level sufficient to protect the defendant and to prevent abuse, and so as not to unreasonably deter recourse to such procedures.
    (b) in the event that its judicial or other authorities appoint experts, technical or otherwise, that must be paid by the plaintiff, such costs should be closely related, *inter alia*, to the quantity of work to be performed and should not unreasonably deter recourse to such relief.

Special Requirements Related to Border Measures Concerning the Enforcement of Intellectual Property Rights

16. Each Party shall provide that any right holder initiating procedures for suspension by the Party's customs authorities of the release of suspected counterfeit trademark or pirated copyright goods[16-16] into free circulation shall be required to provide adequate evidence to satisfy the competent authorities that, under the law of the importing country, there is *prima facie* an infringement of the right holder's intellectual property right and to supply sufficient information that may reasonably be expected to be within the right holder=s knowledge to make the suspected goods reasonably recognizable to the customs authorities.
17. Each Party shall provide that its competent authorities shall have the authority to require an applicant to provide a reasonable security or equivalent assurance sufficient to protect the defendant and the competent authorities and to prevent abuse. Each Party shall provide that the security or assurance shall not unreasonably deter recourse to these procedures.

18. Where its competent authorities have made a determination that goods are counterfeit or pirated, the Party shall grant its competent authorities the authority to inform the right holder of the names and addresses of the consignor, the importer, and the consignee, and of the quantity of the goods in question.

19. Each Party shall provide that its competent authorities may initiate border measures *ex officio*, without the need for a formal complaint from a private party or right holder. Such measures shall apply to shipments of pirated and counterfeit goods imported into or exported out of a Party's territory, including shipments consigned to a local party. For transshipped goods that are not consigned to a local party, each Party shall, upon request, endeavor to examine such goods. For products transshipped through the territory of a Party destined for the territory of the other Party, the former shall cooperate to provide all available information to the latter Party to enable effective enforcement against shipments of counterfeit or pirated goods. Each Party shall ensure that it has the authority to undertake such cooperation in response to a request by the other Party on counterfeit or pirated goods en route to that other Party.

20. Each Party shall provide that goods that its competent authorities have determined to be pirated or counterfeit shall be destroyed, except in exceptional cases. In regard to counterfeit trademark goods, the simple removal of the trademark unlawfully affixed shall not be sufficient to permit the release of the goods into the channels of commerce. In no event shall the competent authorities be authorized to permit the export of counterfeit or pirated goods.

Criminal Procedures and Remedies for the Enforcement of Intellectual Property Rights

21. Each Party shall provide criminal procedures and penalties to be applied at least in cases of willful trademark counterfeiting or copyright or related rights piracy on a commercial scale. Willful copyright or related rights piracy on a commercial scale includes (i) significant willful infringements of copyright or related rights that have no direct or indirect motivation of financial gain, as well as (ii) willful infringements for purposes of commercial advantage or financial gain.
    (a) Specifically, each Party shall provide:
        (i) remedies that include imprisonment as well as monetary fines sufficiently high to deter future acts of infringement consistent with a policy of removing the monetary incentive of the infringer. Also, each Party shall encourage its judicial authorities to impose such fines at levels sufficient to provide a deterrent to future infringements;
        (ii) that its judicial authorities have the authority to order the seizure of suspected counterfeit or pirated goods, any related materials and implements that have been used in the commission of the offense, any assets traceable to the infringing activity, and documentary evidence relevant to the offense that fall within the scope of such order. Items that are subject to seizure pursuant to such order need not be individually identified so long as they fall within general categories specified in the order;

(iii) that its judicial authorities shall, except in exceptional cases, order the forfeiture and destruction of all counterfeit or pirated goods, and, at least with respect to willful copyright or related rights piracy, materials and implements that have been used in the creation of the infringing goods. Each Party shall further provide that such forfeiture and destruction shall occur without compensation of any kind to the defendant; and

(iv) that its authorities may initiate legal action *ex officio*, without the need for a formal complaint by a private party or right holder.

(b) Each Party may provide procedures for right holders to initiate private criminal actions. However, these procedures shall not be unduly burdensome or costly for right holders. Each Party shall ensure that non-private criminal actions are the primary means by which it ensures the effective enforcement of its criminal law against willful copyright or related rights piracy. In addition, each Party shall ensure that its competent authorities bring criminal actions, as necessary, to act as a deterrent to further infringements.

Limitations on Liability for Service Providers

22. Each Party shall provide, consistent with the framework set forth in Article 16.9:

(a) legal incentives for service providers to cooperate with copyright[16-17] owners in deterring the unauthorized storage and transmission of copyrighted materials; and

(b) limitations in its law regarding the scope of remedies available against service providers for copyright infringements that they do not control, initiate, or direct, and that take place through systems or networks controlled or operated by them or on their behalf, as set forth in this subparagraph.[16-18]

(i) These limitations shall preclude monetary relief and provide reasonable restrictions on court-ordered relief to compel or restrain certain actions for the following functions and shall be confined to those functions:[16-19]

(A) transmitting, routing or providing connections for material without modification of its content, or the intermediate and transient storage of such material in the course thereof;

(B) caching carried out through an automatic process;

(C) storage at the direction of a user of material residing on a system or network controlled or operated by or for the service provider; and

(D) referring or linking users to an online location by using information location tools, including hyperlinks and directories.

(ii) These limitations shall apply only where the service provider does not initiate the chain of transmission of the material, and does not select the material or its recipients (except to the extent that a function described in clause (i)(D) in itself entails some form of selection).

(iii) Qualification by a service provider for the limitations as to each function in clauses (i)(A) through (i)(D) shall be considered separately from qualification for the limitations as to each other function, in accordance with the conditions for qualification set forth in subparagraphs (iv) – (vii).

(iv) With respect to functions referred to in clause (i)(B), the limitations shall be conditioned on the service provider:

    (A) permitting access to cached material in significant part only to users of its system or network who have met conditions on user access to that material;

    (B) complying with rules concerning the refreshing, reloading, or other updating of the cached material when specified by the person making the material available online in accordance with a generally accepted industry standard data communications protocol for the system or network through which that person makes the material available;

    (C) not interfering with technology consistent with industry standards accepted in the territory of each Party used at the originating site to obtain information about the use of the material, and not modifying its content in transmission to subsequent users; and

    (D) expeditiously removing or disabling access, on receipt of an effective notification of claimed infringement, to cached material that has been removed or access to which has been disabled at the originating site.

(v) With respect to functions referred to in clauses (i)(C) and (i)(D), the limitations shall be conditioned on the service provider:

    (A) not receiving a financial benefit directly attributable to the infringing activity, in circumstances where it has the right and ability to control such activity;

    (B) expeditiously removing or disabling access to the material residing on its system or network on obtaining actual knowledge of the infringement or becoming aware of facts or circumstances from which the infringement was apparent, such as through effective notifications of claimed infringement in accordance with subparagraph (ix) and

    (C) publicly designating a representative to receive such notifications.

(vi) Eligibility for the limitations in this subparagraph shall be conditioned on the service provider:

    (A) adopting and reasonably implementing a policy that provides for termination in appropriate circumstances of the accounts of repeat infringers; and

    (B) accommodating and not interfering with standard technical measures accepted in the territory of each Party that protect and identify copyrighted material, that are developed through an open, voluntary process by a broad consensus of copyright owners and service providers, that are available on reasonable and nondiscriminatory terms, and that do not impose substantial costs on service providers or substantial burdens on their systems or networks.

(vii) Eligibility for the limitations in this subparagraph may not be conditioned on the service provider monitoring its service, or affirmatively seeking facts indicating infringing activity, except to the extent consistent with such technical measures.

(viii) If the service provider qualifies for the limitations with respect to the functions referred to in clause (i)(A), court-ordered relief to compel or restrain certain actions shall be limited to terminating specified accounts, or to taking reasonable steps to block access to a specific, non-domestic online location. If the service provider qualifies for the limitations with respect to any other function in clause (i), court-ordered relief to compel or restrain certain actions shall be limited to removing or disabling access to the infringing material, terminating specified accounts, and other remedies that a court may find necessary provided that such other comparably effective forms of relief. Each Party shall provide that any such relief shall be issued with due regard for the relative burden to the service provider and harm to the copyright owner, the technical feasibility and effectiveness of the remedy, and whether less burdensome, comparably effective enforcement methods are available. Except for orders ensuring the preservation of evidence, or other orders having no material adverse effect on the operation of the service provider=s communications network, each Party shall provide that such relief shall be available only where the service provider has received notice of the court order proceedings referred to in this subparagraph and an opportunity to appear before the judicial authority.

(ix) For purposes of the notice and take down process for the functions referred to in clauses (i)(C) and (D), each Party shall establish appropriate procedures for effective notifications of claimed infringement, and effective counter-notifications by those whose material is removed or disabled through mistake or misidentification. Each Party shall also provide for monetary remedies against any person who makes a knowing material misrepresentation in a notification or counter-notification that causes injury to any interested party as a result of a service provider relying on the misrepresentation.

(x) If the service provider removes or disables access to material in good faith based on claimed or apparent infringement, each Party shall provide that the service provider shall be exempted from liability for any resulting claims, provided that, in the case of material residing on its system or network, it takes reasonable steps promptly to notify the person making the material available on its system or network that it has done so and, if such person makes an effective counter-notification and is subject to jurisdiction in an infringement suit, to restore the material online unless the person giving the original effective notification seeks judicial relief within a reasonable time.

(xi) Each Party shall establish an administrative or judicial procedure enabling copyright owners who have given effective notification of claimed infringement to obtain expeditiously from a service provider information in its possession identifying the alleged infringer.

(xii) For purposes of the functions referred to in clause (i)(A), **service provider** means a provider of transmission, routing or connections for digital online communications without modification of their content between or among points specified by the user of material of the user=s choosing, and for purposes of the functions referred to in clauses (i)(B) through (i)(D) service provider means a provider or operator of facilities for online services or network access.

Article 16.10: Transitional Provisions

1. Each Party shall implement the obligations of this Chapter within the following periods:
   (a) Each Party shall ratify or accede to the UPOV Convention and give effect to the obligations in paragraph 4 of Article 16.4 within six months of the date of entry into force of this Agreement or December 31, 2004, whichever date is earlier;
   (b) each Party shall ratify or accede to the agreements listed in paragraph 2(a) of Article 16.1(except for the UPOV Convention) and give effect to Articles 16.4 and 16.5 (except for paragraph 4 of Article 16.4) within one year of the date of entry into force of this Agreement; and
   (c) each Party shall implement each of the other obligations of this Chapter within six months of the date of entry into force of this Agreement.
2. Except as otherwise provided in this Chapter, the date of entry into force in paragraph 6(b) of Article 16.1 means the date of the expiry of the six-month period commencing on the date this Agreement enters into force.

Article 17.1: Statement of Shared Commitment

1. The Parties reaffirm their obligations as members of the International Labor Organization (AILO") and their commitments under the ILO Declaration on Fundamental Principles and Rights at Work and its Follow-up.[17-1] Each Party shall strive to ensure that such labor principles and the internationally recognized labor rights set forth in Article 17.7 are recognized and protected by domestic law.
2. Recognizing the right of each Party to establish its own domestic labor standards, and to adopt or modify accordingly its labor laws and regulations, each Party shall strive to ensure that its laws provide for labor standards consistent with the internationally recognized labor rights set forth in Article 17.7 and shall strive to improve those standards in that light.

Article 17.2: Application and Enforcement of Labor Laws

1.
   (a) A Party shall not fail to effectively enforce its labor laws, through a sustained or recurring course of action or inaction, in a manner affecting trade between the Parties, after the date of entry into force of this Agreement.
   (b) The Parties recognize that each Party retains the right to exercise discretion with respect to investigatory, prosecutorial, regulatory, and compliance matters and to make decisions regarding the allocation of resources to enforcement with respect to other labor matters determined to have higher priorities. Accordingly, the Parties understand that a Party is in compliance with subparagraph (a) where a course of action or inaction reflects a reasonable exercise of such discretion, or results from a *bona fide* decision regarding the allocation of resources.
2. The Parties recognize that it is inappropriate to encourage trade or investment by weakening or reducing the protections afforded in domestic labor laws. Accordingly,

each Party shall strive to ensure that it does not waive or otherwise derogate from, or offer to waive or otherwise derogate from, such laws in a manner that weakens or reduces adherence to the internationally recognized labor rights referred to in Article 17.7 as an encouragement for trade with the other Party, or as an encouragement for the establishment, acquisition, expansion, or retention of an investment in its territory.

Article 17.3: Procedural Guarantees and Public Awareness

1. Each Party shall ensure that persons with a legally recognized interest under its law in a particular matter have appropriate access to administrative, quasi-judicial, judicial, or labor tribunals for the enforcement of the Party's labor laws.
2. Each Party shall ensure that its administrative, quasi-judicial, judicial, or labor tribunal proceedings for the enforcement of its labor laws are fair, equitable and transparent.
3. Each Party shall provide that the parties to such proceedings may seek remedies to ensure the enforcement of rights under domestic labor laws.
4. Each Party shall promote public awareness of its labor laws.

Article 17.4: Institutional Arrangements

1. The functions of the Joint Committee established under Chapter 20 (Administration and Dispute Settlement) shall include discussion of matters related to the operation of this Chapter, including the Labor Cooperation Mechanism established under Article 17.5, and the pursuit of the labor objectives of this Agreement. The Joint Committee may establish a Subcommittee on Labor Affairs consisting of officials of the labor ministry and other appropriate agencies or ministries of each Party to meet at such times as they deem appropriate to discuss matters related to the implementation of this Chapter. Each meeting of the Subcommittee shall include a public session, unless the Parties agree otherwise.
2. Each Party shall designate an office within its labor ministry that shall serve as a contact point with the other Party, and with the public, for purposes of implementing this Chapter.
3. Each Party may convene a national labor advisory committee, comprising members of its public, including representatives of its labor and business organizations and other persons, to advise it on the implementation of this Chapter.
4. Each formal decision of the Parties concerning implementation of this Chapter shall be made public, unless the Parties decide otherwise.
5. Each Party's contact point designated under paragraph 2 shall provide for the submission, receipt, and consideration of public communications on matters related to provisions of this Chapter, and shall make such communications available to the other Party and, as appropriate, to the public. Each Party shall review such communications, as appropriate, in accordance with domestic procedures. The Parties, when they consider it appropriate, shall jointly prepare reports on matters related to the implementation of this Chapter, and shall make such reports public.

Article 17.5: Labor Cooperation

Recognizing that cooperation provides enhanced opportunities to promote respect for core labor standards embodied in the ILO Declaration on Fundamental Principles and Rights at Work and its Follow-Up and compliance with ILO Convention 182 Concerning the Prohibition and Immediate Action for the Elimination of the Worst Forms of Child Labor, and to further advance other common commitments, the Parties establish a Labor Cooperation Mechanism, as set out in Annex 17A to this Chapter.

Article 17.6: Labor Consultations

1. A Party may request consultations with the other Party regarding any matter arising under this Chapter. Unless the Parties agree otherwise, consultations shall commence within 30 days of a Party's delivery of a request for consultations to the other Party's contact point designated pursuant to Article 17.4.2.

2. The Parties shall make every attempt to arrive at a mutually satisfactory resolution of the matter and may seek advice or assistance from any person or body they deem appropriate.

3. If the consultations fail to resolve the matter, either Party may request that the Subcommittee on Labor Affairs be convened. The Subcommittee shall convene within 30 days of a Party's delivery of a request to convene the Subcommittee to the other Party's contact point designated pursuant to Article 17.4.2,[17-2] unless the Parties otherwise agree. The Subcommittee shall endeavor to resolve the matter expeditiously, including, where appropriate, by consulting governmental or outside experts and having recourse to such procedures as good offices, conciliation, or mediation.

4. If a Party considers that the other Party has failed to carry out its obligations under Article 17.2.1(a), the Party may request consultations pursuant to Article 20.4.2(a) (Additional Dispute Settlement Procedures) or under paragraph 1 of this Article.

   (a) If a Party requests consultations pursuant to Article 20.4.2(a) at a time when the Parties are engaged in consultations on the same matter under paragraph 1 of this Article or the Subcommittee is endeavoring to resolve the matter under paragraph 3, the Parties shall discontinue their efforts to resolve the matter under this Article. Once consultations have begun under Article 20.4.2(a), no consultations on the same matter may be entered into under this Article.

   (b) If a Party requests consultations pursuant to Article 20.4.2(a) more than 60 days after the commencement of consultations under paragraph 1, the Parties may agree at any time to refer the matter to the Joint Committee pursuant to Article 20.4.2(a).

5. Articles 20.3 (Consultations) and 20.4 (Additional Dispute Settlement Procedures) shall not apply to a matter arising under any provision of this Chapter other than Article 17.2.1(a).

Article 17.7:Definitions

For purposes of this Chapter:

1. **labor laws** means a Party's statutes or regulations, or provisions thereof, that are directly related to the following internationally recognized labor rights:
   (a) the right of association;
   (b) the right to organize and bargain collectively;
   (c) a prohibition on the use of any form of forced or compulsory labor;
   (d) labor protections for children and young people, including a minimum age for the employment of children and the prohibition and elimination of the worst forms of child labor; and
   (e) acceptable conditions of work with respect to minimum wages, hours of work, and occupational safety and health; and

2.
   (a) for Singapore, **minimum wages** means wage guidelines issued by the National Wages Council ("NWC") and gazetted under the Employment Act; and
   (b) for the United States, **statutes or regulations** means acts of the U.S. Congress or regulations promulgated pursuant to an act of the U.S. Congress that are enforceable, in the first instance, by action of the federal government.

Annex 17A. United States – Singapore Labor Cooperation Mechanism

1. **Establishment of a Labor Cooperation Mechanism.** Recognizing that cooperation provides enhanced opportunities to improve labor standards, and to further advance common commitments, including the June 1998 ILO Declaration on Fundamental Principles and Rights at Work and its Follow-up, the Parties establish a Labor Cooperation Mechanism.

2.
   (a) **Organization and Principal Functions.** The contact points established under Article 17.4.2 shall serve as the contact points for the Labor Cooperation Mechanism.
   (b) Officials of the labor ministries and other appropriate agencies and ministries shall cooperate through the Labor Cooperation Mechanism to:
       (i) establish priorities for cooperative activities on labor matters;
       (ii) develop specific cooperative activities in accord with such priorities;
       (iii) exchange information regarding labor law and practice in each Party;
       (iv) exchange information on ways to improve labor law and practice, including best labor practices;
       (v) advance understanding of, respect for, and effective implementation of the principles reflected in the ILO Declaration on Fundamental Principles and Rights at Work and its Follow-up; and
       (vi) develop recommendations for their respective governments for consideration by the Joint Committee.

3. **Cooperative Activities.** Cooperative activities to be undertaken by the Labor Cooperation Mechanism may include the following subjects:

(a) **fundamental rights and their effective application**: legislation, practice, and implementation related to the core elements of the ILO Declaration on Fundamental Rights at Work (freedom of association and the effective recognition of the right to collective bargaining, elimination of all forms of forced or compulsory labor, abolition of child labor including the worst forms of child labor in compliance with ILO Convention No. 182, and elimination of employment discrimination);

(b) **labor-management relations:** forms of cooperation and dispute resolution among workers, management and governments;

(c) **working conditions**: occupational safety and health; prevention of and compensation for work-related injuries and illness; and employment conditions;

(d) **unemployment assistance programs and other social safety net programs**;

(e) **human resource development and life long learning;**

(f) **labor statistics**; and

(g) such other matters as the Parties may agree.

4. **Implementation of Cooperative Activities.**

(a) Cooperative activities agreed upon under paragraph 3 may be implemented through:

(i) exchanges of delegations, professionals, and specialists, including study visits and other technical exchanges;

(ii) exchange of information, standards, regulations and procedures, and best practices, including publications and monographs;

(iii) organization of joint conferences, seminars, workshops, meetings, training sessions, and outreach and education programs;

(iv) development of collaborative projects or demonstrations;

(v) joint research projects, studies, and reports, including through engagement of independent experts with recognized expertise; and

(vi) other forms of technical exchange or cooperation that may be decided.

(b) In identifying areas for cooperation and carrying out cooperative activities, the Parties shall consider views of their respective worker and employer representatives.

18. ENVIRONMENT

Article 18.1: Levels of Protection

Recognizing the right of each Party to establish its own levels of domestic environmental protection and environmental development policies and priorities, and to adopt or modify accordingly its environmental laws, each Party shall ensure that its laws provide for high levels of environmental protection and shall strive to continue to improve those laws.

Article 18.2: Application and Enforcement of Environmental Laws

1.

(a) A Party shall not fail to effectively enforce its environmental laws, through a sustained or recurring course of action or inaction, in a manner affecting trade between the Parties, after the date of entry into force of this Agreement.

(b) The Parties recognize that each Party retains the right to exercise discretion with respect to investigatory, prosecutorial, regulatory, and compliance matters and to make decisions regarding the allocation of resources to enforcement with respect to other environmental matters determined to have higher priorities. Accordingly, the Parties understand that a Party is in compliance with subparagraph (a) where a course of action or inaction reflects a reasonable exercise of such discretion, or results from a *bona fide* decision regarding the allocation of resources.

2. The Parties recognize that it is inappropriate to encourage trade or investment by weakening or reducing the protections afforded in domestic environmental laws. Accordingly, each Party shall strive to ensure that it does not waive or otherwise derogate from, or offer to waive or otherwise derogate from, such laws in a manner that weakens or reduces the protections afforded in those laws as an encouragement for trade with the other Party, or as an encouragement for the establishment, acquisition, expansion, or retention of an investment in its territory.

Article 18.3: Procedural Matters

1. Each Party shall ensure that judicial, quasi-judicial, or administrative proceedings are available under its law to sanction or remedy violations of its environmental laws.

   (a) Such proceedings shall be fair, open, and equitable, and to this end shall comply with the due process of law, and be open to the public (except where the administration of justice otherwise requires).

   (b) Each Party shall provide appropriate and effective remedies or sanctions for a violation of its environmental laws that:

   (i) take into consideration the nature and gravity of the violation, any economic benefit the violator has derived from the violation, the economic condition of the violator, and other relevant factors; and

   (ii) may include remedies or sanctions such as: compliance agreements, penalties, fines, imprisonment, injunctions, the closure of facilities, and the cost of containing or cleaning up pollution.

2. Each Party shall ensure that interested persons may request the Party's competent authorities to investigate alleged violations of its environmental laws and that the competent authorities give such requests due consideration in accordance with its law.

3. Each Party shall ensure that persons with a legally recognized interest under its law in a particular matter have appropriate access to judicial, quasi-judicial, or administrative proceedings for the enforcement of the Party's environmental laws.

4. Each Party shall provide persons appropriate and effective rights of access to remedies, in accordance with its laws, which may include rights such as:

   (a) to sue another person under that Party's jurisdiction for damages;

(b) to seek sanctions or remedies such as monetary penalties, emergency closures, or orders to mitigate the consequences of violations of its environmental laws;

(c) to request the competent authorities to take appropriate action to enforce that Party's environmental laws in order to protect the environment or to avoid environmental harm; or

(d) to seek injunctions where a person suffers, or may suffer, loss, damage or injury as a result of conduct by another person subject to that Party's jurisdiction contrary to that Party's environmental laws, or from tortious conduct that harms human health or the environment.

Article 18.4: Institutional Arrangements

1. In addition to discussions of issues or activities related to the operation of this Chapter that may take place in the Joint Committee established under Article 20.1 (Joint Committee), the Parties shall, at the request of either Party, form a subcommittee consisting of government officials to meet at other times, as they deem appropriate, to discuss matters related to the operation of this Chapter. These meetings shall normally include a session where members of the subcommittee have an opportunity to meet with the public to discuss matters related to the operation of this Chapter. The Parties, when they consider appropriate, shall jointly prepare reports on matters related to the implementation of this Chapter, and shall make such reports public, except as otherwise provided in this Agreement.

2. Each formal decision of the Parties concerning implementation of this Chapter shall be made public, unless the Parties decide otherwise.

Article 18.5: Opportunities for Public Participation

1. To ensure the availability of opportunities for public participation in the discussion of matters related to the operation of this Chapter, and to facilitate the sharing of best practices and the development of innovative approaches to issues of interest to the public with regard to such matters, each Party shall develop or maintain procedures for dialogue with its public concerning the implementation of this Chapter, including:

   (a) the identification of matters to discuss at the meetings of the Joint Committee or the subcommittee described in Article 18.4; and

   (b) opportunities for its public to provide, on an on-going basis, views, recommendations, or advice on matters related to the provisions of this Chapter. Such views, recommendations, or advice shall be made available to the other Party and the public.

2. Each Party may convene, or consult with an existing, national advisory committee, composed of representatives of its environmental and business organizations and other members of its public, to advise it on the implementation of this Chapter, as appropriate.

3. Each Party shall make best efforts to respond favorably to requests for consultations by persons or organizations of its territory regarding that Party's implementation of this Chapter.

Article 18.6: Environmental Cooperation

1. The Parties recognize the importance of strengthening capacity to protect the environment and to promote sustainable development in concert with the strengthening of trade and investment relations between them. The Parties shall, as appropriate, pursue cooperative environmental activities, including those pertinent to trade and investment and to strengthening environmental performance, such as information reporting, enforcement capacity, and environmental management systems, under a Memorandum of Intent on Cooperation in Environmental Matters to be entered into between the Government of Singapore and the United States and in other fora. The Parties also recognize the ongoing importance of environmental cooperation that may be undertaken outside this Agreement.

2. The Parties shall take into account public comment and recommendations regarding cooperative environmental activities undertaken pursuant to this Chapter. Each Party shall also seek opportunities for its citizens to participate in the development and implementation of cooperative environmental activities, such as through the use of public-private partnerships.

3. In addition to the environmental cooperation activities outlined in Paragraph 1 of this Article, the Parties shall, as they deem appropriate, share information on their experiences in assessing and taking into account positive or negative environmental effects of trade agreements and policies.

Article 18.7: Environmental Consultations

1. A Party may request consultations with the other Party regarding any matter arising under this Chapter. Unless the Parties otherwise agree, consultations shall commence within 30 days of a Party's delivery of a request for consultations to the contact point designated by the other Party for this purpose.

2. The Parties shall make every attempt to arrive at a mutually satisfactory resolution of the matter and may seek advice or assistance from any person or body they deem appropriate.

3. If the consultations fail to resolve the matter, either Party may request that the subcommittee described in Article 18.4 be convened. The subcommittee shall convene within 30 days of a Party's delivery of a written request to convene the subcommittee to the other Party's contact point designated pursuant to paragraph 1,[18-1] unless the Parties otherwise agree, and shall endeavor to resolve the matter expeditiously, including, where appropriate, by consulting governmental or outside experts and having recourse to such procedures as good offices, conciliation, or mediation.

4. If a Party considers that the other Party has failed to carry out its obligations under Article 18.2.1(a), the Party may request consultations pursuant to Article 20.4.2(a) (Additional Dispute Settlement Procedures) or under paragraph 1 of this Article.

    (a) If a Party requests consultations pursuant to Article 20.4.2(a) at a time when the Parties are engaged in consultations on the same matter under paragraph 1 of this Article or the subcommittee is endeavoring to resolve the matter under paragraph

3, the Parties shall discontinue their efforts to resolve the matter under this Article. Once consultations have begun under Article 20.4.2(a), no consultations on the same matter may be entered into under this Article.

(a) If a Party requests consultations pursuant to Article 20.4.2(a) more than 60 days after the commencement of consultations under paragraph 1, the Parties may at any time agree to refer the matter to the Joint Committee pursuant to Article 20.4.2(a).

5. Articles 20.3 (Consultations) and 20.4 (Additional Dispute Settlement Procedures) shall not apply to a matter arising under any provision of this Chapter other than Article 18.2.1(a).

Article 18.8: Relationship to Environmental Agreements

The Parties recognize the critical role of multilateral environmental agreements in addressing some environmental challenges, including through the use of carefully tailored trade measures to achieve specific environmental goals and objectives. Recognizing that WTO Members have agreed in paragraph 31 of the Ministerial Declaration adopted on 14 November 2001 in Doha to negotiations on the relationship between existing WTO rules and specific trade obligations set out in multilateral environmental agreements, the Parties shall consult on the extent to which the outcome of those negotiations applies to this Agreement.

Article 18.9: Principles of Corporate Stewardship

Recognizing the substantial benefits brought by international trade and investment as well as the opportunity for enterprises to implement policies for sustainable development that seek to ensure coherence between social, economic and environmental objectives, each Party should encourage enterprises operating within its territory or subject to its jurisdiction to voluntarily incorporate sound principles of corporate stewardship in their internal policies, such as those principles or agreements that have been endorsed by both Parties.

Article 18.10: Definitions

For purposes of this Chapter:

1. **environmental laws** means any statutes or regulations of a Party, or provisions thereof, the primary purpose of which is the protection of the environment, or the prevention of a danger to human, animal, or plant life or health, through:

   (a) the prevention, abatement, or control of the release, discharge, or emission of pollutants or environmental contaminants;

   (b) the control of environmentally hazardous or toxic chemicals, substances, materials, and wastes, and the dissemination of information related thereto; or

   (c) the protection or conservation of wild flora or fauna, including endangered species, their habitat, and specially protected natural areas,

   in areas with respect to which a Party exercises sovereignty, sovereign rights, or jurisdiction, but does not include any statute or regulation, or provision thereof, directly related to worker safety or health; and

2.

   (a) for the United States, **statutes or regulations** means an act of the U.S. Congress or regulations promulgated pursuant to an act of the U.S. Congress that is enforceable, in the first instance, by action of the federal government; and

   (b) for Singapore, **statutes or regulations** means an Act of the Parliament of Singapore and any subsidiary legislation made thereunder. Subsidiary legislation includes proclamations, rules, regulations, orders, notifications, by-laws, or other instruments made under any Act or other lawful authority and having legislative effect.

19. TRANSPARENCY

Article 19.1: Definitions

For purposes of this Chapter:

Administrative ruling of general application means an administrative ruling or interpretation that applies to all persons and fact situations that fall generally within its ambit and that establishes a norm of conduct but does not include:

   (a) a determination or ruling made in an administrative or quasi-judicial proceeding that applies to a particular person, good, or service of the other Party in a specific case; or

   (b) a ruling that adjudicates with respect to a particular act or practice.

Article 19.2: Contact Points

1. Each Party shall designate a contact point or points to facilitate communications between the Parties on any matter covered by this Agreement.

2. On the request of the other Party, the contact points shall identify the office or official responsible for the matter and assist, as necessary, in facilitating communications with the requesting Party.

Article 19.3: Publication

1. Each Party shall ensure that its laws, regulations, procedures, and administrative rulings of general application respecting any matter covered by this Agreement are promptly published or otherwise made available in such a manner as to enable interested persons and the other Party to become acquainted with them.

2. To the extent possible, each Party shall:

   (a) publish in advance any such laws, regulations, procedures, and administrative rulings that it proposes to adopt; and

   (b) provide interested persons and the other Party a reasonable opportunity to comment on such proposed measures.

Article 19.4: Notification and Provision of Information

1. To the maximum extent possible, each Party shall notify the other Party of any actual or proposed measure that the Party considers might materially affect the operation of this Agreement or otherwise substantially affect the other Party's interests under this Agreement.

2. On request of the other Party, a Party shall promptly provide information and respond to questions pertaining to any actual or proposed measure, whether or not the other Party has been previously notified of that measure.

3. Any notification, request, or information under this Article shall be provided to the other Party through the relevant contact points.

4. Any notification or information provided under this Article shall be without prejudice as to whether the measure is consistent with this Agreement.

Article 19.5: Administrative Proceedings

1. With a view to administering in a consistent, impartial, and reasonable manner all measures referred to in Article 19.3, each Party shall ensure that in its administrative proceedings applying such measures to particular persons, goods, or services of the other Party in specific cases that:

   (a) wherever possible, persons of the other Party that are directly affected by aproceeding are provided reasonable notice, in accordance with domestic procedures, when a proceeding is initiated, including a description of the nature of the proceeding, a statement of the legal authority under which the proceeding is initiated, and a general description of any issues in controversy;

   (b) such persons are afforded a reasonable opportunity to present facts and arguments in support of their positions prior to any final administrative action, when time, the nature of the proceeding, and the public interest permit; and

   (c) its procedures are in accordance with domestic law.

Article 19.6: Review and Appeal

1. Each Party shall establish or maintain judicial, quasi-judicial, or administrative tribunals or procedures for the purpose of the prompt review and, where warranted, correction of final administrative actions[19-1] regarding matters covered by this Agreement. Such tribunals shall be impartial and independent of the office or authority entrusted with administrative enforcement and shall not have any substantial interest in the outcome of the matter.

2. Each Party shall ensure that, in any such tribunals or procedures, the parties to the proceeding are provided with the right to:

   (a) a reasonable opportunity to support or defend their respective positions; and

   (b) a decision based on the evidence and submissions of record or, where required by domestic law, the record compiled by the administrative authority.

3. Each Party shall ensure, subject to appeal or further review as provided in its domestic law, that such decision shall be implemented by, and shall govern the practice of, the offices or authorities with respect to the administrative action at issue.

20. Administration and Dispute Settlement

Article 20.1: Joint Committee

1. The Parties hereby establish a Joint Committee to supervise the implementation of this Agreement and to review the trade relationship between the Parties.
    (a) The Joint Committee shall be composed of government officials of each Party and shall be chaired by (i) the United States Trade Representative and (ii) Singapore's Minister for Trade and Industry or their designees.
    (b) The Joint Committee may establish and delegate responsibilities to ad hoc and standing committees or working groups, and seek the advice of non-governmental persons or groups.
2. The Joint Committee shall:
    (a) review the general functioning of this Agreement;
    (b) review and consider specific matters related to the operation and implementation of this Agreement in the light of its objectives, such as those related to customs administration, technical barriers to trade, electronic commerce, the environment, labor, the Medical Products Working Group, and distilled spirits;
    (c) facilitate the avoidance and settlement of disputes arising under this Agreement, including through consultations pursuant to Articles 20.3 and 20.4;
    (d) consider and adopt any amendment to this Agreement or other modification to the commitments therein, subject to completion of necessary domestic legal procedures by each Party;
    (e) as appropriate, issue interpretations of this Agreement, including as provided in Articles 15.21 (Governing Law) and 15.22 (Interpretation of Annexes);
    (f) consider ways to further enhance trade relations between the Parties and to further the objectives of this Agreement; and
    (g) take such other action as the Parties may agree.
3. At its first meeting, the Joint Committee shall consider the review performed by each Party of the environmental effects of this Agreement and shall provide the public an opportunity to provide views on those effects.
4. The Joint Committee shall establish its own rules of procedure.
5. Unless the Parties otherwise agree, the Joint Committee shall convene:
    (a) in regular session every year in order to review the general functioning of the Agreement, with such sessions to be held alternately in the territory of each Party; and
    (b) in special session within 30 days of the request of a Party, with such sessions to be held in the territory of the other Party or at such location as may be agreed by the Parties. A requirement under Article 20.4 that the Joint Committee take any

action with regard to a dispute shall not be interpreted to require the convening of a special session of the Joint Committee.

6. Recognizing the importance of transparency and openness, the Parties reaffirm their respective practices of considering the views of members of the public in order to draw upon a broad range of perspectives in the implementation of this Agreement.

7. Each Party shall treat any confidential information exchanged in relation to a meeting of the Joint Committee on the same basis as the Party providing the information.

Article 20.2: Administration of Dispute Settlement Proceedings

1. Each Party shall:
    (a) designate an office that shall be responsible for providing administrative assistance to panels established under Article 20.4;
    (b) be responsible for the operation and costs of its designated office; and
    (c) notify the other Party of the location of its office.

2. The Joint Committee shall establish the amounts of remuneration and expenses to be paid to panelists.

3. The remuneration of panelists and their assistants, their travel and lodging expenses, and all general expenses relating to proceedings of a panel established under Article 20.4 shall be borne equally by the Parties.

4. Each panelist shall keep a record and render a final account of the panelist's time and expenses, and the panel shall keep a record and render a final account of all general expenses.

Article 20.3: Consultations

1. Except as otherwise provided in this Agreement, either Party may request consultations with the other Party with respect to any matter that it considers might affect the operation of this Agreement by delivering written notification to the other Party's office designated under Article 20.2.1(a). If a Party requests consultations with regard to a matter, the other Party shall afford adequate opportunity for consultations and shall reply promptly to the request for consultations and enter into consultations in good faith.

2. In consultations under this Article, a Party may request the other Party to make available personnel of its government agencies or other regulatory bodies who have expertise in the matter subject to consultations.

3. In the consultations, each Party shall:
    (a) provide sufficient information to enable a full examination of how the matter subject to consultations might affect the operation of this Agreement; and
    (b) treat any confidential information exchanged in the course of consultations on the same basis as the Party providing the information.

Article 20.4: Additional Dispute Settlement Procedures

1. Except as otherwise provided in this Agreement or as the Parties otherwise agree, the provisions of this Article shall apply wherever a Party considers that:
    (a) a measure of the other Party is inconsistent with the obligations of this Agreement;
    (b) the other Party has otherwise failed to carry out its obligations under this Agreement; or
    (c) a benefit the Party could reasonably have expected to accrue to it under Chapters 2 (National Treatment and Market Access for Goods), 3 (Rules of Origin), Chapter 8 (Cross Border Trade in Services), or Chapter 16 (Intellectual Property Rights) is being nullified or impaired as a result of a measure that is not inconsistent with this Agreement.

2.
    (a) The Parties shall first seek to resolve a dispute described in paragraph 1 through consultations under Article 20.3. If the consultations fail to resolve the dispute within 60 days of the delivery of a Party's request for consultations under Article 20.3.1, either Party may, by delivering written notification to the other Party's office designated under Article 20.2.1(a), refer the matter to the Joint Committee, which shall endeavor to resolve the dispute.
    (b) Subject to Article 20.3.3(b), promptly after requesting or receiving a request for consultations related to a matter identified in paragraph 1, each Party shall solicit and consider the views of members of the public in order to draw upon a broad range of perspectives.

3.
    (a) Where a dispute regarding any matter referred to in paragraph 1 arises under this Agreement and under the WTO Agreement, or any other agreement to which both Parties are party, the complaining Party may select the forum in which to settle the dispute.
    (b) The complaining Party shall notify the other Party in writing of its intention to bring a dispute to a particular forum before doing so.
    (c) Once the complaining Party has selected a particular forum, the forum selected shall be used to the exclusion of other possible fora.
    (d) For the purposes of this paragraph, a Party shall be deemed to have selected a forum when it has requested the establishment of, or referred a matter to, a dispute settlement panel.

4.
    (a) If the Joint Committee has not resolved a dispute within 60 days after delivery of the notification described in paragraph 2(a) or within such other period as the Parties may agree, the complaining Party may refer the matter to a dispute settlement panel by delivering written notification to the other Party's office designated under Article 20.2.1(a).[20-1] Unless the Parties otherwise agree:
        (i) The panel shall have three members.
        (ii) Each Party shall appoint one panelist, in consultation with the other Party, within 30 days after the matter has been referred to a panel. If a Party fails to appoint a panelist within such period, a panelist shall be selected by lot from

the contingent list established under subparagraph (b) to serve as the panelist appointed by that Party.

(iii) The Parties shall endeavor to agree on a third panelist who shall serve as chair.

(iv) If the Parties are unable to agree on the chair of the Panel within 30 days after the date on which the second panelist has been appointed, the chair shall be selected by lot from the contingent list established under subparagraph (b).

(v) The date of establishment of the panel shall be the date on which the chair is appointed.

(b)

(i) By the date of entry into force of this Agreement, the Parties shall establish a contingent list of five individuals who are willing and able to serve as a panelist or chair.

(ii) Each such individual shall have expertise or experience in law, international trade, or the resolution of disputes arising under international trade agreements; shall be independent of, and not be affiliated with or take instructions from, any Party; and shall comply with the code of conduct to be established by the Joint Committee.

(iii) Individuals on the contingent list shall be appointed by agreement of the Parties for terms of three years, and may be reappointed.

(c) Panelists other than those chosen by lot from the contingent list shall meet the criteria set out in subparagraph (b)(ii) and have expertise or experience relevant to the subject matter that is under dispute.

(d) The Parties shall establish by the date of entry into force of this Agreement model rules of procedure, which shall ensure:

(i) a right to at least one hearing before the panel, which, subject to clause (vi), shall be open to the public;

(ii) an opportunity for each Party to provide initial and rebuttal submissions;

(iii) that each Party's written submissions, written versions of its oral statement, and written responses to a request or questions from the panel will be made public within ten days after they are submitted, subject to clause (vi);

(iv) that the panel shall consider requests from nongovernmental entities in the Parties' territories to provide written views regarding the dispute that may assist the panel in evaluating the submissions and arguments of the Parties;

(v) a reasonable opportunity for each Party to submit comments on the initial report presented pursuant to paragraph 5(a); and

(vi) the protection of confidential information.

Unless the Parties agree otherwise, the panel shall follow the model rules of procedure and may, after consulting the Parties, adopt additional rules of procedure not inconsistent with the model rules.

5.

(a) Unless the Parties agree otherwise, the panel shall, within 150 days after the chair is appointed, present to the Parties an initial report containing findings of fact and its determination as to whether:

(i) the measure at issue is inconsistent with the obligations of this Agreement;

(ii) a Party has otherwise failed to carry out its obligations under this Agreement; or

(iii) the measure at issue causes a nullification or impairment described in subparagraph 1(c); as well as any other determination requested by both Parties with regard to the dispute.

(b) The panel shall base its report on the submissions and arguments of the Parties. The panel may, at the request of the Parties, make recommendations for the resolution of the dispute.

(c) After considering any written comments by the Parties on the initial report, the panel may modify its report and make any further examination it considers appropriate.

(d) The panel shall present a final report to the Parties within 45 days of presentation of the initial report, unless the Parties agree otherwise. The Parties shall release the final report to the public within 15 days thereafter, subject to the protection of confidential information.

Article 20.5: Implementation of the Final Report

1. On receipt of the final report of a panel, the Parties shall agree on the resolution of the dispute, which normally shall conform with the determinations and recommendations, if any, of the panel.

2. If, in its final report, the panel determines that a Party has not conformed with its obligations under this Agreement or that a Party's measure is causing nullification or impairment in the sense of Article 20.4.1(c), the resolution, whenever possible, shall be to eliminate the nonconformity or the nullification or impairment.

Article 20.6: Non-Implementation

1. If a panel has made a determination of the type described in Article 20.5.2, and the Parties are unable to reach agreement on a resolution pursuant to Article 20.5.1 within 45 days of receiving the final report, or such other period as the Parties agree, the Party complained against shall enter into negotiations with the other Party with a view to developing mutually acceptable compensation.

2. If the Parties:

(a) are unable to agree on compensation within 30 days after the period for developing such compensation has begun; or

(b) have agreed on compensation or on a resolution pursuant to Article 20.5.1 and the complaining Party considers that the other Party has failed to observe the terms of such agreement, the complaining Party may at any time thereafter provide written notice to the office designated by the other Party pursuant to Article 20.2.1(a) that it intends to suspend the application to the other Party of benefits of equivalent effect. The notice shall specify the level of benefits that the Party proposes to suspend. Subject to paragraph 5, the complaining Party may begin suspending benefits 30 days after the later of the date on which it provides notice to the other Party's designated office under this paragraph or the panel issues its determination under paragraph 3, as the case may be.

3. If the Party complained against considers that:
   (a) the level of benefits that the other Party has proposed to be suspended is manifestly excessive; or
   (b) it has eliminated the non-conformity or the nullification or impairment that the panel has found, it may, within 30 days after the complaining Party provides notice under paragraph 2, request that the panel be reconvened to consider the matter. The Party complained against shall deliver its request in writing to the office designated by the other Party pursuant to Article 20.2.1(a). The panel shall reconvene as soon as possible after delivery of the request to the designated office and shall present its determination to the Parties within 90 days after it reconvenes to review a request under subparagraph (a) or (b), or within 120 days for a request under subparagraphs (a) and (b). If the panel determines that the level of benefits proposed to be suspended is manifestly excessive, it shall determine the level of benefits it considers to be of equivalent effect.

4. The complaining Party may suspend benefits up to the level the panel has determined under paragraph 3 or, if the panel has not determined the level, the level the Party has proposed to suspend under paragraph 2, unless the panel has determined that the Party complained against has eliminated the non-conformity or the nullification or impairment.

5. The complaining Party may not suspend benefits if, within 30 days after it provides written notice of intent to suspend benefits or, if the panel is reconvened under paragraph 3, within 20 days after the panel provides its determination, the Party complained against provides written notice to the other Party's office designated pursuant to Article 20.2.1(a) that it will pay an annual monetary assessment. The Parties shall consult, beginning no later than ten days after the Party complained against provides notice, with a view to reaching agreement on the amount of the assessment. If the Parties are unable to reach an agreement within 30 days after consultations begin, the amount of the assessment shall be set at a level, in U.S. dollars, equal to 50 percent of the level of the benefits the panel has determined under paragraph 3 to be of equivalent effect or, if the panel has not determined the level, 50 percent of the level that the complaining Party has proposed to suspend under paragraph 2.

6. Unless the Joint Committee otherwise decides, a monetary assessment shall be paid to the complaining Party in U.S. currency, or in an equivalent amount of Singaporean currency, in equal, quarterly installments beginning 60 days after the Party complained against gives notice that it intends to pay an assessment. Where the circumstances warrant, the Joint Committee may decide that an assessment shall be paid into a fund established by the Joint Committee and expended at the direction of the Joint Committee for appropriate initiatives to facilitate trade between the Parties, including by further reducing unreasonable trade barriers or by assisting a Party in carrying out its obligations under the Agreement.

7. If the Party complained against fails to pay a monetary assessment, the complaining Party may suspend the application to the Party complained against of benefits in accordance with paragraph 4.

8. This Article shall not apply with respect to a matter described in Article 20.7.1.

Article 20.7: Non-Implementation in Certain Disputes

1. If, in its final report, a panel determines that a Party has not conformed with its obligations under Article 17.2.1(a) (Application and Enforcement of Labor Laws) or Article 18.2.1(a) (Application and Enforcement of Environmental Laws), and the Parties:
   (a) are unable to reach agreement on a resolution pursuant to Article 20.5.1 within 45 days of receiving the final report; or
   (b) have agreed on a resolution pursuant to Article 20.5.1 and the complaining Party considers that the other Party has failed to observe the terms of the agreement, the complaining Party may at any time thereafter request that the panel be reconvened to impose an annual monetary assessment on the other Party. The complaining Party shall deliver its request in writing to the office designated by the other Party pursuant to Article 20.2.1(a). The panel shall reconvene as soon as possible after delivery of the request to the designated office.

2. The panel shall determine the amount of the monetary assessment in U.S. dollars within 90 days after it reconvenes under paragraph 1. In determining the amount of the assessment, the panel shall take into account:
   (a) the bilateral trade effects of the Party's failure to effectively enforce the relevant law;
   (b) the pervasiveness and duration of the Party's failure to effectively enforce the relevant law;
   (c) the reasons for the Party's failure to effectively enforce the relevant law;
   (d) the level of enforcement that could reasonably be expected of the Party given its resource constraints;
   (e) the efforts made by the Party to begin remedying the non-enforcement after the final report of the panel; and
   (f) any other relevant factors.
   The amount of the assessment shall not exceed 15 million U.S. dollars annually, adjusted for inflation as specified in Annex 20A.

3. On the date on which the panel determines the amount of the monetary assessment under paragraph 2, or at any other time thereafter, the complaining Party may provide notice in writing to the office designated by the other Party pursuant to Article 20.2.1(a) demanding payment of the monetary assessment. The monetary assessment shall be payable in U.S. currency, or in an equivalent amount of Singaporean currency, in equal, quarterly installments beginning on the later of:
   (a) 60 days after the date on which the panel determines the amount; or
   (b) 60 days after the complaining Party provides the notice described in this paragraph.

4. Assessments shall be paid into a fund established by the Joint Committee and shall be expended at the direction of the Joint Committee for appropriate labor or environmental initiatives, including efforts to improve or enhance labor or environmental law enforcement, as the case may be, in the territory of the Party complained against, consistent with its law. In deciding how to expend monies paid

into the fund, the Joint Committee shall consider the views of interested persons in the Parties' territories.

5. If the Party complained against fails to pay a monetary assessment, and if the Party has created and funded an escrow account to ensure payment of any assessments against it, the other Party shall, before having recourse to any other measure, seek to obtain the funds from the account.

6. If the complaining Party cannot obtain the funds from the other Party's escrow account within 30 days of the date on which payment is due, or if the other Party has not created an escrow account, the complaining Party may take other appropriate steps to collect the assessment or otherwise secure compliance. These steps may include suspending tariff benefits under the Agreement as necessary to collect the assessment, while bearing in mind the Agreement's objective of eliminating barriers to bilateral trade and while seeking to avoid unduly affecting parties or interests not party to the dispute.

Article 20.8: Compliance Review

1. Without prejudice to the procedures set out in Article 20.6.3, if the Party complained against considers that it has eliminated the non-conformity or the nullification or impairment that the panel has found, it may refer the matter to the panel by providing written notice to the office designated by the other Party pursuant to Article 20.2.1(a). The panel shall issue its report on the matter within 90 days after the Party complained against provides notice.

2. If the panel decides that the Party complained against has eliminated the non-conformity or the nullification or impairment, the complaining Party shall promptly reinstate any benefits it has suspended under Article 20.6 or 20.7 and the Party complained against shall no longer be required to pay any monetary assessment it has agreed to pay under Article 20.6.5 or that has been imposed on it under Article 20.7.

Article 20.9: Five-Year Review

The Joint Committee shall review the operation and effectiveness of Articles 20.6 and 20.7 not later than five years after the date of entry into force of this Agreement, or within six months after benefits have been suspended or monetary assessments have been imposed in five proceedings initiated under this Chapter, whichever occurs first.

Article 20.10: Private Rights

Neither Party may provide for a right of action under its domestic law against the other Party on the ground that a measure of the other Party is inconsistent with this Agreement.

Annex 20A. Inflation Adjustment Formula for Monetary Assessments

1. An annual monetary assessment imposed before December 31, 2004 shall not exceed 15 million U.S. dollars.

2. Beginning January 1, 2005, the 15 million U.S. dollar annual cap shall be adjusted for inflation in accordance with paragraphs 3 through 5.

3. The period used for the accumulated inflation adjustment shall be calendar year 2003 through the most recent calendar year preceding the one in which the assessment is owed.

4. The relevant inflation rate shall be the U.S. inflation rate as measured by the Producer Price Index for Finished Goods published by the U.S. Bureau of Labor Statistics.

5. The inflation adjustment shall be estimated according to the following formula:

$$\$15 \text{ million} \times (1 + \Pi i) = A$$

Πi = accumulated U.S. inflation rate from calendar year 2003 through the most recent calendar year preceding the one in which the assessment is owed.

A = cap for the assessment for the year in question.

21. GENERAL AND FINAL PROVISIONS

Article 21.1: General Exceptions

1. For purposes of Chapters 2 through 6 (National Treatment and Market Access for Goods, Rules of Origin, Customs Procedures, Textiles, Technical Barriers to Trade), GATT 1994 Article XX and its interpretive notes are incorporated into and made part of this Agreement, *mutatis mutandis*. The Parties understand that the measures referred to in GATT 1994 Article XX(b) include environmental measures necessary to protect human, animal, or plant life or health, and that GATT 1994 Article XX(g) applies to measures relating to the conservation of living and non-living exhaustible natural resources.

2. For purposes of Chapters 8, 9, and 14 (Cross Border Trade in Services, Telecommunications, and Electronic Commerce[21-1]), GATS Article XIV (including its footnotes) is incorporated into and made part of this Agreement, *mutatis mutandis*.[21-2] The Parties understand that the measures referred to in GATS Article XIV(b) include environmental measures necessary to protect human, animal, or plant life or health.

Article 21.2: Essential Security

Nothing in this Agreement shall be construed:

(a) to require a Party to furnish or allow access to any information the disclosure of which it determines to be contrary to its essential security interests; or

(b) to preclude a Party from applying measures that it considers necessary for the fulfillment of its obligations with respect to the maintenance or restoration of international peace or security, or the protection of its own essential security interests.

Article 21.3: Taxation

1. Except as set out in this Article, nothing in this Agreement shall apply to taxation measures.

2. Nothing in this Agreement shall affect the rights and obligations of either Party under any tax convention. In the event of any inconsistency between this Agreement and any such convention, that convention shall prevail to the extent of the inconsistency. In the case of a tax convention between the Parties, the competent authorities under that convention shall have sole responsibility for determining whether any inconsistency exists between this Agreement and that convention.

3. Notwithstanding paragraph 2:

   (a) Article 2.1 (National Treatment) and such other provisions of this Agreement as are necessary to give effect to that Article shall apply to taxation measures to the same extent as does GATT 1994 Article III; and

   (b) Article 2.4 (Export Tax) shall apply to taxation measures.

4. Subject to paragraph 2:

   (a) Article 8.3 (National Treatment) and Article 10.2 (National Treatment) shall apply to taxation measures on income, capital gains or on the taxable capital of corporations that relate to the purchase or consumption of particular services, except that nothing in this subparagraph shall prevent a Party from conditioning the receipt or continued receipt of an advantage relating to the purchase or consumption of particular services on requirements to provide the service in its territory, and

   (b) Article 15.4 (National and Most-Favored-Nation Treatment), Articles 8.4 (National Treatment) and 8.4 (Most-Favored-Nation Treatment) and Articles 10.2 (National Treatment) and 10.3 (Most-Favored-Nation Treatment) shall apply to all taxation measures, other than those on income, capital gains, or on the taxable capital of corporations, taxes on estates, inheritances, gifts and generation-skipping transfers, except that nothing in those Articles shall apply:

   (c) to any most-favored-nation obligation with respect to an advantage accorded by a Party pursuant to a tax convention;

   (d) to a non-conforming provision of any existing taxation measure;

   (e) to the continuation or prompt renewal of a non-conforming provision of any existing taxation measure;

   (f) to an amendment to a non-conforming provision of any existing taxation measure to the extent that the amendment does not decrease its conformity, at the time of the amendment, with any of those Articles;

   (g) to the adoption or enforcement of any taxation measure aimed at ensuring the equitable or effective imposition or collection of taxes (as permitted by GATS Article XIV(d)); or

   (h) to a provision that conditions the receipt, or continued receipt of an advantage relating to the contributions to, or income of, a pension trust, fund, or other arrangement to provide pension or similar benefits on a requirement that the Party maintain continuous jurisdiction over such trust, fund, or other arrangement.

5. Subject to paragraph 2 and without prejudice to the rights and obligations of the Parties under paragraph 3, paragraphs 2, 3, and 4 of Article 15.8 (Performance Requirements) shall apply to taxation measures.

6. Article 15.15 (Submission of a Claim to Arbitration) shall apply to a taxation measure alleged to be a breach of an investment agreement or an investment authorization. Articles 15.6 (Expropriation) and 15.15 shall apply to a taxation measure alleged to be an expropriation. However, no investor may invoke Article 15.6 as the basis for a claim where it has been determined pursuant to this paragraph that the measure is not an expropriation. An investor that seeks to invoke Article 15.6 with respect to a taxation measure must first refer to the competent authorities described in paragraph 7, at the time that it gives notice under Article 15.15.2, the issue of whether that taxation measure involves an expropriation. If the competent authorities do not agree to consider the issue or, having agreed to consider it, fail to agree that the measure is not an expropriation within a period of six months of such referral, the investor may submit its claim to arbitration under Article 15.15.4.

7. For purposes of this Article,
   (a) **competent authorities** means
       (i) in the case of Singapore, Director (Taxation), Ministry of Finance; and
       (ii) in the case of the United States, the Assistant Secretary of the Treasury (Tax Policy), Department of the Treasury; and
   (b) **investment agreement** and **investment authorization** have the meanings ascribed to them in Chapter 15 (Investment).

Article 21.4: Disclosure of Information

Nothing in this Agreement shall be construed to require a Party to furnish or allow access to confidential information, the disclosure of which would impede law enforcement, or otherwise be contrary to the public interest, or which would prejudice the legitimate commercial interests of particular enterprises, public or private.

Article 21.5: Anti-Corruption

1. Each Party reaffirms its firm existing commitment to the adoption, maintenance, and enforcement of effective measures, including deterrent penalties, against bribery and corruption in international business transactions. The Parties further commit to undertake best efforts to associate themselves with appropriate international anti-corruption instruments and to encourage and support appropriate anti-corruption initiatives and activities in relevant international fora.

2. The Parties shall cooperate to strive to eliminate bribery and corruption and to promote transparency in international trade. They will look for avenues in relevant international fora to address these issues and build upon the potential anti-corruption efforts in these fora.

Article 21.6: Accession

1. Any country or group of countries may accede to this Agreement subject to such terms and conditions as may be agreed between such country or countries and the

Parties and following approval in accordance with the applicable legal procedures of each country.

2. This Agreement shall not apply as between any Party and any acceding country or group of countries if, at the time of the accession, either does not consent to such accession.

Article 21.7: Annexes

The Annexes to this Agreement constitute an integral part of this Agreement.

Article 21.8: Amendments

This Agreement may be amended by agreement in writing by the Parties and such amendment shall enter into force after the Parties have exchanged written notification certifying that they have completed necessary internal legal procedures and on such date or dates as may be agreed between them.

Article 21.9: Entry Into Force and Termination

1. This Agreement shall come into force 60 days after the date when the Parties have exchanged written notification that their respective internal requirements for the entry into force of this Agreement have been fulfilled, or such other date as the Parties may agree.
2. Either Party may terminate this Agreement by written notification to the other Party, and such termination shall take effect six months after the date of the notification.
3. Within 30 days of delivery of a notification under paragraph 2, either Party may request consultations regarding whether the termination of any provision of this Agreement should take effect at a later date than provided under paragraph 2. Such consultations shall commence within 30 days of a Party's delivery of such request.

IN WITNESS WHEREOF, the undersigned, being duly authorized by their respective Governments, have signed this Agreement.

Done at Washington, in duplicate, this sixth day of May, 2003.

FOR THE GOVERNMENT OF THE   FOR THE GOVERNMENT OF THE
UNITED STATES OF AMERICA: REPUBLIC OF SINGAPORE:

End Notes

[3-1] Such consultations may include meetings of the Joint Committee pursuant to Article 20.1 (Joint Committee).

[4-1] For Singapore, this level of administrative review may include the Ministry supervising the Customs authority.

[5-1] For purposes of this paragraph, the term "resolution of the matter" means, with regard to the violation or other act of circumvention in question, (1) a decision by Singapore not to prosecute, (2) a judgment, or (3) a settlement in accordance with the law.

[5-2] Singapore shall ensure that its officials have the authority to examine textile and apparel goods imported into Singapore, exported from Singapore, processed or manipulated in a free trade zone, or transshipped in Singapore en route to the United States, to ascertain that these goods correctly identify their country of origin, that the documents accompanying the goods correctly describe the goods, and that information that Singapore officials discover in the course of such examinations may be shared with the United States.

[5-3] With regard to transshipped textile or apparel goods that are not claimed to be originating goods or products of Singapore, and that do not undergo processing or manipulation in a free trade zone, Singapore is not required to take any action other than to share information about such goods with the United States.

[5-4] A Party is not required to take action under this paragraph if it finds that an enterprise's failure to maintain or produce records is the result of clerical error or inadvertence.

[5-5] For purposes of this paragraph, the term "principal" means a person with principal ownership or control of an enterprise.

[7-1] The Parties understand that "safeguard measure" does not include antidumping or countervailing measures.

[8-1] The Parties understand that **seeks to supply or supplies a service** has the same meaning as **supplies a service** as used in GATS Article XXVIII(g). The Parties understand that for purposes of Articles 8.3, 8.4, and 8.5 of this Agreement, **service suppliers** has the same meaning as **services and service suppliers** as used in GATS Articles II, XVI, and XVII.

[8-2] The Parties understand that nothing in this Chapter, including this paragraph, is subject to investor-state dispute settlement pursuant to Section C of Chapter 15 (Investor-State Dispute Settlement).

[8-3] This paragraph does not cover measures of a Party which limit inputs for the supply of services.

[8-4] The Parties understand that this Article does not extend to Singapore's requirements in relation to the Central Provident Fund regarding the withdrawal of monies from individual accounts.

[8-5] The Parties understand that "regulation" includes regulations establishing or applying to licensing authorization or criteria.

[9-1] For greater certainty, Singapore's obligations under this Chapter shall not apply to measures adopted or maintained relating to broadcasting services as defined in Singapore's Schedule to Annex 8B.

[9-2] This Article does not apply to access to unbundled network elements, including access to leased circuits as an unbundled network element, which is addressed in Article 9.4.3.

[9-3] For the purpose of the United States' obligations, Article 9.4 does not apply to rural telephone companies, as defined in section 3(37) of the Communications Act of 1934, as amended by the Telecommunications Act of 1996, unless a state regulatory authority orders otherwise. Moreover, a state regulatory authority may exempt a rural local exchange carrier, as defined in section 251(f)(2) of the Communications Act of 1934, as amended by the Telecommunications Act of 1996, from the obligations contained in Article 9.4.

[9-4] Article 9.4 does not apply to suppliers of commercial mobile services.

[9-5] In the United States, a wholesale rate set pursuant to domestic law and regulation shall be considered to be reasonable for purposes of subparagraph (a). In Singapore, wholesale rates are not required by the telecommunications regulatory body and therefore are not factored into a determination of what is considered to be reasonable for the purposes of subparagraph (a).

[9-6] In the United States, a reseller that obtains at wholesale rates a telecommunications service that is available at retail only to a category of subscribers may be prohibited from offering such service to a different category of subscribers. In Singapore, where national law and regulation provides for this, resellers that obtain public telecommunications services available at retail only to a category of subscribers at particular rates may be prohibited from offering such service to a different category of subscribers at that particular rate.

[9-7] In the United States, this obligation may not apply to those states that regulate such rates as a matter of state law.

[9-8] These costs may include the cost of physical or virtual co-location referenced in Article 9.4.4.

[9-9] The obligation under this article is not an obligation to provide leased circuits as an unbundled network element, which is addressed in Article 9.4.3.

[9-10] This shall include any submarine cable landing facilities included as part of that authorization.

[9-11] The Parties understand that decisions on allocating and assigning spectrum, and frequency management are not measures that are *per se* inconsistent with Article 8.5 (Market Access) and Article 15.8 (Performance Requirements). Accordingly, each Party retains the right to exercise its spectrum and frequency management policies, which may affect the number of suppliers of public telecommunications services, provided that this is done in a manner that is consistent with the provisions of this Agreement. The Parties also retain the right to allocate frequency bands taking into account existing and future needs.

[9-12] Because the United States does not classify services described in 47 U.S.C. § 153(20) as public telecommunications services, these services are not considered public telecommunications services for the purposes of this Agreement. This does not prejudice either Party's positions in the WTO on the scope and definition of these services.

[9-13] (a) For purposes of Singapore's obligations in Articles 9.3, 9.4.1, 9.4.5, 9.4.8, and 9.13, the phrase **supplier of public telecommunications services** means a facilities-based licensee or services-based licensee that uses switching or routing equipment, in accordance with the Singapore Code of Practice for Competition in the Provision of Telecommunications Services, 2000.

(b) For purposes of Singapore's obligations in Articles 9.4.3, 9.4.4, 9.4.6 and 9.5, the phrase **supplier of public telecommunications services** means a facilities-based licensee in accordance with the Singapore Code of Practice for Competition in the Provision of Telecommunications Services, 2000.

[9-14] Including by photonic means.

[10-1] For greater certainty, the letters referred to in Article 15.26 (Status of Letter Exchanges), to the extent relevant, are applicable to Article 15.6 (Expropriation) as incorporated into this Chapter.

[10-2] For purposes of this Article, the term "financial institutions of the other Party" includes financial institutions that are located within the territory of the other Party and controlled by persons of the other Party that seek to establish financial institutions within the territory of the Party.

[10-3] The Parties understand that nothing in Article 10.6 prevents a financial institution of a Party from applying to the other Party to consider authorizing the supply of a financial service that is supplied in neither Party's territory. Such application shall be subject to the law of the Party to which the application is made and, for greater certainty, shall not be subject to the obligations of Article 10.6.

[10-4] For purposes of this Article, the term "financial institutions of the other Party" includes financial institutions that are located within the territory of the other Party and controlled by persons of the other Party that seek to establish financial institutions within the territory of the Party.

[10-5] It is understood that the term "prudential reasons" includes the maintenance of the safety, soundness, integrity or financial responsibility of individual financial institutions or cross-border financial service suppliers.

[10-6] The Federal Deposit Insurance Corporation of the United States and any entity that administers a deposit insurance scheme in Singapore shall be deemed to be within the definition of public entity for purposes of Chapter 12 (Anticompetitive Business Conduct, Government Monopolies, and Government Enterprises).

[1] As defined in relation to intra-corporate or company transferees in each Party's Schedule of Commitments to the GATS.

[12-1] Singapore shall enact general competition legislation by January 2005, and shall not exclude enterprises from that legislation on the basis of their status as government enterprises.

[12-2] The Parties recognize that shareholders do not oversee the day-to-day operations of enterprises. Nothing in this provision is intended to require or encourage action that would be inconsistent with applicable U.S. or Singapore law.

[13-1] For greater certainty, nothing in this Chapter shall be construed as incorporating U.S. General Note 8.

[14-1] Paragraph 1 of this Article does not preclude a Party from imposing internal taxes or other internal charges provided that these are imposed in a manner consistent with this Agreement.

[14-2] For greater clarity, digital products do not include digitized representations of financial instruments.

[15-1] Where an asset lacks the characteristics of an investment, that asset is not an investment regardless of the form it may take. The characteristics of an investment include the commitment of capital, the expectation of gain or profit, or the assumption of risk.

[15-2] Some forms of debt, such as bonds, debentures, and long-term notes, are more likely to have the characteristics of an investment, while other forms of debt, such as claims to payment that are immediately due and result from the sale of goods or services, are less likely to have such characteristics.

[15-3] Whether a particular type of license, authorization, permit, or similar instrument (including a concession, to the extent that it has the nature of such an instrument) has the characteristics of an investment depends on such factors as the nature and extent of the rights that the holder has under the domestic law of the Party. Among the licenses, authorizations, permits, and similar instruments that do not have the characteristics of an investment are those that do not create any rights protected under domestic law. For greater certainty, the foregoing is without prejudice to whether any asset associated with the license, authorization, permit, or similar instrument has the characteristics of an investment.

[15-4] The term "investment" does not include an order or judgment entered in a judicial or administrative action.

[15-5] Actions taken by an agency of a Party to enforce laws of general application such as competition law do not come within this definition.

[15-6] For purposes of this definition, "national authority" means (1) for Singapore, a ministry or other government body that is constituted by an Act of Parliament; and (2) for the United States, an authority at the central level of government.

[15-7] Actions taken by an agency of a Party to enforce laws of general application such as competition law do not come within this definition.

[15-8] Article 15.5 is to be interpreted in accordance with the letter exchange on customary international law.

[15-9] Article 15.6 is to be interpreted in accordance with the letter exchange on customary international law and the letter exchange on expropriation, and is subject to the letter exchange on land expropriation.

[15-10] Article 15.7 is subject to Annex 15A.

[15-11] Article 15.8 is subject to Annex 15B and Annex 15C.

[15-12] Article 15.15 is subject to the letter exchange on land expropriation.

[15-13] For greater certainty, payments pursuant to a loan or bond shall exclude capital account transactions relating to inter-bank loans, including loans to or from Singapore licensed banks, merchant banks, or finance companies.

[16-1] Singapore is not obligated to give effect to Articles 6 and 7 of the Trademark Law Treaty.

[16-2] For purposes of Articles 16.1.3 and 16.5.1, a national of a Party shall also mean, in respect of the relevant right, entities located in such Party that would meet the criteria for eligibility for protection provided for in the agreements listed in Article 16.1.2 and the TRIPS Agreement.

16-3 For the purposes of paragraphs 3 and 4, "protection" shall include matters affecting the availability, acquisition, scope, maintenance, and enforcement of intellectual property rights as well as matters affecting the use of intellectual property rights specifically covered by this Chapter. For the purposes of paragraphs 3 and 4, "protection" shall also include the prohibition on circumvention of effective technological measures pursuant to paragraph 7 of Article 16.4 and the provision concerning rights management information pursuant to paragraph 8 of Article 16.4.

16-4 "Benefits derived therefrom" refers to benefits such as levies on blank tapes.

16-5 Neither Party is obligated to treat certification marks as a separate category in domestic law, provided that such marks are protected.

16-6 A geographical indication shall be capable of constituting a trademark to the extent that the geographical indication consists of any sign, or any combination of signs, capable of identifying a good or service as originating in the territory of a Party, or a region or locality in that territory, where a given quality, reputation or other characteristic of the good or service is essentially attributable to its geographical origin.

16-7 This provision is not intended to affect the use of common names of pharmaceutical products in prescribing medicine.

16-8 For the application of paragraph 1 of Article 16.5, fixed means the finalization of the master tape or its equivalent.

16-9 The definition of phonogram provided herein does not suggest that rights in the phonogram are in any way affected through their incorporation into a cinematographic or other audiovisual work.

16-10 A Party may limit such cause of action to cases where the product has been sold or distributed only outside the Party's territory before its procurement inside the Party's territory.

16-11 AUse" in this provision refers to use other than that allowed in paragraph 3.

16-12 The Parties recognize that an intellectual property right does not necessarily confer market power upon its owner.

16-13 Periods attributable to actions of the patent applicant shall include such periods of time taken to file prescribed documents relating to the examination as provided in the laws of the Party.

16-14 Where a Party, on the date of its implementation of the TRIPS Agreement, had in place a system for protecting pharmaceutical or agricultural chemical products not involving new chemical entities from unfair commercial use that conferred a different form or period of protection shorter than that specified in paragraph 1 of Article 16.8, that Party may retain such system notwithstanding the obligations of that paragraph.

16-15 For the purpose of Article 16.9 concerning the enforcement of intellectual property rights, the term Aright holder@ shall include exclusive licensees as well as federations and associations having the legal standing to assert such rights; and the term "exclusive licensee" shall include the exclusive licensee of any one or more of the exclusive rights encompassed in a given intellectual property.

16-16 For the purposes of this Chapter:

(a) **counterfeit trademark goods** shall mean any goods, including packaging, bearing without authorization a trademark which is identical to the trademark validly registered in respect of such goods, or which cannot be distinguished in its essential aspects from such a trademark, and which thereby infringes the rights of the owner of the trademark in question under the law of the country of importation; and

(b) **pirated copyright goods** shall mean any goods which are copies made without the consent of the right holder or person duly authorized by the right holder in the country of production and which are made directly or indirectly from an article where the making of that copy would have constituted an infringement of a copyright or a related right under the law of the country of importation.

16-17 For purposes of Article 16.9.22, "copyright" shall also include related rights.

16-18 It is understood that this subparagraph is without prejudice to the availability of defenses to copyright infringement that are of general applicability.

16-19 Either Party may request consultations with the other Party to consider how to address future functions of a similar nature under this paragraph.

17-1 The Parties recall that paragraph 5 of this ILO Declaration states that labor standards should not be used for protectionist trade purposes.

17-2 If, on the date a Party delivers a request, the Parties have not established the Subcommittee, they shall do so during the 30-day period described in this paragraph.

18-1 If, on the date a Party delivers a request, the Parties have not established the subcommittee, they shall do so during the 30-day period described in this paragraph.

19-1 For greater certainty, the correction of final administrative actions includes a referral back to the body that took such action for corrective action.

20-1 This paragraph is subject to the letter referred to in Article 15.26(c) (Status of Letter Exchanges).

21-1 This is without prejudice to the classification of digital products as a good or a service.

21-2 If GATS Article XIV is amended, this Article shall be amended, as appropriate, after consultations between the Parties.

CHAPTER SOURCES

The following chapters have been previously published:

Chapter 1 – This is an edited, reformatted and augmented version of a Congressional Research Service publication, report RL34315, dated March 26, 2010.

Chapter 2 – is an edited, reformatted and augmented version of a Organization of American States, Foreign Trade Information System on United States-Singapore Free Trade Agreement.

INDEX

D

G

H

I

N

O

P

Q

R

S

T